RESTLESS

A radical journey through Scotland's history

Volume One (500AD–1914)

Alan McCombes & Roz Paterson

Alan McCombes was the founding editor of the *Scottish Socialist Voice*, and was a founding member of both the Scottish Socialist Party and the Scottish Independence Convention. He has written a number of books and booklets including *Downfall* (Birlinn, 2011); *Two Worlds Collide* (SSP, 2005); *Reclaim Our Railways* (RMT, 2004); *Imagine* (Canongate, 2000) and *How to Fight the Poll Tax* (SML, 1988).

Roz Paterson is a teacher and writer. She has written for the *Sunday Herald*, the *Daily Record*, *The Scotsman* and *Scotland on Sunday,* and writes regularly for the *Scottish Socialist Voice* and *Red Pepper.* She lives in the Highlands with her husband and children.

For Robbie

First published in July 2014 by Calton Books
159 London Road, Glasgow G1 5BX • www.calton-books.co.uk

ISBN 978-0-9928983-1-1

A CIP catalogue record for this book is available from the British Library

Typeset and cover design by Simon Whittle • @revolbiscuit

Distributed by AK Press & Distribution
33 Tower Street, Edinburgh EH6 7BN • www.akuk.com

Printed and bound by Forward Graphics
100 Elderpark Street, Glasgow G51 3TR • www.forwardgraphics.co.uk

CONTENTS

Acknowledgements

Many, many thanks to the following for their time and effort in helping us get this book out. Simon Whittle, who has handled the typography and design with his customary quiet professionalism. Robert Rae and Brian Lewis, who run the best bookshop in Glasgow, Calton Books, for taking on the publishing of this book. Carolyn Leckie for her astute observations after reading various drafts of the manuscript, and her organisational support. Shona McCombes for final proof-reading and skilful honing of the manuscript. Katie McCombes for her adept work in creating the index. Malcolm McDonald for his strength and support. Susan Wright for some valuable insights and marketing expertise. Tony Philipsz and the rest of the team at Forward Graphics in Govan, for stepping in at the last minute (following a technical crisis elsewhere) to get this book printed at lightning speed.

Foreword

It's October 2001, and I've just arrived in the Pakistani frontier city of Peshawar to report on the political and social repercussions of the bombing of Afghanistan.

A short drive away, up beyond the Khyber Pass, American B52 bombers roar over the Hindu Kush mountains of Eastern Afghanistan, turning villages into mass graves at the flick of a switch. Down here in the crowded marketplace of the Sadaar Bazaar, I'm startled by a magazine front cover on sale on the book and newspaper stalls.

It's a familiar image from back home – *Braveheart* actor Mel Gibson, glowering defiantly from the front cover of a Pashtun magazine, his sword flashing, his face daubed with blue and white warpaint. Except for one detail. Courtesy of Photoshop, William Wallace has a black Taliban-style turban wrapped around his head.

Every nation has its legends, its heroes and its villains, its glories and tragedies. Scotland may be a small country – 0.07 per cent of the world's population at the last count – but from the Wars of Independence to the melodrama of Mary Queen of Scots, from the massacre of Glencoe to the Parcel of Rogues, from Bonnie Prince Charlie to Red Clydeside, we have an almost embarrassing surplus of colourful, if not garish, history.

Great storybook stuff. But as Scotland stands on the threshold of the biggest decision the people of the nation have ever taken, what does it matter?

In one sense, it doesn't. The debate electrifying Scotland right now is not about the battles or betrayals, the triumphs or the injustices of centuries past.

It is about the years, the decades and the centuries to come. For good or ill, the decision made by the people of Scotland at the ballot box will affect not just the generations who live in this country, but the generations yet to be born.

Yet history does matter. Just as individual human beings are shaped by their own accumulated experiences, so societies and nations are moulded by their past. The repercussions of events in one period don't just stop dead. They reverberate down through the years, the generations, the centuries even, influencing politics, culture and ideology far into the future. To even begin to understand Scottish politics today, our relationship with the United Kingdom, and our sometimes obsessive focus on matters of nationhood and identity, it is helpful to first try to make some kind of sense of our history.

All history, however, is controversial – even the recent, two-hours ago variety. Just tune into any Saturday evening radio phone-in during the football season and hear the airwaves crackle with conflict. No-one will dispute the final score, the number of corner kicks, the names of the players shown the red card. But move beyond the bare facts and you stray into stormy waters. Should that penalty have been disallowed? Did that foul deserve a red card? Was that first goal offside? Did the losers deserve a kicking, or was they robbed?

A House of Commons debate on the pros and cons of entering a world war is but a gentle disagreement compared to the Saturday night fever that rages throughout the football season. If a 90-minute game, played out that same day on a small patch of grass with 20,000 witnesses (not to mention officials and TV cameras) can fire such passionate debate, we can hardly expect polite consensus over heroics and horrors whose finer details are lost under the dust of centuries.

The historian EH Carr once compared history to angling. The facts are not laid out like dead fish on a supermarket counter, he explained; they are more akin to creatures swimming around in a vast and unfathomable ocean. What you discover very much depends upon which part of the ocean you dip into, and what you use as bait.

Invariably, even the most fair-minded historian will select and emphasise the importance of those historical facts which vindicate his or her own political standpoint. History is never fully objective, no matter how exalted the professor, or how many pages the appendix runs to.

In this book, we have tried to be absolutely scrupulous over the facts. We have checked, double-checked, triple-checked where necessary. We have relied heavily, especially in the earlier centuries, upon the research of professional academic historians. In later chapters we have also used newspapers, court transcripts and other first-hand records. The facts, we hope, are as accurate as it is possible to be.

But we do not stand aloft and aloof from the facts. We venture opinions and draw conclusions. We take sides. Some of our analysis directly challenges conventional history, and not just the version taught in universities or printed in scholarly tomes. It also presents a contrary view to some left-wing versions of Scottish history.

Scotland has always been a restless land, in conflict with itself as much as with anyone else. This book, volume one of a two part history, tries to chart and explain that conflict from a radical and working class standpoint all the way from 500AD to August 1914, when the world was turned upside down by the greatest cataclysm in history.

In the interests of disclosure, I should say that both authors intend to vote Yes. Both of us stand on the political left. Neither of us are members or supporters of the SNP.

We would, however, like to think this book will be read across the political spectrum, and has something to say to both sides in the referendum debate, and to those who have yet to make up their minds. Not because this referendum is about the past, but because the past helps us better understand the present and the future.

Alan McCombes, July 2014

1

BIRTH OF A MONGREL NATION

The misty millennium

The first ones are lost from the record. Their roots, their deeds, their language, all scratched from the face of history. We can say that the Picts were here, but the rest is fragments.

There are no surviving native historical texts or documents written before the second half of the eleventh century. Most were destroyed in Viking raids, and thus what little we have learnt of Scotland's first-known inhabitants has been gleaned mainly from archaeological remains and a few isolated texts.

From the remnants of the ancient Pictish language that still survive in place-name prefixes such as Aber (as in Aberdeen, Aberfoyle, Aberfeldy) and Pit (Pitlochry, Pittenweem, Pittodrie), we know that Pictish was a Celtic language, but of the Brythonic strand, making it more akin to Welsh and Cornish than to Scottish or Irish Gaelic.

Until recently, the Picts were imagined by historians as primitive warriors, famed chiefly for halting the Roman occupation of Britannia in its tracks at the Antonine Wall. Even their name – from the Latin word pictus, which means painted – conjures up a vision of terrifying, woad-dyed savages. But excavations between 1994 and 2008 of a sixth century Pictish monastery in the village of Portmahomack in Easter Ross uncovered unexpected evidence of a highly sophisticated culture, capable of producing magnificent art and extraordinary architecture.

The monastery itself was built on the principle of what would become known, centuries later, as the 'Divine Proportion': a ratio of dimensions – 1.618 to one – which appears in nature, including in seashells and in the faces of people considered beautiful. During the fourteenth century, the ratio was used to construct Notre Dame Cathedral in Paris and the Alhambra Palace in Spain. But the mysterious Picts had been there and done that, eight centuries earlier. According to Martin Carver, a professor of archaeology at York University, 'They were the most extraordinary artists. They could draw a wolf, a salmon, an eagle on a piece of stone with a single line and produce a beautiful naturalistic drawing. Nothing as good as this is found between Portmahomack and Rome. Even the Anglo-Saxons didn't do stone-carving as well as the Picts did. Not until the post-Renaissance were people able to get across the character of animals just like that.'

Another distinctive feature of Pictish society was its matrilineal system of succession – probably a common-sense arrangement if you believe in royal bloodlines, because legitimacy is never in contention.

But how and why Pictavia was transformed into Gaelic-speaking Alba – or Scotland, as it was renamed by the Anglo-Saxons – remains a mystery. We know that the Scoti Gaels, who gave the land its modern name, came across the narrow stretch of sea that separates Scotland from the north of Ireland, and built settlements across Argyll, Galloway and Strathclyde. In the fifth century, they formed their own kingdom, Dalriada, along the western seaboard, which for the next four centuries co-existed alongside the Pictish kingdom that comprised most of the landmass north of the Forth and Clyde, including what is now Central Scotland, Fife, Perthshire, Grampian, Easter Ross, Caithness, Sutherland and Orkney.

Sometime around the end of the ninth century, Pictavia turned into Alba. Were they ethnically cleansed? Most historians now reject that theory. There is no evidence, nor even folklore, pointing to great battles between the two ethnic groups. The fact that the Pictish royal line, the MacAlpine dynasty, simply changed the name of their land from the Kingdom of the Picts to the Kingdom of Alba suggests that this was a peaceful transition. We don't know exactly how it happened because there is no explicit account of the demise of the Picts. But we can speculate.

Emeritus Professor John Foster of the University of the West of Scotland has argued convincingly that the two peoples were first thrown together to protect themselves from Viking plunder and terror. Modern Scandinavians may have acquired a reputation for easy-going liberalism, but their Norse ancestors did not arrive across the North Sea as polite tourists speaking perfect English. At the height of Viking power, their feared longships wreaked terror across the Baltic, North Sea and English Channel. They even reached down into the Mediterranean and pillaged the shorelines of southern Europe, North Africa and Asia Minor. Their military might was based on advanced marine technology: with access to abundant quantities of timber and iron, the Vikings perfected the craft of shipbuilding in the fjords of Norway.

When they first took to the seas in pursuit of plunder, Scotland, just a few hundred miles from the west coast of Scandinavia, was a prime target. The northern Vikings could make the voyage within one day. And this was a brutal, slave-trading empire, which carried out human trafficking on a mammoth scale. In a single raid, they seized thousands of Scots in Dumbarton, and transported them in hundreds of longships to their pirate base in Dublin. The Vikings would also ship their human treasure to the slave markets of Constantinople to be traded for gold and silver. Modern DNA techniques suggest that many inhabitants of modern Iceland are probably descended from slaves captured in the Hebrides. Those who tried to resist were punished mercilessly: the children massacred, the women raped and the men castrated. Torture techniques included the grisly Blood Eagle, in which a live victim would have their heart and lungs torn from their chests, then spread out on the ground to resemble the wings of a giant bird of prey.

The Norsemen also began the ecological destruction of Scotland's landscape that would accelerate down through the centuries. In these pre-feudal times Scotland's greatest natural resource was the Great Forest of Caledon, vast woodlands of oak, pine, birch, alder, hazel, aspen, willow and rowan, teeming with wildlife and vegetation, which in turn provided an abundance of food, shelter and natural materials. From the Viking invasions onwards, that precious asset was relentlessly slashed and burned until it was finally stripped almost bare to make way for sheep farms and deer forests by the Georgian and Victorian landlords and capitalists.

The west coast was especially vulnerable. In contrast to the stark and open North Sea coast, the secluded inlets, islands and peninsulas of the Atlantic seaboard provided a multitude of hidden natural harbours. For three centuries, from the first raid on the holy island of Iona in 798 AD, these scattered coastal communities were terrorised. This in turn seems to have provoked a major population shift within Scotland, from west to east, as Gaelic refugees fled into the heartlands of Pictavia. Although their languages were different, they were both Celtic – and probably not mutually incomprehensible.

The two communities of Scotland had other things in common. They were peaceful farmers, combining livestock and crops. Their society was egalitarian, for the practical reason that this was a subsistence economy, with no great surplus produced that could be creamed off by a privileged class. Furthermore, the Celtic system of 'partible inheritance', in which land was divided equally between sons, then further sub-divided with each successive generation, prevented individuals from amassing great estates.

Both ethnic groups were also united by the distinct version of Christianity that had taken root in Scotland and Ireland from the sixth century. The term 'Celtic Church', used by some historians, is not strictly accurate. Christianity in Scotland and Ireland was, from the beginning, formally part of the Catholic Church. Yet from its spiritual HQ in Iona, it developed independently of Rome, at least until the mid-twelfth century when the church, as part of a wider advance of feudalism, became more centralised. Before then, instead of a hierarchy of archbishops and bishops, it was based on a looser network of monasteries and missionaries. It was more ascetic, with none of the ostentation of Rome. Its philosophy included sanctity of the clan and family, and opposition to slavery. It used ancient druid symbolism, as seen in Govan Old Parish Church today, which has a remarkable collection of Celtic crosses and hogback memorial tombstones, all carved between 800 and 1000 AD.

All of these elements – social, cultural, economic, religious – meant resistance to the invaders would not only unite Picts and Scots, but would also blossom into a socially progressive struggle to defend basic rights and liberties.

For a time, the Vikings did manage to annex big chunks of territory, including Caithness, Sutherland, the Hebrides and the Northern Isles. Gradually, over centuries, these areas were freed from Norse control. Many descendants of Viking settlers, however, remained in Scotland to become peaceful farmers and fishermen. They intermarried, converted to Christianity and embraced Gaelic culture. Within a few generations, all that was left in mainland Scotland of the Viking invasions were the strange-sounding place names, such as Staxigoe, Occumster, Skrithe, that pepper the maps and road signs of the far north-east to this day. But the biggest single legacy of the Norsemen was to force the native peoples together, laying the basis for the rise of a single, united Gaelic-speaking kingdom.

Creeping feudalism

From the beginning, Scotland was largely shaped by its own geography. At a time when overland travel was difficult and dangerous, this narrow kingdom was always easily accessible to outsiders. At its furthest point, it is just 45 miles from the sea, and comprises 10,000 miles of coastline, 790 islands, plus innumerable peninsulas, bays and natural harbours. To the west, the Irish Sea functioned as a broad highway connecting Scotland with Ireland, England, Wales, Cornwall, and kingdoms further afield, across the Bay of Biscay. To the east, a multitude of links were forged down the east coast of England, and to Scandinavia, the Baltic and the Low Countries.

By the start of the second millennium, Scotland was already a multicultural confederation, including Gaelic Celts in the north and west; Brythonic or Welsh-speaking Celts in the south-west; Anglo Saxon and Flemish settlers in the south-east; and the descendants of Norse settlers to the far north. In the twelfth century, there was an influx of Anglo-Norman knights and barons, including the Balliols, the Stuarts, the Bruces and the Comyns, who had been awarded land by the King of Scots, David I, in return for military service.

Historical records report that in 1138, at the Battle of the Standard, over disputed lands in Northumberland, the English were astonished at the diversity of the Scots armies. These included, according to the historian Michael Lynch, 'Normans, Germans, English, Northumbrians and Cumbrians, men of Teviotdale and Lothian, Galwegians [from Galloway] and Scots'. So how, why and when was this sundry ragbag of peoples moulded into a single nation?

As a general rule, nations do not ignite in the minds of visionary kings, priests or poets. And, unlike ships and babies, their entrance to the world can rarely be pinned down to a single date. They emerge slowly and uncertainly, into the dim and fitful light of history, either in response to internal social change, to external danger, or to both.

By the thirteenth century, Scotland was again under threat – this time from a force so cohesive, disciplined and efficient, it made the Vikings look like a chaotic rabble. The Normans, descendants of a band of Viking warriors who had established the world's first fully-fledged feudal state in the Seine Valley, had conquered England following the Battle of Hastings in 1066. This was an unprecedented and formidable military machine, and it proceeded to crush all resistance with clinical brutality.

From the English Channel to the River Tweed, the Normans atomised the older, looser Anglo-Saxon class structures, and imposed instead a rigid, hierarchical regime of total subjugation. Two hundred Norman barons grabbed half of all English land, turning the peasantry into their own personal property, while building a chain of mighty stone castles across the land to consolidate their supremacy. Within two decades, the entire English ruling class of church and state spoke French, the adopted language of the Normans.

This was the third full-scale foreign military occupation of England in a thousand years. The Romans, followed by the Anglo-Saxons, had already ravaged the old Celtic system and language, driving it out to the Western fringes of Wales and Cornwall. None of these invading forces had ever conquered the land that the Romans called Caledonia – more, perhaps, for geographical than military reasons. The result was that, other than in those pockets colonised by the Vikings, Celtic society had survived and flourished north of the Tweed for the best part of a millennium. But in the south the old ways were dying. Society was changing fast. Feudalism was ascendant.

The pre-feudal Celtic kings and chieftains never claimed personal ownership of the soil, which was always regarded as the common property of the clans who lived on it. Nor did clan chiefs inherit their position on the basis of primogeniture, where power was handed down from father to eldest son. Instead, in the tradition called Tanistry, the successor to the clan chieftain was elected at a general clan assembly from a group of male candidates deemed eligible by bloodline. The Tanist, who was both deputy and heir to the current chieftain, was elected on the basis of qualities such as bravery, intelligence, fairness and good judgment.

While the triumph of feudalism in England had involved a cataclysmic transformation, the advance of the new system into Scotland was a more subtle, gradual and piecemeal process, begun by an influx of immigrants. But these weren't poverty-stricken refugees fleeing famine and torture; they were wealthy young men embarking on the great scramble for Scotland. Many were the younger sons of feudal barons, disinherited because they happened to be born a bit later than their brothers. Deprived of landed estates in England, they headed north in a quest for land and power. Others were military professionals, Anglo-French and Flemish knights, who had first arrived in England after 1066 as part of a mass invasion of colonists. Thousands subsequently spread northwards into Scotland, where they used their wealth and military expertise to establish a foothold for feudalism.

To be fair, they were encouraged by the new Scottish elite that had begun to crystallise in the south and east of the country, where fertile farmlands and a reasonable climate ensured a burgeoning prosperity. In contrast to the subsistence economy across most of the Highlands and Islands, the Lowlands was now producing a surplus, allowing for the rise of a privileged class at the top, especially around the royal court.

When David I ascended the throne in 1124, with the support of his brother-in-law Henry I of England, he began to assume legal ownership of the land. This break with Celtic tradition was the first step on the road to feudalism. The process accelerated with the king using land to reward allies and buy off enemies. The Stuarts, for example, were originally the 'Stewards' – henchmen, in other words, who hired themselves out to the royal court in return for land. This emerging aristocracy didn't overthrow the old Celtic system so much as gradually erode it from within. The feudal nobility never openly conquered Scotland. They just wheeled and dealed, intimidated and ingratiated, plundered and murdered their way to power.

Nonetheless, when feudalism finally emerged dominant in Scotland, it was more diluted and restrained than its southern counterpart. It was also geographically restricted to the Borders and Lowlands. By the end of the twelfth century, there were over 200 motte-and-bailey castles glaring down at the peasantry south of the Great Glen. But to its north? Not one.

Even in the Lowlands, the new lords were constrained by deep-rooted Celtic traditions. Feudal Scotland, unlike feudal England, was considerably less inclined to throw its weight about on the international stage. As a general rule, smaller nations, especially those with larger, more powerful neighbours, tend to desist from imperial conquest. Thus, Scotland's medieval campaigns were either defensive in character, or confined to more localised battles in the disputed border territories of Northumberland and Cumbria. By contrast, England was knee-deep in relentless, expansionist wars against France, Spain, the Low Countries, Wales and Ireland. Then it began to look to the north.

Scotland's troubles with England began with the death of a little girl in 1290. Margaret, the Maid of Norway, had fallen ill after a stormy voyage across the North Sea to attend a coronation – her own. Under the rules of feudalism, she had inherited the throne after her grandfather, Alexander III, was killed in a riding accident in Fife leaving no male heirs. Her mother – Alexander's daughter – had married King Eric of Norway, and then died in childbirth. As the only living descendant of Alexander, the seven-year-old Margaret was next in line to the throne of Scotland.

Having to settle for a queen rather than a king was always a serious inconvenience to the feudal establishment of any country. Women were deemed barely fit to rule, but the men in grey suits of armour would sometimes temporarily tolerate a female monarch to ensure the continuity of the royal bloodline. A queen would be more figurehead than genuine monarch, performing ceremonial duties while the real business of government was carried out by big, serious men over her head. But when this child queen died in Orkney, the entire royal line – the House of Dunkeld – came to a full stop. Scotland became a kingdom without a monarch. Worse, there were 13 contenders, all male, and every last one of them claiming to have the right mixture of blood and genes. As the country slithered towards civil war, the bishops began to panic – so much so that they invited King Edward of England to adjudicate. It was the first step along the road to a long, bloody war that for most of the next 60 years would convulse the borderlands straddling the two kingdoms.

Hammer of the Scots

Prior to his accession to the English throne, Edward Plantagenet had distinguished himself during the Crusades for laying waste to the entire population of Nazareth. Soon afterwards, as Edward I, he deported the entire Jewish population of his kingdom. He also pioneered an early form of colonialism by invading Wales, dividing it into six counties, and imposing English laws and customs on this Celtic stronghold.

Under the strict feudal rules of primogeniture, it was unlikely that this classical Norman king would choose anyone other than John Balliol to take the throne of Scotland. The fact that Balliol was notoriously weak-willed wouldn't have harmed his chances either. For three years, King John was monarch in name only. Edward forced him to pay homage to the English throne, appointing himself the final legal arbitrator in any disputes that arose between the Scottish king and his subjects, and extorting large sums of money from the Scottish exchequer to pay for his relentless wars against France.

But then Edward overstepped the mark, by demanding that King John raise an army to join England's military campaign against France. Under pressure from his advisers – a panel of twelve 'Guardians' – Balliol found the courage to defy his overlord and signed a treaty with the French king, initiating what became known as the 'Auld Alliance'.

When Edward staged a series of cross-channel invasions, Scotland responded by sending a force over the border to attack the English garrison at Carlisle. It was both a gesture of solidarity with France and an attempt to reassert Scottish power while Edward's attention was focused on Europe. To the furious English king, this was unforgivable. Scotland would have to pay the price. He dispatched a 30,000-strong invasion force to Berwick, Scotland's main port, centre of its wool industry, and most vibrant and prosperous town. His vengeful army butchered its way through Berwick's narrow streets and wynds. More than half the population of 13,000 was slaughtered – 'falling like autumn leaves', according to one contemporary chronicle.

Edward's armies then advanced up the east coast, occupying town after town from Dunbar all the way to Aberdeen, Banff and Elgin. At Edinburgh Castle, they looted Scotland's holiest relics. And at Scone Palace, in Perthshire, Edward seized the Stone of Destiny, the ancient slab of red sandstone that symbolised Scottish sovereignty.

Balliol was dragged in person before Edward, where he abjectly confessed to an 'unlawful rebellion', blaming 'unwise counsel' from his advisers and his own dull-mindedness in accepting their advice. His tabard, inscribed with the royal arms of Scotland, was stripped theatrically from his body, and from then on, King John would be known as 'Toom Tabard', meaning empty coat – King Nobody, King of Nothing. With Balliol exiled to the continent, Scotland was again a kingdom without a monarch, and Edward looked invincible.

Five hundred years later, Robert Burns wrote 'Wha will be a traitor knave? Wha will fill a coward's grave? Wha sae base as be a slave?' The poet knew his history: faced with Edward's brutal display of power and bloodlust, the Scots' ruling elite – earls, knights, barons and bishops – chose to be traitors, cowards and slaves. In total, over 2,000 Scots signed their name to the Ragman Roll manuscript, pledging eternal homage and fealty to Edward. The sheer number of signatories extended way beyond the nobility, suggesting that many had been pressurised into adding their names by their feudal superiors.

A typical Ragman Roll signatory was the Borders racketeer Richard le Scott, who would pillage, bribe and slaughter his way across the south of Scotland, finally becoming one of the most feared warlords in the business. His legacy was lasting: le Scott's descendant, the Duke of Buccleuch, is the largest private landowner in Britain today, with 430 square miles of prime agricultural land, stretching from the Solway to the Forth.

In the looming Wars of Independence, the main concern of the Scottish nobility was to be on the winning side. Devoid of loyalty to anyone but themselves, their personal wealth and ambition was always paramount. Their prostration before Edward could have extinguished the emerging flame of national consciousness, and Scotland could have become simply another region of England, alongside Yorkshire or Northumberland. But there were pockets of resistance: the Bishop of Glasgow, Robert Wishart, refused to surrender, as did 22-year-old Robert Bruce, whose grandfather – also Robert Bruce – had been overlooked by Edward I for the crown of Scotland in favour of John Balliol. Isolated from the rest of their social class, however, these mutineers were petrified in their tracks.

The wealth and power of the feudal aristocracy on both sides of the border was built on violence. These were the medieval equivalents of today's gangland godfathers, who prey on the weak and mercilessly liquidate their rivals. Yet the national struggle to maintain the liberty of Scotland was more than just an extension of these personal power struggles. As King of England, Edward represented a more draconian, more oppressive and more commercial form of feudalism than had ever taken root in Scotland.

The Scottish rebellion would come, eventually, but its origins would be way down the social scale.

2

CRY FREEDOM

Enigmatic outlaw

Because he was an obscure commoner who died an outlaw, there is a dearth of documentation regarding the life of William Wallace, leaving the door wide open for the most romantic of interpretations. Like Jesus of Nazareth, Wallace's story would be worked and woven with artistry and passion by successive generations of writers, transforming this plain man of the people into a saviour in spun gold. Almost 300 years after his death, the poet Blind Harry would pen an epic, 11-volume rhyming narrative, which in turn would become the basis of innumerable biographies and the foundation stone of the 1996 Hollywood epic, *Braveheart*.

Blind Harry remains something of a mystery. We don't even know his surname. Furthermore, his vivid geographical descriptions suggest that Harry wasn't even very blind. Most serious historians reject his poem, *The Wallace*, as an admirably graphic and gripping work of historical fiction, based loosely on real events. According to Harry, Wallace was a seven-foot tall giant, who once killed a lion in France with his bare hands.

> 'He was very fair in his judgements... he was most compassionate in comforting the sad... he was very patient... he was a distinguished speaker... he hunted down falsehood and deceit and detested treachery.'

Modern historians have managed to piece together a more plausible account of Wallace's role in the defence of the Scottish kingdom. We cannot be definitive, but his name suggests he was either a native Strathclyde Brythonic Celt, or possibly of Welsh descent. His exact birthplace has never been established beyond reasonable doubt, but recent research points to Ayrshire – which means that all those commemoration marches and rallies through the town of Elderslie, in Renfrewshire, have been staged in the wrong location. Nor was Scotland's rebel hero the son of a landowner called Malcolm Wallace, as most historians previously believed. In fact, it seems his father was Alan Wallace, a crown tenant in Ayrshire, and thus a man of considerably more lowly status.

We do know for sure that in May 1297, while Scotland was under military occupation, Wallace and his accomplices attacked an English garrison in Lanark – which, as it happens, is much closer to Ayrshire than to Renfrewshire – and assassinated the English sheriff in charge of the burgh. According to Blind Harry, and *Braveheart*, this execution was an act of revenge for the murder of Wallace's wife or sweetheart by English soldiers. There is no evidence to either support or contradict this claim. Nevertheless, the incident was a turning point in the life of this previously unknown young man.

By this time, Southern Scotland was bridling angrily at English occupation, accompanied not only by punitive taxation to fund England's foreign wars, but also military conscription to provide the manpower to fight them. A network of sheriffs, lords, sergeants, tax collectors, rent collectors and customs officials was established to keep this once prosperous region under an iron thumb. It was proved a promising time for an outlaw with nothing to lose, and Wallace escalated his mutiny against English oppression into an all-out guerrilla war. With every successful raid and ambush, his small militia grew stronger.

Meanwhile, the Scots nobility had abandoned any notion of an independent Scottish kingdom. Some had gone into hiding; others had enlisted to fight France as officers in the English army; and some were even assisting Edward's occupation of Scotland. This was more than just a matter of cowardice on the part of the Scottish elite; land and wealth were at stake. Large swathes of the aristocracy, particularly in the far south, held properties on both sides of the border. Any hint of dissent and their estates in England would be forfeited. So they did the opposite of dissent.

The nobility were essentially medieval devolutionists: although they believed in a Scottish kingdom, they simultaneously acknowledged English supremacy. Perhaps Balliol, or a successor, could be restored to the throne of Scotland; but that would be a decision for Edward, the royal overlord of both kingdoms. Wallace, on the other hand, stood firm for full-blooded independence. His movement was drawn from the common people: agricultural labourers, poor peasants, craftsmen from the burghs, and dispossessed small landholders whose properties had been plundered by the Norman warlords.

They were poorly armed, with makeshift spears, axes and knives. They wore no helmets or armoured plating, only tunics of leather and cloth, and survived on a frugal diet of oatmeal and lentils. But they were fired with the zeal of a rebel army challenging oppression and injustice. In stark contrast to the hocus-pocus propagated by right wing groups in America, who treated the film *Braveheart* as a celebration of Celtic racial purity, Wallace's army included Irish, French, Flemish and English immigrants as well as Gaelic-speaking Highlanders and English-speaking Lowland Scots. What had started as a local revolt now began to develop into a national movement.

As Wallace's men marched towards Perth and Dundee, another army was being mustered in the far north by Andrew Murray, a nobleman's son who had broken ranks with his social class. After the sacking of Berwick, Murray had fought with his father against Edward's army at the Battle of Dunbar, where he was captured. He then escaped back to the Highlands, where his private army drove the English garrison out of Urquhart Castle, on the shores of Loch Ness. This seemingly unstoppable force then seized Inverness, before sweeping through Aberdeenshire towards Perth, where it is believed he met Wallace for the first time.

There, the two young men formed what they called 'the Army of the Kingdom of Scotland' and marched south, over the Ochil Hills, onto the Carse of Stirling and up onto Abbey Craig, where the Wallace Monument now stands, to do some serious battle. Far below, the formidable English army, its infantry bolstered by heavy cavalry and troops of archers, assembled on the south bank of the River Forth at Stirling Bridge.

The action began with a catastrophic blunder by the English commander, the Earl of Surrey, who ordered his cavalry to advance two abreast across the narrow bridge and onto the causeway that stretched for a mile over the flood plain. For hour after hour they proceeded to the north bank, while Wallace and Murray watched and waited from their elevated vantage point. Once the English frontline troops had separated themselves from the massed battalions on the other bank, the Scots swooped down. There was no place to run, no place to hide. The bridge was too narrow, either for retreat or to bring across reinforcements. And they were hemmed in on three sides by a loop in the river, where now stand the playing fields of Stirling County Rugby Club. The vanguard of the English army was annihilated, while the rearguard fled in disarray. In all, perhaps as many as 5,000 English cavalrymen and infantry were either cut down or drowned as they tried to escape back across the river.

Andrew Murray was gravely wounded in the battle, and several months later died of those wounds. But the events of that day, 11 September 1297, electrified Scotland. A raggle taggle horde of ill-equipped amateurs had routed the most fearsome military machine in Europe. Patriotism was back in fashion, and suddenly the nobility rediscovered the Scottish cause. William Wallace, a commoner whose name had been unknown outside of his own village just four months earlier, was appointed Guardian of Scotland– the *de facto* leader of the entire kingdom, in the absence of the exiled John Balliol.

Operating on the principle that the best form of defence is attack, Wallace pushed down over the border into Cumberland, Northumbria and Durham. Unlike Edward, Wallace had no colonialist ambitions. His aim was neither to rule England, nor even to annex its northern territories. This was simply a preemptive strike, a warning shot to the English to desist, or else.

If Blind Harry would later transform Wallace into something of a saintly superhero, contemporary English propaganda did quite the reverse – 'filthy swine, malignant savages, murderers', it said of this Scottish warrior and his trusty fighters. That said, medieval warfare was a brutal business, and it's highly likely that, having crossed the border, Wallace's army sought retribution for the persecution of Scotland. On a more strategic, less emotional level, Wallace's troops would certainly have been inclined to create a climate of terror and spread demoralisation across the north of England, in a Dark Ages version of the Dresden bombings or the nuclear obliteration of Hiroshima and Nagasaki.

But Edward, who would later have the words 'Malleus Scotorum'– Hammer of the Scots – engraved on his tomb, wasn't a man to run up the white flag. The white-haired warrior-king returned in person to Scotland the following year, along with a mighty phalanx of cavalry, knights, and archers, to meet a Scots army at Falkirk. It was a bloodbath. Most of the Scots nobility fled early from the Falkirk battlefield, including one of the strongest claimants to the throne of Scotland, John Comyn. His main rival, Robert the Bruce, wasn't even there.

Wallace himself survived the battle and managed to escape to the Trossachs. Reputedly angry at the cowardice of the nobility, he resigned his post as Guardian of Scotland and pledged himself again to the common people. Now a fugitive, he is reputed to have lived in forests and caves, from whence he launched his guerrilla hit-and-run campaigns against the English occupation. Fanciful biographies of Wallace suggest he was the archetypal noble savage, a Caledonian Hawkeye from *Last of the Mohicans*. But the real Wallace was rather more sophisticated. As Guardian of Scotland, he had tried to re-open trade links between Scotland and Germany. As a refugee, he travelled through Europe to Norway, Germany, Rome and France, seeking international allies in the struggle for Scottish sovereignty. On his return to Scotland, he no longer commanded an army, but a band of insurgents. And he was now being hunted down, not only by the English occupying forces, but by the Scottish ruling elite.

In a deal negotiated by John Comyn in 1304, the nobility had once again surrendered to Edward. For three months, a small garrison at Stirling Castle held out as an outpost of defiance, until it finally fell to siege engines supplied to Edward by the man who would later become an icon of Scottish national independence – Robert the Bruce.

Wallace's days were numbered, and on 5 August 1305, he was captured by a Scots nobleman, Sir John Menteith, the keeper of Dumbarton Castle and sheriff of the town. Paraded past jeering crowds in London, Wallace then faced a show trial in the grand surroundings of Westminster Hall. He was subsequently hanged, disembowelled, beheaded and tortured, the various parts of his body put on public display in town centres across Scotland as a warning to any future potential rebels. Some of the more starry-eyed versions of medieval Scottish history suggest that the martyrdom of Wallace was a turning-point, the catalyst that turned quiescence into rebellious, unstoppable fury, and brought on Bannockburn. More sober accounts mention no uprisings or protests of any kind. Far from provoking a backlash, the death of Wallace seems to have left Scotland demoralised and pacified.

Like the leaders of Vichy France, those who regarded themselves as Scotland's natural-born leaders were in league with the occupiers. Surprisingly, then, the next leader of the Scottish resistance would spring from the treacherous heart of this very same, self-serving elite.

From pariah to saviour

Robert Bruce was born in Turnberry Castle in Ayrshire, his father a wealthy nobleman of Norman origin and royal lineage, his mother from the old Celtic aristocracy in the Gaelic speaking south-west. The Bruce dynasty owned vast estates on both sides of the border, including land in what is now the London Borough of Haringey. In contrast to the incorruptible Wallace, Bruce was cynical, calculating and driven by a burning personal ambition rather than the searing pinpricks of injustice. In the early years of the Wars of Independence, he had performed a series of bewildering zig-zags between the oppressors and the rebels. When the tide of independence was surging high, he backed the rebels, but in 1302, with Wallace on the run, the future hero of Bannockburn made his peace with Edward and received a royal pardon. He was even appointed Sheriff of Lanark.

In 1304, he assisted the English king in the recapture of Stirling Castle, the last stand of the rebel army. Yet even with the fight in full fray, Bruce slipped away to hold clandestine discussions with church leaders in Cambuskenneth Abbey, just outside Stirling, where they agreed a secret pact to install Bruce as King of Scotland when the time was ripe – probably after the death of the ageing Edward.

Bruce was a brilliant strategist and a cunning tactician, and would eventually prove his mettle as a military commander *par excellence*. His defenders maintain that he ultimately succeeded where Wallace failed precisely because of this flexibility and pragmatism: he knew when to advance and when to retreat; his wheeling and dealing was necessary for his own survival; and his apparent treachery was a manoeuvre to buy time and live to fight another day. Whatever his motives, an incident one cold February day in 1306 forced him out of the shadowy world of double-dealing and into open revolt.

Bruce had arranged to meet John Comyn – his main rival for the future throne of Scotland – in a Dumfries churchyard. No-one knows what was on the agenda. Perhaps they intended to thrash out who would be Scotland's next leader? Maybe Bruce wanted to offer Comyn a consolation prize in return for his support? And maybe the Red Comyn, who was still loyal to the exiled John Balliol, refused to countenance such treachery? Whatever they said, they said it within the walls of Greyfriars Kirk while their bodyguards waited outside. Voices were raised and angry words exchanged until, in a sudden flash of anger, Bruce drew a blade and fatally stabbed Comyn. Even for these violent times, this was a shocking and sacrilegious murder. And by taking out his main rival, Bruce had also killed his own chances of persuading Edward to crown him king.

With Scotland's two most powerful figures now out of the picture – one in his grave, the other on the run – the astute Edward seized the chance to consolidate his power over the unruly north. In Westminster Hall, before hundreds of English nobles, he vowed to bring the killer to justice. But he never did. In the summer of the following year, the 68-year-old king died of dysentery at a military camp just south of the border, *en route* to Scotland. He was replaced by his son, Edward II.

Bruce may have turned the bravado dial right up to 11 by declaring himself king, but he was now a pariah within his own social class. The slaying of a rival to the throne was a rather clumsy breach of social etiquette, to say the least, especially as it had taken place on consecrated ground. The Scottish elite ditched him, and the English occupying forces went after his blood. Cornered thus, he was damned if he did and damned if he didn't – and so his all-out struggle for independence was launched. As the writer and historian John Prebble puts it, 'the liberty of Scotland was now the only cause that might preserve his own', and to further that cause, he turned to the same social forces that Wallace and Murray had mobilised a decade earlier: the common people.

Much of what we know of Bruce's campaign comes from the epic poem *The Bruce* by John Barbour, an eminent scholar who studied at Oxford and Paris before becoming an Archdeacon in Aberdeen. Written 60 years after Bannockburn, it is considered a more reliable account than Blind Harry's *Wallace*. Whatever motives and ambitions impelled Bruce into action, what is clear is that the struggle itself was much more than a war between two medieval kings.

The name of Robert the Bruce may be a byword for Scottish liberation, but his victory could never have been achieved had it not struck a deep and resonant chord with the people of Scotland. The Battle of Bannockburn was not simply declared one fine summer's day, like a duel or a wrestling match. For seven long years previously, guerrilla war had raged across Scotland, as members of the English occupying forces found themselves subject to ambush, raid and assassination. This, he found, was a much more successful ploy than the ruinous policy, as seen at Falkirk, of engaging the English military machine in direct battle. With thousands of men under his control, Bruce marched from the south-west to the north-east, capturing one key fortress after another whilst avoiding any head-on conflict. Other armies were raised by allies of Bruce in Galloway, the Borders and the north of Scotland. It was, as they say, all happening.

Nonetheless, a confrontation was inevitable, and when Bruce's army came face-to-face with the mightiest army in Europe on the banks of the Bannock

Burn, the result should have been a foregone conclusion. On one side, perhaps 10,000 footsoldiers armed with spears and broadswords; on the other, 30,000 crack troops, with chainmail, cavalry battalions and massed ranks of archers. One reason for the gross imbalance is offered by historian David Cornwell, an authority on Bannockburn, who states it was 'partly a product of the Scottish feudal system, which, where it existed, was less developed than its English equivalent. Scottish knights were far fewer in number than their English counterparts and generally were in possession of less wealth and fewer resources.'

Another reason was that Bruce had no state machine behind him, and no colossal war chest to fund his campaign. What he did have, however, was a risen people who had suffered decades of occupation and oppression. The Scots army was an irregular volunteer force drawn from the depths of society. It included, according to one account, 'all the men of Carrick, of Argyll and Kintyre, and of the isles, and a great host of men from the Lowlands'. Although heavily outnumbered, proportional to the Scottish population of perhaps half a million it was a mobilisation on the scale of the great demonstrations that marched through Glasgow and London in the run-up to the Iraq war.

Seven hundred years on, the date 1314 has become to Scotland as resonant as 1066 to England, or 1789 to France. The battlefield is not the most pristinely preserved historical site in Scotland, much of it lying submerged beneath a jumble of houses, schools, roads, and a disused railway line. Nonetheless, every year, on the last Saturday in June, a boisterous tartan-clad procession weaves its way through the backstreets of Stirling, flags flying and pipes skirling, before proceeding to a patch of land on the southern outskirts of the town, where the giant statue of King Robert stands triumphant.

Many modern Scots, even of a nationalist disposition, would prefer to leave the past behind. Prominent SNP politician Kenny MacAskill, for example, spoke out against the Bannockburn annual celebration in 2003, writing in *The Sunday Times* that 'it's time for Scotland to take a long, hard look at itself and move on from defining ourselves against past glories, illusionary or otherwise'. This is understandable. Hollywood movies, folk songs and even history books tend to sanitise the wars of long ago; Bannockburn was anything but a pretty sight. According to contemporary accounts, the scene was one of carnage. Where now stand quiet suburban streets, then lay thousands of bloody, mutilated corpses, rotting in the fierce midsummer sun. They had been stripped naked by hordes of scavengers, while carrion crows feasted on the carcasses of dead horses and the gory entrails of the remnants of the English army. Scotland would do well, in future, not to glorify bloodshed.

Bannockburn did not mark the end of the Wars of Independence; they had another nine years to run before peace was declared, for four years, before the second war erupted. But the battle was a turning point. After 1314, Bruce's army swelled in numbers and confidence. They appeared to be invincible, at one point driving Edward II's forces out of Edinburgh and chasing them deep into Yorkshire. They marched through the north of England as far south as Lancashire, using violence to force a peaceful recognition of Scotland's independent status.

The strategy proved successful, with a defeated Edward II ending his campaign to rule Scotland. It was pragmatic retreat. He still claimed sovereignty over Scotland, but the liberated kingdom now began a process of coalescence into a rudimentary nation-state, with its own social hierarchy, legal system, church, currency, and parliament.

Yet this was no isolationist outpost. Scotland had always been a maritime kingdom, but more now than ever before, its survival depended on forging links across the sea. Locked in a cold war with its larger, more powerful neighbour, Scotland reached outwards, to Scandinavia and the Low Countries, and south, beyond England, to France and mainland Europe. Independence was secured by internationalism.

The nature of the struggle that set Scotland on the road to freedom also created a new internal balance of forces within. In times of all-out war, ruling elites are always forced to rely on the lower classes, who in turn become more conscious of their own strength and power. This was demonstrated in dramatic fashion in the aftermath of the two world wars of the twentieth century, when mass radicalisation spread across Europe, shaking the old order to its foundations. On a more rudimentary scale, the same process affected Scotland after the Wars of Independence.

Scotland was born a rebel nation, resisting outside oppression. The common people, though scattered and disorganised, became a force to be reckoned with. Meanwhile the nobility, who had covered themselves with shame, found their position weakened. It was no coincidence that within 50 years of Bannockburn, Scotland became the first part of Europe to rid itself of serfdom. It took England a further hundred years to do likewise.

The progressive character of Scotland's national independence struggle was most eloquently expressed in the wording of the 1320 Declaration of Arbroath, agreed by the Scottish Parliament six years after Bannockburn. This document reflects, above all, a sense that the Scottish elite, including even Robert the Bruce himself, could not be fully trusted to defend Scotland's independence, given the slipperiness, selfishness and, at times, outright cowardice they had displayed over the preceding decades. Amidst the rambling medieval mysticism and the pious appeals to the Pope, one passage stands out, not only for its defiant assertion of national sovereignty, but also, almost half a millennium before the French Revolution, its renunciation of the divine right of kings:

> 'Yet if he [Bruce] should give up what he has begun, and agree to make us or our kingdom subject to the King of England or the English, we should exert ourselves at once to drive him out as our enemy and a subverter of his own rights and ours, and make some other man who was well able to defend us our King; for, as long as but a hundred of us remain alive, never will we on any conditions be brought under English rule. It is in truth not for glory, nor riches, nor honours that we are fighting, but for freedom – for that alone, which no honest man gives up but with life itself.'

3

THE CALVINIST REVOLUTION

Culture wars

The Cambridge historian Eric Hobsbawn once observed that trying to define a nation is like trying to define a cloud. Unlike fixed features of the landscape, such as mountains and valleys, nations are ephemeral – 'fuzzy, shifting, ambiguous'.

Europe, for example, has been shape-shifting for over a thousand years. Most of the continent was, for many hundreds of years, submerged under The Holy Roman Empire, which at its peak stretched from Tuscany to the Baltic Sea. Spain was divided into the kingdoms of Aragon and Castille until the late fifteenth century. The shape of modern France only began to emerge with the annexation of Brittany in the sixteenth century. And Germany, Italy and Belgium didn't even start taking shape as unitary political states until the nineteenth century.

By contrast, Scotland has endured as a remarkably stable geographical unit throughout the centuries. It has only one 60-mile stretch of land border, which to this day follows closely the line of Hadrian's Wall, built by the Roman Army to keep out the Pictish tribes of ancient Caledonia. Apart from the far-flung and sparsely populated Northern Isles, which were ruled from Norway until the fifteenth century, the physical shape of Scotland has remained unchanged, its territorial boundaries distinct and undisputed.

But nations and societies are not just tracts of land. They are shaped and reshaped from one generation to the next. Language and culture evolves. People come and go, and with each new wave of migration, the elusive ingredients that make a nation, at any given time, are lost and gained in equal measure. Technological and economic progress breaks down the power of tradition and challenges the established structures. As a result, every society, every nation, is forever in a state of flux.

Scotland's borders may have stabilised, but as with an old building whose interior has been repeatedly reconstructed and redecorated, the façade tells only part of the story.

Even in the four centuries between Bannockburn and the Act of Union, Scotland was transformed internally, with the old culture, language and religion swept out to the margins. The slow strangulation of the Gaelic language began centuries before the Act of Union, Culloden and the Highland Clearances. And it began, not with some English overlord with overweening ambitions, but with a homegrown Stuart monarch.

Unlike some other members of the dynasty, James IV – who inherited the throne in 1473 when he was just 15 – generally gets a good press from historians. Dubbed the Renaissance King, he encouraged a culture of learning and literacy, wrote poetry, practised dentistry, founded the Royal College of Surgeons, dabbled in alchemy, and was fluent in a number of European languages. He was also a notorious womaniser, with eight illegitimate children by four mistresses, and a lavish spendthrift who squandered fortunes on grandiose vanity projects, including a new royal palace at Holyrood, the opulent Great Halls in the castles of Stirling and Edinburgh, and a puffed-up navy whose flagship was the fearsome Great Michael, designed to carry 300 men and 27 cannons.

James also had visionary ambitions to turn Scotland into a single, unified feudal state, speaking one common language. And that common language was not going to be Gaelic, the common tongue of the common people.

At the time, over half the population, mainly in the poorer parts of the country, spoke Gaelic. The Celtic clans had played a decisive role in securing Scottish independence, notably at Bannockburn, and had been rewarded with land and power by Robert the Bruce.

Out in the islands and peninsulas of the western seaboard, the Lordship of the Isles had flourished after Scotland's independence was secured. This quasi-autonomous Gaelic state within a state, run by the mighty Clan MacDonald from its HQ in Finlaggan, on the island of Islay, was rooted in an older, tribal civilisation that pre-dated feudalism. Like the culture of modern gypsy travellers – but on a grand scale – its very existence was seen as a threat to so-called progress. From being the heart and soul of the Scottish nation, the Gàidhealtachd under James IV became gradually ostracised, its language sidelined in favour of the Scots tongue, its culture demonised. In the eyes of the prosperous feudal establishment, the Celtic inhabitants of the poor, wild and mountainous west and north were the riff-raff of Scotland, an outlaw underclass, a throwback to the dark past of the old world. The final *coup de grace* against the Gaels was delivered in 1493 when King James dismantled the Lordship of the Isles in favour of centralised feudal rule by the royal court in distant Edinburgh.

The rose against the thistle

James IV also signed what was supposed to be a permanent peace deal with England, symbolised by the 'Marriage of the Thistle and the Rose', when the 30-year-old King of Scots wed the 13-year-old Margaret Tudor, the daughter of King Henry VII of England. Today such an arrangement would be regarded as child abuse, but for the feudal ruling classes, marriage was nothing to do with love and romance, and everything to do with politics and power. How Margaret felt about it, no-one knows, but James and his new father-in-law certainly lived happily ever after – or at least, up until the death of the elderly English king.

For a brief moment there, England and Scotland had enjoyed an era of peaceful coexistence. One of the many problems with feudalism, however, was its volatility. When absolute power is concentrated in the hands of the crown, the fate of that society is dictated by the prejudices, temperament and judgement of a single, all-powerful monarch. Thus, when Henry VII died, the cards were, once again, thrown into the air.

His son, the flamboyant and grandiose Henry VIII, would become the most infamous of all the Tudor monarchs, best remembered as a bloated misogynist who broke with the Church of Rome in order to acquire a string of wives. By all accounts, he appears to have been a psychopathic egomaniac who built 55 palaces in honour of himself, while conducting a foreign policy that made the Hammer of Scots look like a religious missionary. Henry expanded the Royal Navy tenfold, invaded France, and took England to the brink of bankruptcy with his reckless warmongering. He also declared himself overlord of Scotland, turning the calendar back several centuries to the unlamented days of Edward I.

James IV responded to Henry's provocation by invading the disputed territory of Northumberland. It was a catastrophic blunder, opposed at the time by his young wife whose opinion was, naturally, ignored. At the Battle of Flodden, in 1513, James's army was routed and he was killed on the battlefield along with 10,000 other Scots, including hundreds of nobles and clan chieftains. Broken, humiliated and fearing an English invasion, Scotland built the Flodden Wall, parts of which stand to this day, along the southern edges of Edinburgh city centre.

The invasion did come, but not for almost 30 years. One of the most turbulent and bloody periods in Scottish history would be triggered by a birth and a death within a single week.

On 8 December 1542, a baby girl was born in Linlithgow Palace. Her father was King James V of Scotland; her uncle, Henry VIII of England. With the blood of two royal dynasties flowing through her veins, Mary Stuart was surely destined for a life of pampered opulence. But her gender, her religion and a series of personal calamities would curdle this early promise, rendering it an epic tragedy beyond the imagination of even the most hysterical historical hagiographer.

It all began when she was just six days old. That was the day her father died, leaving Mary as his sole surviving legitimate child, and heir to the throne of Scotland. Nine months later, the infant was crowned Queen of Scots.

In her 1987 play *Mary Queen of Scots Got her Head Chopped Off*, Liz Lochhead, a republican socialist from a Presbyterian background, paints an unexpectedly sympathetic portrait of the Catholic monarch. Perhaps more powerfully than any historical tome, the play illustrates the bigotry, ridicule and misogyny that would haunt Mary from her ill-starred infancy to her lonely execution, 44 years later. In one early scene, three Scots nobles squabble over whether the orphaned infant should be married off to a Hamilton, a Douglas or a Gordon, while a posse of European ambassadors compete to fix her up with their own royal offspring. Just days old, the infant queen had become a prize to be fought over by power-hungry elites from Iberia to Scandinavia.

Five hundred miles to the south, Henry VIII had his own plans for his grand-niece. In 1544, he decided that Mary Queen of Scots belonged to him, and that she would make an ideal bride for his baby son. This would effectively give Henry control of Scotland, enabling him to annex the northern kingdom as a colony of England. To make his proposition of marriage more persuasive, shall we say, he dispatched a Nazi-style invasion force, tens of thousands strong, across the border, with orders to exterminate all opposition. This expeditionary force ingratiated themselves by putting the great Borders' abbeys to the torch, as well as Holyrood Palace, before ransacking Edinburgh and Leith in an orgy of murder and rape. His generals also set about nurturing collaborators.

With Scotland on its knees, and the corpses of the commoners piling high, 400 nobles switched sides, demonstrating once again their unwavering loyalty, not to their country, nor to the people whose lives they controlled, but to their own wealth and possessions.

Knox and the Queen of Scandal

For the next five years, Mary was smuggled around Scotland, from draughty castle to shivering stately home, in a bid to prevent her abduction by Henry's forces. She was then spirited away to France where, aged just 15 years, she became the bride of the French Dauphin, the heir to the French throne.

Accounts suggest she was a gifted child, fluent in six languages, a talented writer of prose and poetry, and an accomplished horsewoman. Her husband, Francis, was even younger than Mary, and ascended the throne of France aged 15. Tragically for Mary, he died 18 months later. The teenage widow was childless, so her services were no longer required. She was cast out of the French royal family and forced to return to Scotland, a place she hardly knew, and was even less certain of her place in.

By her mid-20s, Mary had been twice widowed, thrice married, and had witnessed the slaying of her young, Italian, male private secretary at the hands of her violent, power-hungry second husband, Lord Darnley. Shortly afterwards, he too was dead, his strangled corpse found lying beside the smoking ruins of his house, which had been blown up with gunpowder. Three months later, Mary married the man accused of this murder, the Earl of Bothwell, who had divorced his wife 12 days earlier.

Mary was doubly unfortunate. First, she was a woman. Second, she was a Roman Catholic. And in sixteenth century Scotland, neither of these things was an asset. Women, as we know, were considered wholly inadequate as monarchs, and the Catholic Church in Scotland had, by the mid-sixteenth century, lost all moral authority and become instead a hated symbol of tyranny, corruption and vice.

Since the reign of Mary's grandfather, James IV, the church hierarchy had become more and more enmeshed with the monarchy and the feudal system. The first qualification for any position of power or influence in the church hierarchy was total subservience to the reigning monarch. James himself had appointed his illegitimate 11-year-old son to the lofty position of Archbishop of Saint Andrews, presumably not on the basis of his deep theological wisdom. And just to rub it in, he appointed his other four illegitimate sons to key positions as abbots and priors, effectively putting them in charge of some of Scotland's greatest abbeys.

By the time Mary arrived back in Scotland, the bishops of the church had roughly the same popularity ratings as the directors of the Royal Bank of

Scotland would achieve five and a half centuries later in the depths of the financial meltdown. From top to bottom, the institution was riven with corruption and greed. Across the land, the clergy imposed punitive tithes – or 'tenths' – on their impoverished congregations to maintain themselves in ostentatious luxury. 10 per cent of all farm animals, food and other products, and the same cut of all profits from trade, had to be handed over to the church. Bereaved families were forced to pay 'mortuary dues' and 'corpse presents' – which meant handing over the most expensive possession of the dead person to the church. Then there were Easter Pennies, Sunday Pennies, baptism fees, marriage fees and a host of other taxes, none of which were ever used to provide public services. They were not even used to maintain church buildings; indeed, by Mary's time, negligence had reduced to ruins many of the once-magnificent cathedrals, churches and abbeys.

Debauchery was also rampant among the clergy. In the years 1548 to 1556, it was recorded that 40 per cent of all illegitimate births were the offspring of priests, despite the fact they only accounted for four per cent of the population. One Jesuit scholar of the time was moved to denounce these pious and supposedly celibate pillars of Christianity as 'extremely licentious and scandalous'. The carpenter of Nazareth, if the stories of his life are anything to go by, drove the moneylenders from the temple and stood up for the poor against the henchmen of the mighty Roman Empire. Scroll some 1,600 years onwards, and the Christian church, in Europe certainly, appears to have switched sides and taken up with the tyrants.

The exception was Ireland. There the bishops, subservient to their English colonial masters, had defected almost en masse to the Church of England during the reign of Henry VIII. The grassroots clergy and their congregations, however, stayed with the old church. As a result, the Catholic Church in Ireland became a rebel religion, on the side of the people against their Anglo-Irish oppressors, which is why it remained popular for centuries thenceforward. By contrast, Scottish Catholicism was hopelessly compromised by its association with corrupt elements of the aristocracy.

Although led by scholarly academics and radical clergy, the Reformation was driven as much by politics and economics as by theology. The Catholic Church was part of the feudal establishment, which stood in the way of scientific and social progress. Half of Europe had already broken with the

Church of Rome as the reformist theology of the radical priest Martin Luther swept all before it in Scandinavia, the Low Countries and across swathes of what is now Germany.

The merchants and seafarers of Scotland's burghs and ports had for centuries traded across the North Sea, and were thus wide open to new influences from Northern Europe. They were also increasingly hostile to their own church hierarchy, which they viewed as a parasitical caste siphoning off 10 per cent of their profits. It was no accident that the burghs were the first strongholds of the Reformation. But it was only when the movement spread into the farms, hamlets and villages of rural Scotland, where the broad mass of the population lived, that the old order began to crumble.

The small lairds and farmers simmered with resentment at those they regarded as producers of nothing but consumers of everything. The high tide of their indignation was well-nigh unstoppable. Eventually, even a significant proportion of the nobility joined the Protestant cause – not least because of the potentially lucrative spoils to be had through the confiscation of the church's vast landed estates.

In contrast to England, where Protestantism had been orchestrated from above by Henry VIII, the Scottish Reformation was a ground-up revolution that combined fanatical Calvinism with social radicalism. Like the political revolutions of Russia and China in the twentieth century, this sixteenth century religious transformation combined progressive ideals with tyrannical reaction. The founding manifesto of the Scottish Reformation was the *First Book of Discipline*, whose slightly menacing title conveyed just a hint of the fanaticism to come. It was a brutal backlash against the hedonism and decadence of the old church; 'Fornication', 'Drunkenness', 'Ostentation', 'Swearing' and 'Brawling' were all banned. The author, the fierce and bearded John Knox, whose life-size statue continues to grimace at the populace from its perch just inside St Giles Cathedral on Edinburgh's Royal Mile, was the symbol and chief evangelist of this great turbulence. He would sooner have supped with the Devil than make any compromise with his Papish enemies.

He was a Calvinist to the marrow of his bones, unyielding in his support for the ideas of the French theologian who made the modern Taliban look positively free and easy. Under John Calvin's spiritual leadership, the city-state of Geneva had introduced the death penalty for blasphemy, heresy, adultery and witchcraft.

Dancing was banned, theatres demolished, and even the colour of people's clothing was rigidly regulated. John Knox would gladly have turned the whole of Scotland into the Geneva of the north, but despite mass support for sweeping change, there was less appetite in Scotland for wholesale violent oppression.

Rampaging mobs, often whipped up by the demagogy of Knox and other preachers, could be relied upon to attack Catholic churches, vandalising and desecrating altars, statues and other religious icons. But there were no religious massacres in Scotland as there had been in England and Europe. The language of Scottish Protestantism was ferocious and the dogma rigid, but the early days of the Reformation were not marked by bloodshed. While the majority of Lowland Scots went with the new religion, the monarch, Mary Queen of Scots, along with sections of the nobility, clung to the old, using their power and wealth to protect the Catholic clergy. Consequently, the Scottish Reformation was constrained to a vitriolic war of words. The new religious regime was grey and authoritarian, but sinners were punished with public humiliation, excommunication and isolation, not execution.

That is, except for one group of people, who would become the victims of the most shameful, vindictive and senseless series of atrocities in the history of the nation. These were no threat to the state, being mainly poor and powerless, and they would become to Calvinist Scotland what the Jews became to Nazi Germany.

Burning times

In all recorded Scottish history prior to the Reformation, a bare handful of people had ever been executed for sorcery. But after the triumph of Protestantism, the Witchcraft Act of 1563 opened the door to charges of 'Sorcery, Witchcraft and Incantation', which flew out at the weak, the maimed, the dissenting, like a hailstorm of poisoned darts.

In the hundred years leading up to the eighteenth century, thousands of innocent people were burned at the stake for the imaginary crime of witchcraft. This was mob hysteria on a grand scale, driven by both misogyny and class prejudice, and directed against those at the margins of society. Some men became victims, including travelling pipers whose strange, haunting music was offensive to sombre Calvinistic decorum. But the vast majority were women, targeted for all manner of specious reasons. Some were healers and herbalists.

A fair few probably suffered from mental health problems or alcoholism. Others were singled out by spiteful neighbours or jealous, vindictive husbands. Many more were rounded up as part of a suspected coven, often after being named under torture by a friend or neighbour interrogated for witchcraft.

King James VI of Scotland (who would later also become King James I of England) was obsessed with witchcraft, and even wrote a book on the subject. The *Daemonologie* justified the persecution of 'these detestable slaves of the Devil, the Witches or enchaunters'. In one notorious episode in 1590, the king was returning home across the North Sea with his new 14-year-old bride when his fleet was caught up in a storm at the mouth of the Firth of Forth. One ship, carrying wedding gifts for the new queen, was sunk. In his fevered imagination, inflamed by his sycophantic advisers, the King convinced himself he had been the victim of a satanic conspiracy.

A year later, a local dignitary in the town of Tranent, near the East Coast, accused his servant of witchcraft. After being sadistically tortured, the young woman, Gelie Duncan, confessed to having been part of a group of over 200 witches who had gathered on the seafront at North Berwick on Hallowe'en, 1590. There, the Devil had preached a sermon while the witches danced, sang and put a spell on the doomed ship.

The North Berwick Witchcraft Trials raged for two long years and, in the end, scores of people are believed to have been executed, including the ringleader, Agnes Sampson, who was strangled and burned at the stake.

Medieval Catholic Scotland had been a cauldron of superstition. Belief in ghosts and fairies, saints and devils, witches and warlocks, was woven into the fabric of Celtic culture. But those suspected of sorcery, Satanism and witchcraft were rarely persecuted. Instead, they were feared and placated with bowls of oatmeal and milk – a tradition that continued in Celtic Scotland long after the Reformation. In the Highlands and Islands, even at the height of the hysteria which held the rest of Scotland (and parts of both Protestant and Catholic Europe) in thrall, witch-trials and executions were almost unheard of. But under the new religious regime that held sway across Lowland Scotland, bribing a witch was tantamount to collusion with an agent of Satan. They were now to be liquidated rather than tolerated. It is estimated by historians that in the course of a century, up to 5,000 suspected witches were executed – five times more per head of population than in England.

Although the Church of Scotland and the Church of England were part of the same Protestant family, theologically they were oceans apart. Anglicanism preached the doctrine of what it called 'mediocrity' – a moderate halfway house between what it viewed as the extremism of Catholicism, on the one hand, and of Calvinism, on the other. Scottish Protestantism was a fire and brimstone religion, uncompromising and at times brutal. Its sectarianism, misogyny, intolerance and cultural repression would sear the Scottish psyche for centuries to come.

4

UNDER ONE KING

The invention of Britain

In October 2002, Jack McConnell, the Labour First Minister of Scotland, announced a year-long programme of celebrations to commemorate the 400th anniversary of the Union of the Crowns in 1603. This had been, he declared, a momentous turning point in history, leading, he added gushingly, 'to the best known Royal Family in the world'.

In the event, the celebrations were a damp squib. Forget carnivals, concerts and flag-waving cacophony; this royal knees-up boiled down to a posh meal for several hundred hand-picked dignitaries at the Royal Museum in Edinburgh, and a specially-commissioned fanfare – *The Union of the Crowns* – for the Edinburgh Military Tattoo. In short, an affair that pretty much passed under the radar of pretty much most of the people.

Yet the event it commemorated was far from a harmless piece of ceremonial trivia. First of all, it dragged Scotland into the frontline of England's centuries-long war of conquest against Ireland, leaving a legacy of hatred and conflict, the scars of which disfigure both Scotland and Ireland to this day. Second, it plunged the country into decades of internal cultural strife, creating bitter enmity between the Highlands and Lowlands, which would almost fatally erode the rich, vibrant culture of the Gàidhealtachd. Third, it drove Scotland to the brink of economic ruin. And fourth, it reduced the country to the status of stateless nation whose destiny would be shaped for centuries to come by a bigger, more powerful, more aggressive neighbour. And all this despite Scotland retaining its own parliament, before the Treaty of Union, a century later, would force Scotland's hand in binding marriage.

The affair began with the death of the childless Queen Elizabeth, ruler of England for 45 years. English monarchs had wreaked destruction in pursuit of the Scottish throne for centuries but, in a quirk of a history, it would be under a Scottish king that unity – of sorts – would finally be attained. And without the traditional, late-medieval pile of dead bodies either.

James Stuart, son of Mary Queen of Scots, was the last king of Scotland – and the first of 'the United Kingdom of Scotland and England'. He acceded to the Scottish throne at the tender age of 18 months, following his mother's forced abdication, and was subsequently brought up to despise the woman that Scottish high society now vilified as a wicked harlot, a scheming fanatic and an enemy of progress.

To promote the narrative of a clean new broom sweeping out the evils of the old, this high society had to turn a blind eye to the idiosyncrasies of James's character. On the plus side, as far as his supporters were concerned, he appeared learned, and was not his mother. Less positive, however, was his gluttony and his taste for paedophilia, in which he indulged frequently with a procession of young boys. Despite his sophistication and education, he was said to be exceedingly vulgar and uncouth of speech. And he had a crazed obsession with what he called 'these detestable slaves of the Devil, the Witches or enchaunters'. This almost hysterical hatred towards women may have been born of the rage and dislike instilled in him from infancy towards his absent mother. His singular views were not confined to witchery, however.

His follow-up to the infamous *Daemonologie* was a book called *The True Law of Free Monarchies*, published in 1598, in which he expounded his belief in the divine right of kings. In this work, he boldly asserts that kings are higher human beings than all other men and, no matter their villainy or tyranny, must not be removed by anyone other than God. 'Kings are justly called gods for they exercise a manner or resemblance of divine power upon earth', he explained. This theological justification flew in the face of the Declaration of Arbroath, suggesting that the intervening three centuries of culture and progress were entirely lost on the young king.

It was an assertion that set him at odds with his own national church, then moving in quite the opposite direction. The seeds of democracy and egalitarianism were beginning to germinate within the Church of Scotland. It had recently adopted Presbyterianism, a form of church government where key decisions are taken by representative assemblies of the membership, rather than handed down from on high. It held hierarchies in disdain, despised pomp and insisted that the General Assembly – rather than the king – was the ultimate religious authority.

James was Protestant to the core. He hated Gaelic and the old religion that his mother had defended with her dying breath. But he also feared Presbyterianism. His grandiose sense of destiny was more suited to Anglicanism, an altogether more pliant faith, more attuned to the people in power than the power of the people. Moreover, James had ambitions beyond his own land.

As Queen Elizabeth grew old, and with no prospect of children, it could hardly have escaped his attention that he was next in line to the throne of England. Despite the preceding centuries of cross-border turmoil, James VI's accession to the throne of England went ahead quietly and peacefully. Unperturbed by the lack of cheering mobs, James toyed with the idea of styling himself Emperor, but ultimately settled for the slightly less exalted 'King of Great Britain' – though no such state actually existed, as yet.

Scotland and England were very much nations apart. North of the border – despite the Reformation, whose language was Scots – half the population still spoke Gaelic. The legal systems of the two countries were, if anything, becoming even more at variance as English common law warped into an increasingly rigid and conservative system. The two parliaments were distinct, for now, but James had every intention of wreaking change.

He was a pioneering British nationalist before such a political entity existed. From the starting gun of 1603 onwards, a torrent of propaganda poured forth from the royal court, in the form of poems, essays and documents, advocating union not just of the crowns, but of the parliaments too. From the outset, the idea of a united Britain was a monarchist project, driven by the king and his close disciples. His vision was not an equal union, but a greater England, with Scotland relegated to the status of northern annex.

Although he was born and raised in Scotland, James was contemptuous of his homeland, a nation he was convinced was divided between religious fanatics in the south and primitive savages in the north. It was a feature shared by the Georgian-born dictator of the Soviet Union, Josef Stalin, who grew to despise the small nationalities imprisoned within a master-state that became, under his rule, a Russian tyranny.

Though the Union of the Crowns failed to create a unified state, it profoundly altered the nature of the relationship between the two countries. The Scots Parliament retained control of domestic affairs, but for the rest of the seventeenth century, foreign policy was to be dictated by the monarch.

With his northern flank now secured, James turned outwards to take the first tentative steps towards building what would eventually become a global empire. He had developed a taste for colonial adventure before he even ascended the throne of England. In 1597, at his behest, the Scottish Parliament passed an act to encourage 'civility' in the Hebrides and remote parts of the mainland Highlands. The people of the Isle of Lewis, in particular, were pronounced 'devoid of any knowledge of God or his religion' and behaved with 'barbarity and inhumanity'.

The solution was not to open a string of genteel Sunday schools specialising in the teaching of polite manners, but to dispatch gangs of Lowland settlers to 'develop [the area's] extraordinary rich resources for the public good and the king's profit'. An acute observer may already surmise from these words that James's interest in Lewis had more to do with extracting riches than discouraging rude behaviour. The island in the far north-west was blessed and cursed with an abundance of natural resources. Its surrounding seas teemed with fish, and its interior was covered with rich peat bogs – the seventeenth century equivalent of Middle Eastern oil wells.

Meanwhile the far south of Scotland, from Galloway to the eastern Borders, was bursting at the seams, and plagued with starvation and violent disorder. In 1598, the first shipload of southern settlers disembarked at Stornoway with instructions to 'ruit out the barabarous inhabitants' – an invite, for all intents and purposes, to genocide. This was supposed to mark the start of the taming of the Highlands and Islands, but the scheme soon unravelled as the plantation ran into intense and righteous resistance. The homes of the colonisers were razed to the ground, their livestock killed, and their boats hijacked. When a garrison then sent to protect them was slaughtered, James abandoned his prototype colonial adventure.

Later, however, after the Union of the Crowns, with the power and resources of both England and Scotland at his disposal, his colonial ambitions were rekindled, and the first foundations were laid for what would become the biggest and bloodiest empire the world had ever known. It all began next door, in Ireland.

Celtic colony

It's a strange thing, if you're not from Glasgow.

Celtic fans, decked out in emerald green, wave the Irish tricolour, while Rangers, wearing royal blue, wave the Union Flag and the Red Hand of Ulster. Not only that, but the songs they sing in the stands – or did sing, until they were banned recently by the Scottish Government – hark back to battles of long ago. In Ireland. Which is not in Glasgow.

And just to even things up, many young men can be seen on the streets of Belfast wearing green and white hooped jerseys, or royal blue tops, in homage to Glasgow Celtic and Glasgow Rangers Football Clubs.

The links between Scotland and Ireland predate all written history. In later chapters we explore the more recent connections in more detail. But to begin to understand how the troubles of our Gaelic neighbour entered the DNA of the urban West of Scotland, you need look no further than James VI, the man who would be king, not only of Scotland and England, but of Ireland too.

The conquest of the north east of Ireland, the fertile lands of Antrim and beyond, was orchestrated by King James, and implemented on the ground mainly by his own Scottish people. To this day, Protestant communities in Northern Ireland fly the Saltire alongside the Union flags in the run-up to the annual Orange Order parade on 12 July. Their names are Scottish and their dialect they call Ulster-Scots. Yet contrary to popular mythology, Ulster was never a Scottish colony, nor even, for that matter, a British colony.

As early as the twelfth century, the English Crown had harboured ambitions to conquer and control the Celtic land across the sea. In 1541, Henry VIII went so far as to proclaim himself the King of Ireland, even though his rule was restricted to the Pale, a 60-mile stretch of the east coast running from Dublin to Dundalk. From this narrow ribbon of conquered land came the expression 'beyond the pale' – a reference to the rebellious Irish further west, who could not be subdued.

For the rest of the sixteenth century, England strived to take control of the whole island. It cleared the native population and established plantations in a range of locations, including Wicklow, Offaly, Laois, Cork, Kerry, Limerick and Tipperary. Among the colonists were the poet Edmund Spenser, author of *The Faerie Queene*, and Walter Raleigh, who was awarded 100 square miles of prime land by the Crown for his part in driving the native Irish from their land.

In the decade running up to the Union of the Crowns, England waged the Nine Years' War in a sustained attempt to break out of the Pale and conquer the whole island. The resistance – almost 20,000 strong – was led by the rebel Ulster earls, Red Hugh O'Donnell of Tyrconnell and Hugh O'Neill of Tyrone. The only Scots involved were the so-called Redshanks – mercenaries from the Hebrides and West Highlands who fought in kilts on the side of their Gaelic kinsmen, against the English occupation forces.

The rebellion was finally defeated at the Battle of Kinsale, in 1601. The ancient legal system of Ireland – Brchon Law, based on principles of morality and the will of the people, rather than coercion, and which emphasised justice, fairness and equality – was ripped up and replaced by the English feudal legal system. The final surrender, by Hugh O'Neill, the Earl of Tyrone, was signed on 31 March 1603, just four days after the death of Queen Elizabeth, and five days before King James left Scotland for London.

Politically, Ireland was reduced to a region of England, while economically it was a colony, its resources plundered by the English ruling classes. The Scots were there literally to make up the numbers. James, whose focus had by now shifted to England, conceived the plan to create a dense plantation in the north of Ireland, with Scots as the bridgehead.

By this time, there was no appetite in England to settle in Ireland, a hostile land peopled by natives speaking a barbaric tongue. Scotland, on the other hand, had no history of warfare with Ireland. There was, if anything, a strong cultural affinity between the two countries. For centuries, indeed, there had been waves of migration back and forth across the short stretch of the Irish Sea which divides the two territories. Though southern and eastern Scotland had lost touch with their Celtic origins, half the population of Scotland was still Gaelic-speaking, including large concentrations in some of the regions closest to Ireland.

It was a case, thought James, of pushing at an open door. A mass plantation in Ulster would rid Scotland of its hordes of dissidents and troublemakers. And there were plenty of them, including hardline Presbyterians hostile to the Church of England; dispossessed Gaelic clansmen, such as the MacDonalds of Kintyre, who had lost their land to the Campbells; and the lawless reivers who terrorised both sides of the England-Scotland border. The plantation of Ulster involved exploiting the poverty of one people, the Lowland Scots, order to crush another people, the native Irish.

The exodus began around 1609. In the course of a century, over 200,000 Scots arrived in northern Ireland. Before they were eligible to purchase land, they were required to take an oath of allegiance to the British crown, making them, legally, English subjects in Ireland, irrespective of their nationality.

The Irish did rise, notably in 1641, when they drove the settlers out of a number of areas. They, in turn, were driven back by an army composed mainly of Scots. Generations of conflict between the native Irish and the settlers from across the North Channel would breed the myth that Ulster was Scotland's colony. In fact, from the beginning, the whole show was run from England and financed by a consortium of a dozen London companies who built a chain of towns across the province, including Enniskillen, Omagh and Londonderry, originally a village called Derry. Their motive was greed: Ulster was rich in natural resources, including extensive native woodland (which would be reduced by 90 per cent over the next 200 years), lush agricultural land, and rich fishing in its plentiful rivers and loughs.

For the crown, there was a further dimension. Ireland had long been feared as a potential back door into England, through which powerful enemies such as France and Spain might one day stage an invasion. The Scots in Ulster were the pawns who could be sacrificed in the interests of more important pieces on the grand chess board of European imperial rivalry.

Without the Union of the Crowns, Irish history would have been different. And so too would Scottish history. We are where we are because of the ambitions of James VI, funded by English gold, whose legacy today is the contorted border that looks like a drunken scribble on a piece of paper, the thousands of gravestones of those killed during the late twentieth century Troubles, and in the anthems of war that echo back and forth from Belfast Lough to the River Clyde.

5

FIRE AND SWORD

Countdown to civil war

James VI died in 1625. The absentee monarch had once boasted to the English Parliament of his ability to rule Scotland by remote control: 'Here I sit and govern it with my pen; I write and it is done; and by a Clerk of the Council I govern Scotland now, which others could not do by the sword.'

Somehow, he muddled through. Which is more than can be said for his son and successor, Charles I.

James had contrived to tiptoe through the minefields of politics and religion, without tripping any violent explosions. Charles floundered across the same hazardous terrain like a myopic drunk; he was, to be sure, a walking, talking billboard for the absurdity of the principle of hereditary rule. If he had reigned during a period of general peace and prosperity, he might have survived; but this was an era of blood and thunder.

During his 18-year rule, the three kingdoms of Scotland, England and Ireland – Wales, at this time, was regarded as an adjunct of England – was to be sucked into a maelstrom of murderous destruction. Like the Poll Tax 350 years later, the trouble kicked off in Scotland before spreading south of the border – and with even further-reaching consequences. Margaret Thatcher was only removed from power in an internal Tory Party coup; Charles I lost his head, literally.

King Charles' first mistake – of many – was a piece of legislation called the Act of Revocation. He was keen to continue the imperialist expansion begun by his late father, but the costs of going to war had soared, as bows and arrows were replaced by muskets and cannons. On top of which, he was simply living beyond his means. Thus, he found himself facing a cash short-fall, in the region of £1 million, the equivalent of almost £32 billion in today's money.*

---

* There are different ways to measure the relative value of money over time; when dealing with state expenditure we use 'economic power', which is wealth relative to the total output of the economy. We use a different method, based on purchasing power, when dealing with everyday consumer items.

He looked to Scotland, casting an avaricious eye over the lands and properties that had been expropriated by the nobility from the Catholic Church during the Reformation, almost a century earlier. Charles now decided it would do nicely in the hands of the crown. You could call it a pioneering bit of land nationalisation, but for the benefit of the monarch rather than the people. The modern equivalent might be the Westminster government renationalising without compensation all the industries privatised since the 1980s, not to pay for welfare or public services, but to fund the Tory Party.

From the standpoint of accountancy it all looked good on paper. But it was a political disaster. Scotland's feudal landowners, who should have been the king's most loyal allies in the north, were incandescent at this threat to their wealth. In their eyes, Charles was a land-grabbing tyrant, the Robert Mugabe of his day. A prolonged power struggle broke out between the English crown and the Scottish nobility. For the great mass of people, the conflict might have remained a squabble at the top, of no consequence to their everyday lives, the equivalent of a turf war between the Triads and the Mafia. But like his father before him, Charles truly believed he had been placed on this earth by God himself, to direct the lives of the little people. He had inherited all James VI's sense of destiny, but none of his flexibility or tactical nous.

Nor had he any feel for Scotland. Although born in Dunfermline Palace, Charles had been taken south at the age of two, when his father assumed the English throne. Not for another 30 years did he foot in the land of his birth, and only for a symbolic Scottish coronation, eight years after he had already assumed the throne of Scotland and England. This belated ceremony in St Giles Cathedral was a provocative tour de force of arrogance and pomposity. Conducted according to Anglican rites, complete with choirs, music, candles and crucifix, the event could hardly have been more calculated to ignite the outrage of Scotland's Calvinist national church. The Lowlands erupted in fury, with kirk ministers and congregations joining the embittered nobility in what was fast becoming a mass movement against the king.

Yet Charles, suffering from a severe case of self-regard, blundered on regardless, alienating Scotland every time he opened his mouth. His imposition of the Anglican Prayer Book on Presbyterian Scotland was the spark that lit the blue touch paper. Pamphlets circulated, protests flared, and in some areas, riots exploded onto the streets. This fuming discontent crystallised in the National Covenant, a kind of cross between a manifesto and a mass public petition. Its launch in Edinburgh's Greyfriars Church, in February 1638, was what people might now describe as a defining moment, a historical turning point that would trigger the countdown to civil war.

Which side are you on?

A number of modern Scottish nationalists and republicans sympathise retrospectively with the Covenanters. After all, this was a mass movement of Scots in opposition to the absolutism of an English monarch. It defended religious rights and liberties against royal interference, stood up for the rule of law and parliament against the crown, and ignited a constitutional revolution that brought about the collapse of the institution of monarchy across Britain and Ireland, albeit temporarily.

However, these achievements were not quite what the original Covenanters had in mind. This was a movement instigated and led by the Scottish aristocracy. The first signature on the National Covenant was that of the Earl of Sutherland, James Gordon. Another key figure was the Marquis Montrose, James Graham, who would later switch sides – with far-reaching consequences. The Covenant itself praised 'the King's greatness and authority', and promised that 'we will to the uttermost of our power, with our means and lives, stand to the defence of our dread sovereign the King's Majesty'. Some radical, quasi-republican currents would later emerge within the Covenanters, but in the 1640s, any progressive political dimension to the movement was very much secondary to its dark and destructive religious fanaticism, a tendency that would cast its malignant shadow over the Scottish psyche for centuries to come.

Much of the 4,000-word document is devoted to a diatribe against 'the Roman Anti-Christ' and his 'tyrannous laws... corrupted doctrine... bastard sacraments... blasphemous litany... devilish mass... strange language... wicked hierarchy'. It does defend religious liberties – for Calvinists – against the crown, but threatens savage persecution for other faiths.

Religious fundamentalism wasn't unique to Scotland in the seventeenth century, of course, nor was it an exclusive trait of Calvinism. In Spain, the 300,000-strong Morisco population – people of Berber and Arab origin who had converted from Islam to Catholicism at the height of the Inquisition – were expelled en masse, on pain of death, from the lands they had lived in for centuries, because they were suspected of having Muslim sympathies. In France, in 1685, King Louis XIV ordered the torching of Huguenot churches and the closure of Protestant schools, whilst terrorising families who refused to convert by billeting armed dragoons in their households. By the following year, the self-styled 'Sun King' would boast that he had reduced the Protestant population of France by up to 900,000. And all in the name of religious harmony.

In England, the Penal Laws enforced a form of religious apartheid on the Catholic minority, who were banned from public office and forced to pay fines for failing to attend Anglican services. The same laws, made in England, were imposed on the Catholic majority in Ireland, and were ratcheted up in ferocity as the century progressed.

By contrast, Islamic states such as the Ottoman Empire were paragons of pluralism, where Christians and Jews had the right to worship, and were not subject to Muslim law.

The Covenanters could never unite Scotland. The messianic Calvinism of the movement was infused with a quasi-racist fear and hatred of that half of the population which resided north of the Clyde and Tay, and had held true to the old language, culture and religion. This would prove to be the Covenanters' Achilles heel.

Nonetheless, in the early days, the movement had been unstoppable, strolling to victory in the two Bishops' Wars of 1639 and 1640, and forcing Charles I to make sweeping concessions. He ratified resolutions of the General Assembly of the Church of Scotland, banishing episcopacy; he promised no retribution against Covenanters; he agreed to return all Scottish property and ships captured during the war; he agreed to suppress all anti-Covenant books and publications; and he pledged to compensate Scotland to the tune of £300,000 (the equivalent of £9 billion) for losses incurred during the wars.

But out of that victory was born a new and more brutal war, complex and confusing, that would rage across the three kingdoms of Scotland, England and Ireland. The humiliation of Charles by the Covenanters exposed his weakness and galvanised the diverse opposition to the king in England, ranging from jealous nobles excluded from the royal court to religious dissenters, and from prosperous merchants to factory workers in the growing clothing industry. By the summer of 1642, England was engulfed in civil war.

Ireland was also in state of turmoil. In 1641, the old English Catholic aristocracy launched a failed coup against the Protestant parliament in Dublin, which was soon followed by a second uprising in the north of the country, by Catholic peasants who had been driven off their land during the plantations.

At the same time, the unity of the Scottish Covenanters was beginning to unravel. What perhaps began as a power struggle between two egotistical leaders broke down into a brutal and bloody rupture, fatally weakening the movement and paving the way for an English occupation of Scotland. Archibald Campbell, the Marquis of Argyll, had come late to the movement; James Graham, Marquis of Montrose, became personally jealous and politically hostile to the upstart from the west, whose star was now on the rise. Montrose was a moderate by instinct, and feared that the movement was escalating out of control under the influence of a man he regarded as a populist demagogue. After several years of factional intrigue, he broke away to become the king's Lieutenant-General in Scotland and the Covenanters' most feared enemy. The rivalry of Argyll and Montrose, and the violence of their struggle, would have terrible consequences for Scotland.

As noted by Woody Guthrie during the ferocious struggles of the miners in Kentucky during the American Depression, there were no neutrals here. But which side people took in this seventeenth century conflict was dictated, not by class, but by geography, culture and religion. In the Lowlands, the Covenanters had mass support, with some estimates putting the signatories to the Covenant at 600,000 – around half Scotland's total population. But most of the Highlands trembled before the spectre of these men in black, with their fire-and-brimstone religion and their hatred of the Gaels.

There were elements of right and wrong on both sides. Argyll's intransigent opposition to Stuart absolutism was in tune with Scotland's traditional view of the monarchy. The idea that kings were divinely appointed by God alone, and that subjects had no right to resist, had already been rejected in Scotland 300 years before, in the Declaration of Arbroath. Although associated in people's minds with Catholicism, the idea that the King was God's representative on earth was actually an invention of the Protestant King Henry VIII, an altogether immodest man who had set himself up as a kind of Hampton Court alternative to the Pope. But a century after his death, royal blood no longer commanded unflinching devotion, no doubt because of the abuses perpetrated by those who had it coursing through their veins. In that sense, Argyll represented the future.

But in the Highlands, the future as represented by the Covenanters was terrifying, promising as it did the crushing of the old ways of life, and the centuries-old traditions of language, lore and belonging. Historians, including those from a left-wing tradition, have tended to oversimplify the wars that convulsed the British Isles during the seventeenth century as a titanic struggle between reaction and progress, with most of Highland Scotland and Gaelic Ireland, in alliance with the Stuart dynasty, pitching itself against the forward march of progress. But progress is not always straightforward.

In the 1980s, much of the international left defended the Soviet occupation of Afghanistan on the basis that it would drag the old country out of the dark ages and into a modern world of electricity and running water. Hollywood, for much of the twentieth century, glorified the wars of extermination against the Native American population, the genocide that paved the way for the rise of United States capitalism. Even fascism in pre-war Italy and Germany portrayed itself as a movement dedicated to burying the past and building a new future. And, lest you imagine that kind of thinking is in the past, consider how Tony Blair, George Bush and their cohorts used the language of progress, enlightenment and modernisation to justify the catastrophic twenty-first century invasions of Afghanistan and Iraq. Or how globalisation and the removal of all restrictions on the power of capital, no matter the dreadful repercussions for peoples, places, and the global environment, is hailed by certain economists as a great leap forward for civilisation.

Most academic historians, including those of a left-wing persuasion, take pride in their objectivity. They deal in the currency of facts, figures and processes, and tally these up like auditors analysing profit and loss accounts. Such history – rigorous, detached and impassive – does add immensely to our knowledge of the past and to our understanding of the present. But its absence of humanity effectively photoshops out of history the authentic experiences of real people.

Some of those on the left who have argued, for example, that Culloden and the destruction of the Gàidhealtachd was a necessary stage in the evolution of society might take a deep breath before applying the same approach to the smashing of the print trade unions in the 1980s, which led to the communications revolution. Or to the great miners' strike of 1984, in defence of an industry built on the most destructive of all fossil fuels.

In Scotland, it has been left to popular historians such as the late John Prebble, Maggie Craig and James Hunter – a community land activist as well as an expert in Highland history – to bring the human victims of progress into focus, thus redressing the imbalance perpetrated by the universities. Hunter takes as his guiding light the great English Marxist historian, EP Thomson, who sought to rescue the victims of history from 'the enormous condescension of posterity'. In a splendid polemic against the arrogance of establishment academics, Hunter mocks the pretensions of Hugh Trevor-Roper – who was made Baron Dacre of Glanton by Margaret Thatcher – for his dismissal of African history as 'the unrewarding gyrations of barbarous tribes in picturesque but irrelevant corners of the globe'.

For their struggles against the Covenanters and their century-long link with the Stuart dynasty, the Highland clans have been both romanticised and demonised. To some, they represented the heart and soul of Scotland; to others, they symbolised feudal absolutism against freedom and enlightenment. Neither of these interpretations tells the whole story.

History, like life itself, is a ball of contradictions. Not black lines on a blank white canvas, so much as hazy grey scribbles against a backdrop of deepest mist. Progress can generate its own oppression, while resistance to that oppression can itself be progressive.

Drenched red with blood

The uprising of the Highland clans against the Covenanters in the 1640s was driven by hatred of their most fearsome oppressor, the Marquis of Argyll. This aggressive feudal overlord had driven rival clans from their ancestral lands. He had been awarded a 'Royal Commission of Fire and Sword' against the outlaw clan MacGregor, whose very name was now banned in Scotland. He had made enemies of the MacDonalds, the MacLeans and the Camerons in the west, and the Clan Chattan confederation which dominated the east, by grabbing their lands and generally brutalising them.

Meantime, the Campbell chiefs had further secured their power and wealth by marrying their sons into the Lowland aristocracy, thus ingratiating the clan into the heart of the Scottish ruling elite. They now occupied the position once held by the Stewarts, as Masters of the Royal Household.

Elsewhere in the Highlands, especially on the eastern and southern fringes, feudalism had also gained a solid foothold, mainly through the agency of Anglo-Norman families such as the Morays, Stewarts and Chisholms. But in the heart of the Gàidhealtachd, crown power remained weak. Across these rugged mountain chains, sundered by raging rivers, and fragmented into a myriad of islands and peninsulas, clan chiefs were able to operate as a law unto themselves.

Feudalism had first taken root in the fertile soil of Normandy before evolving further in arable, well-populated lands with easy communications, such as England, the Scottish Lowlands and the eastern coastal strip of Ireland. The Highlands, especially the north-west and the islands, was always an inhospitable environment for the system. In this harsh landscape, with its volatile weather of sunshine and storm, matched by its unstable economy of feast and famine, the values and obsessions of the clan chieftains were very different to those of the landowning classes in the south. The goal of feudal landowners was to maximise profit by extracting as much production from the land as possible with as little labour as necessary. Exploitation was intense and, where expedient, men and women were replaced by machines. Profits were then turned into hard cash by selling produce at market.

By contrast, the dispersed geography and the unyielding soil of the north-west ensured that the economy rarely rose above subsistence level. Production across large tracts of the Highlands was geared towards internal consumption rather than external markets, and in these wild lands, where rival tribes were forced to compete for meagre resources, clan chiefs required maximum manpower, not a slimmed-down labour force. The primitive communism of clan society had long since been eroded by the tides of the outside world, but many of the old customs and values lived on. Not that this should be confused with sepia-tinted postcards of rosy-cheeked lassies sitting spinning by cottage doors – life in the Highlands was basic and brutal, and communities, particularly remote communities, lived in terrible isolation. From the infamous rocks of St Kilda to the far flung shores of Caithness, handfuls of families struggled to stay alive through the harsh winters and hungry springs, hobbled by almost superstitious adherence to tradition and lack of any external contact or assistance.

There were, however, aspects of Highland life that are lamented still. The clan system, kitted up by nostalgic nineteenth century authors such as Walter Scott as a tartan-fest of hairy men and dancing ladies in tight wee pumps, was in fact a functional network of social organisation. It ensured that the old and weak were housed and fed, and that the able-bodied had land to work, reasonable rents, and a sense of community and place. In return, they were expected to take up arms in clan clashes and keep the lord's table groaning under the weight of cream and mutton. But it wasn't such a heavy price to pay, not by seventeenth century standards.

Whereas conventional feudal barons ruled their fiefdoms by power and fear, clan chiefs could not exercise supreme authority without consent. Debates were the currency of clan gatherings. As historian John Prebble puts it, 'the chief's title to land was no more tangible than the approval of his tribe'. Nor did clan leaders seek to impose their own religious beliefs; some Catholic clans even had Protestant chiefs. Kinship and community, collectivism and solidarity co-existed – uneasily at times – alongside hierarchical power and privilege.

In this hybrid society, the old Gaelic culture continued to thrive. Its language was rooted in nature and landscape rather than commerce and law, the letters of the alphabet each named after a tree, the months of the calendar descriptive of the fluctuating natural world. Songs and poetry, piping and dancing, drinking and story-telling, hospitality and festivity, religious tolerance and acceptance of unconventional lifestyles – these were all part of a culture that was now under siege from the southern men who sought to rule Scotland with a mailed fist.

The Calvinist commissars were themselves permeated with contradictions. The regime they had established was an incongruous mix of progressive social policies and religious tyranny. Legislation to provide care for the poor, the sick and the elderly, and for every parish in the land to have a school funded by local landowners, had been promoted by ministers and lay preachers who were close to the common people of the towns, villages and hamlets. This reformist component provided Presbyterianism with a solid base of mass support among the lower orders. But it had an authoritarian counterweight, designed to keep these same lower orders in their place. Draconian laws were enacted against 'fornication, swearing, drunkenness, clandestine marriages, scandalous persons, fishing on the Sabbath day'. Death was decreed for 'blasphemy, idolatry, parent cursing, incest and witchcraft'.

In this fevered atmosphere, a new epidemic of paranoiac misogyny convulsed the land. In Fife alone, over 30 women accused of witchcraft were executed in a single year, with hundreds more massacred across the country. The regime that was supposed to be leading a revolt against the superstitious backwardness of a monarch with a messianic complex was itself burning women and girls at the stake for supposedly casting wicked spells and concocting evil potions. The Covenanters may have carried through elements of constitutional and religious reform, but as the rear-view mirror of history reveals, revolutionaries can rapidly turn into despots.

His personal flaws and hostility towards Argyll notwithstanding, Montrose may well have been disturbed by the increasing belligerence of his old movement, which was now trying to impose Calvinism on England and Ireland too. This shrewd aristocrat turned to the Highlands, in the sure knowledge that, in the Marquis of Argyll, he had a ready-made hate figure that would rally support for his anti-Covenanter cause.

Meanwhile, the Covenanters were severely stretched. They had by now joined the English Civil War, on the side of parliament against the crown. And they had sent an army to Ireland – paid for, in a rare show of unity, by the English Parliament and Crown – to help defend their Presbyterian kith and kin in the Plantation of Ulster against an uprising of the native Irish. On the principle that my enemy's enemy is my friend, and fearful of a future under a regime dedicated to the stamping out all religious and cultural dissent, much of the Highlands mobilised behind Montrose. Joined by a contingent of MacDonalds from Ireland, who had been driven from their lands in Kintyre and Islay, the Gaelic royalist forces won a stunning series of victories in 1644 and 1645. Argyll fled the battlefield at Inverlochy and 1,500 of his men were killed. The Covenanters were soon routed everywhere north of Perth, and Montrose's army even conquered the Campbell stronghold of Inverary, in Argyll. Even further south, in Kilsyth, the royalists were triumphant.

By all accounts, the Highland clansmen had little interest in saving the king, conquering the Lowlands or invading England. So, while Montrose continued to push southwards, his army began to unravel in his wake, his infantry returning home to their glens after having wreaked vengeance on their old enemies and carried out a fair amount of looting and plundering. At last, Montrose met his match at Philiphaugh, in the Borders, in 1645, just one month after his victory at Kilsyth, when a force of Covenanters under General David Leslie was sent back up from England to confront the threat from the north. Leslie's force was available for such military housekeeping because the

English civil war was all over bar the shouting, and Charles had lost. Within two years, the king's neck would be bared to the executioner's axe.

If the Covenanters had any endearing qualities, magnanimity in defeat was not one of them. According to a sympathetic historian, Church of Scotland minister James King Hewison, the God-fearing Covenanters now set about exacting wretched revenge on the Irish and Highlanders who had dared oppose them. In one incident, 300 women – widows of Irish troops killed at Philiphaugh – were systematically slaughtered. At Linlithgow, Leslie had 80 women and children thrown over a bridge and drowned. At Dunavery Castle in Kintyre, 300 MacDougalls, MacDonalds and MacAlisters – men, woman and children – agreed to surrender to Argyll and Leslie, after they were surrounded and their water supply cut off. As the prisoners of war left the castle, the chaplain of the Covenanters, the Rev John Naves, demanded of General Leslie that the prisoners of war, in God's name, be duly slaughtered. Leslie obliged, but as he walked among the corpses with Argyll and Naves, ankle deep in blood, the general turned to the chaplain and asked, 'Now John, have you not for once had your fill of blood?'

In these middle decades of the seventeenth century, for the greed and glory of their masters, the working people had been slaughtered like grouse on the moor. Some estimates put the death toll in Scotland during the civil war at 60,000 – equating to more than 1 in 10 of the male population. Those who suffered the most, however, were not the men who bled to death on battlefields by the thousand, but the women and children they left behind.

Women are the forgotten phantoms of pre-industrial society. Almost all historical sources were written by men, who assiduously chronicled the daily minutiae of the rich and powerful lords and their lady friends, whilst trivialising, marginalising or ignoring the lives of ordinary men, and failing even to acknowledge those of ordinary women. There are no surviving diaries or journals written by women; their stories, voices, significance, have all slipped through the cracks of history. Even their names are scratched from the record, their identities subsumed into the lives of husbands, brothers and fathers. After the dust settled on decades of military carnage, tens of thousands of widowed mothers found themselves struggling in the teeth of starvation. No longer legitimised by a male head of the household, they were feared and hated by the local elites.

For all of Scotland, the middle decades of the seventeenth century had been traumatic and violent. As the labour historian, Tom Johnston, wrote in the early twentieth century: 'The Montroses, Leslies, Moncks and Cromwells drenched Scotland red with blood in the few succeeding years before a king sat on the throne again.'

6

THE KILLING TIMES

A terrible beauty

By now, Scotland was a sideshow. The revolution had begun north of the border, but a new force had arisen in the south that would annihilate everything in its path, including the Royalists in England, the Covenanters in Scotland and the Catholic rebels in Ireland. 'A terrible beauty is born,' wrote the twentieth century Anglo-Irish poet, WB Yeats, of the Easter Rising in Dublin. Oliver Cromwell's New Model Army was the seventeenth century's terrible beauty.

On the face of it, this was a religious movement dedicated to Puritanism, a fundamentalist Protestant creed. But in the seventeenth century, religion was more than a set of private beliefs; it was a statement of identity, and an instrument of political domination. In every country, the church was an arm of the state; in every locality, the clergy were the chief enforcers of law and morality; from every pulpit, ministers preached political as well as religious propaganda.

In the mid-seventeenth century, both England and Scotland had state churches. The Church of England, created by Henry VIII, was a top-down operation. The more radical Church of Scotland had been established in opposition to the crown, but was subsequently embraced by most of the feudal nobility, who in turn diluted its militancy. More subversive were the nonconformist religious groupings that emerged south of the border, in opposition to the Church of England. These sects, including the Baptists, Quakers and Congregationalists – and later, the Methodists, especially strong in Wales – became vehicles of political as well as religious dissent. Oliver Cromwell was a Congregationalist – a denomination which insists to this day that each local church is fully self-governing, without a dominant, external hierarchy.

During this period of religious and political chaos, England leapfrogged over Scotland in the matter of radical politics. The reason, paradoxically, was that England was a wealthier country with a more developed economy and a population five times greater than that of Scotland, making it the biggest single market in the world. It also had eight times more fertile land than Scotland, and a gentler climate. More important still, the imperial war machine, handed down through the generations from Henry VIII, had helped it prosper. England had defeated the Spanish Armada in 1588 and had by now supplanted Spain as the foremost plunderer of the planet. Joint-stock companies were created to further England's interests overseas, with circles of investors pooling their resources for a series of foreign ventures. The East India Company, which would eventually run riot in South Asia, was established in London in 1600, and now had 23 factories in India and sundry ports in China.

All of which helped agriculture, trade and manufacturing to flourish back home. Industries proliferated – clothing, shipbuilding, furniture, housing, paper, armaments and fuel – thus creating an embryonic proletariat. Middlemen supplied the factories with raw materials, and itinerant merchants would travel around towns and villages selling finished consumer goods. By 1640, London had grown into a metropolis of 200,000 people, the value of whose exports had more than trebled since the start of the century. Across England, there emerged a large middle class of richer artisans, successful merchants, and the yeomanry – those beef-eating, beer-drinking, well-to-do farmers. This strata had enough property to stand on its own two feet, and was well-educated to boot. Yet it had none of the privileges or power of the established aristocracy.

The ruling elite feared this rising capitalist class, who in turn loathed the parasitical monarchy and its entourage of thousands who imposed punitive taxes to fund their own extravagant lifestyles. Meanwhile, down in the depths of society, growing armies of unemployed vagrants began to plague the towns in search of subsistence.

England was ripe for revolution, and Cromwell was the man to turn the wheel. Oliver's Army was recruited from the middle and lower ranks of society: the small traders, the peasantry, the town and rural labourers. He claimed to be on the side of the common people, the 'meaner sort' as he called them. Yet he was, as the University of Edinburgh historian William Ferguson notes, 'a conservative revolutionary, if ever there was one, who was driven reluctantly along by the popular agitations'.

Cromwell and his henchmen were landowners. They mobilised the poor and dispossessed as cannon-fodder – until the lower orders began to organise themselves politically, in groups such as the Levellers, which called for universal male suffrage, annual parliaments, freedom of speech, religious tolerance and the abolition of class distinction based on land ownership. Despite their invaluable assistance in smashing the royalist forces, Cromwell's response was to crush this left-wing flank of his New Model Army by shooting its leaders.

England became a republic, and Cromwell was to go down in history as the man who began to dismantle feudalism. To this day, he is a hero of English progressive liberalism, with more roads named after him than any other English figure in history, barring Queen Victoria, and a statue erected in his honour outside the House of Commons. On paper, his achievements look impressive and progressive. The overthrow of a feudal monarch in favour of a republic – a 'commonwealth' no less – should surely have ushered in an era of progress and enlightenment. But that's not how it went. Like many revolutionaries to come, 'Old Ironsides' turned into a tyrant as soon as he donned the mantle of power. He may be revered in England, but in Ireland and, to a lesser extent, in Scotland, he is reviled as a mass-murderer and cold-blooded war criminal, who carried out atrocities shocking even by seventeenth century standards.

In 1649, he invaded Ireland, fearing that this stubbornly Catholic country might become the rallying point for a royalist renaissance. Whilst he was about it, he took the opportunity to exact murderous revenge for the 1641 uprising, in which the dispossessed O'Neills, O'Donnells, O'Dohertys and Maguires had routed the Ulster plantationists, killing thousands. At Drogheda, he pitched 12,000 of his men against a royalist garrison of 3,000, and personally supervised the slaughter of 2,500 soldiers and an unknown number of civilians. Some were incinerated, others clubbed to death. Known royalists were decapitated, and their heads dispatched to Dublin to be displayed on pikes in the streets. At Wexford, the unstoppable Cromwell conducted a massacre of 2,000 troops and 1,500 civilians. 'I am persuaded that this is a righteous judgement of God upon these barbarous wretches', he wrote in a letter to the Speaker of the House of Commons.

On Cromwell's watch, 40 per cent of Ireland's population died or were killed, while Catholic ownership of land in Ireland plummeted from 60 per cent of the total to just 8 per cent. If there had ever been any prospect of an Irish Reformation, it was killed off by Cromwell. The man nicknamed 'God's Executioner' by one of his biographers ensured that the people of Ireland would for centuries cleave to the Catholic Church. After 'liberating' Ireland from the evils of royalism, with muskets, pikes and cannons, Cromwell turned his sights on Scotland, a nation by no means ready for republicanism.

Scotland, at this stage, was still in the hands of the old aristocratic families whose war against Charles I was staged in the name of reform, not revolution. Even at the height of the struggle, they had repudiated republicanism. They might have thrown a tantrum against Charles, but no sooner had they got what they wanted from him – a promise to promote Presbyterianism in England and Ireland, as well as in Scotland – they made their peace with the royalists.

Unlike England, with its imperial war machine and its booming agriculture to support a burgeoning population, Scotland was still too underdeveloped to have bred the kind of capitalist middle-class that might agitate for political revolution. The power of the aristocracy remained intact, while other social classes were weak and atomised. One of Scotland's three major industries – linen – was organised on a domestic, hand-working scale, which meant that the workforce was scattered and powerless. The other two – coal and salt – were controlled by feudal landowners commanding the Firths of Forth and Clyde. Along these coastlines, where place names such as Saltcoats and Prestonpans hint at their economic origins, rich seams of coal were mined and burned to boil sea water in pans to extract the salt, the only food preservative of its time. Conditions for the men who worked down the pits, and for the women and children who produced the salt, were unimaginably grim. Yet both industries needed a massive, dedicated labour force. Obligingly, an Act of Parliament in 1606 reintroduced serfdom for colliers and saltworkers. Thus, several centuries after Scotland had led the world in abolishing slavery, it brought it back. Tens of thousands of men, woman and children suddenly became the private property of the local landowners, to be bought and sold alongside the land on which they laboured. Workers who tried to escape were hunted down like animals.

News that Charles I had lost his head to Cromwell set Scotland's ruling elite into a tailspin. If England was now a republic, where did that leave Scotland? It was unthinkable that the Scottish nobility would carry on without a king – it would be like the Catholic Church failing to replace a dead Pope. But if they defied Cromwell by crowning Charles's son and successor King of Scotland, they knew there would be all hell to pay. In a desperate throw of the dice, they went for broke, proclaiming Charles II the King of Great Britain, France and Ireland. It was a forlorn attempt to rouse the royalist allies outwith Scotland. And if Cromwell had ever needed an excuse to invade, this was it.

At Dunbar, he smashed the army of the Covenanters. Five thousand Scottish prisoners-of-war were marched south to Durham, where they perished in their droves through starvation and disease, before being dumped in mass graves. Of the 1,200 who survived, most were sold as slaves to the English colonies in the Caribbean. Over the next eight years, tens of thousands more would, in the parlance of the day, be 'Barbadoed'. The first slaves to work the plantations of the West Indies were not African, but Scots and Irish prisoners and rebels deported during the Cromwellian era. Some went on to run the slave plantations. Others failed to thrive. To this day, their descendants, nicknamed 'redlegs', live in dirt-poor shanty towns on the west side of the island of Barbados. It is one of history's rich ironies that Scotland's involvement in slavery and empire was kick-started by rebels banished overseas for standing up to oppression and imperialism.

Back home, as in the days of Edward I and Henry VIII, Scotland was now under military occupation. General George Monck, the commander of Cromwell's forces in Scotland, built a chain of fortresses from Ayr to Inverness. Scotland was now an annexed colony, along the lines of Wales, which had suffered this ignominy for centuries. Cromwell did introduce some reforms, including the abolition of elements of feudal law and a ban on patronage within the church, which had given the nobility the right to appoint ministers. He also guaranteed religious freedom, but only for Protestant sects and denominations.

Yet his rule in Scotland was no more progressive than most military occupations tend to be. Any elements of enlightenment were mere spoonfuls of sugar lacing barrels of toxic waste. Taxes rose tenfold. Plunder and looting was conducted on an industrial scale, including the seizure and destruction of all of Scotland's public records. Scotland's parliament was declared redundant, and a bill was prepared asserting 'the right of England to Scotland'. Foreshadowing one of the many repressive practices in apartheid South Africa, the new regime introduced pass laws to prevent the free movement of the people.

Modern Scottish historians, notably Tom Devine, have rightly exposed Scotland's role in the British Empire and the slave trade in the eighteenth and nineteenth centuries. But as Devine also points out: 'In 1707, the Scots joined in parliamentary union with a bellicose nation which was already building the fiscal, political and military foundations for imperial expansion.'

That bellicosity had been evident for centuries, as kings from Edward I onwards sought to conquer and subdue their neighbours at all points of the compass, whilst pick-pocketing them mercilessly.

But Oliver Cromwell took commercial imperialism to a new height. In 1655, his navy conquered the sparsely populated island of Xamayaca – the land of wood and springs – from Spain, anglicising its name to Jamaica. Three years previously, he had declared war on England's old ally, the Netherlands, eventually destroying the Dutch navy, then the most powerful in the world, thus providing the springboard for England's eventual domination of world trade.

Then, suddenly, history turned on a sixpence. Without warning, and at the height of his power, Cromwell collapsed and died, of malaria and pneumonia. Within 18 months, the republic he had founded was also dead and buried.

Cromwell's Commonwealth had been imposed from above, by terror and fanaticism. As with most military dictatorships, it had relied on a single iron man to impose his will on the army, and on society as a whole. And when that man died suddenly of natural causes, the whole structure disintegrated like a sandcastle. In 1660, without a hitch, the son of the executed king returned to the throne of England and, this time officially, to the throne of Scotland.

Misery under the Merrie Monarch

The portrayal of the life and times of Charles II in drama and literature paints a generous picture of a happy-go-lucky, Jack the Lad-type who dispelled the gloom and lifted the oppression of the grim Cromwellian era. Lady Antonia Fraser, the popular historian and widow of the acclaimed playwright Harold Pinter, described him as 'witty and kind, grateful, generous, tolerant, and essentially lovable'. Other, rather more rigorous, academic historians have described him a little differently – as mean, dishonest, cynical and brutal, for instance. The biographer Ronald Hutton confessed that Charles was so repulsive, he found researching his life to be 'genuinely depressing'.

His lifestyle was as hedonistic as a 1960s rock superstar. He raced yachts, drank copious amounts of wine, hosted sumptuous feasts and fathered at least 14 illegitimate children by a string of mistresses. He later showered aristocratic titles on his male offspring, some of whose descendants sat in the House of Lords right up to the twilight of the twentieth century. But while the king pursued his dissolute lifestyle, Scotland entered a new dark age.

A new epidemic of women-burning spread across the Lowlands like a disease; according to one account, 'for some years, the Castlehill in Edinburgh and the heights in the vicinity blazed with the dry carcasses of the miserable victims'. Within a single month, August 1661, 120 women were burned at the stake in the area around Musselburgh and Dalkeith, according to one traveller. At a time when even supposed intellectuals agreed that pacts with the devil and evil spells were quite probable amongst the lower orders of womenfolk, it was probably easier to fly through the sky on a broomstick than gain a fair hearing for charges of witchcraft.

Take the case of Margaret Hutchinson from Duddingston village, just below Arthur's Seat in Edinburgh, who was accused of dancing with the devil and sundry other unlikely activities. Legal records report that 'the young laird of Duddingston deponed that a witch who had lately suffered for sorcery had mentioned that Hutchinson was as great a witch as herself and had attended several of the devil's select parties. Upon this, she was found guilty, strangled and burned.'

Meanwhile, episcopacy was once again foisted upon the Church of Scotland, replacing the democracy of elected presbyteries with a top-down hierarchy, run by bishops who were in turn appointed by the monarch. In a grand display of crown power, Archbishop Sharp rode into St Andrews to take up his post, accompanied by an entourage of 600 horsemen, including most of the big landowners in Fife. But this time there would be no rebellion of the Scottish elites. They had resisted Charles I when he encroached on their privileges – and had then paid a draconian price at the hands of Oliver Cromwell. They had played with fire and unleashed an inferno. If they could, they would gladly have pressed the rewind button and gone back to the start.

They had already made their peace with the House of Stuart, and in turn, Charles II, the Restoration monarch, restored the Scottish Parliament that had been abolished by Cromwell. It was, however, a token gesture. The great institutions of the Scottish state – parliament, the judiciary, the church – were now effectively run by the crown in England.

During the Cromwellian occupation, Scotland had been stripped of political autonomy and reduced to a *de facto* region of England. But at least it had access to English markets. Now, along with Ireland, Scotland was treated as an alien country, banned from trading freely with England and its colonies.

It was the worst of all worlds. For the remainder of the seventeenth century, Scotland was compelled to compete with England in the European economic free-for-all, while the crown in London controlled Scotland's foreign policy and all but controlled its domestic policy too, via an enfeebled parliament in Edinburgh. England thrived, but Scotland slid, slowly but relentlessly, into a black peat bog of depression.

With God on our side

In times of conflict, social, national and religious credos are often fused together. In Ireland and Poland, for example, a sense of national oppression was merged with ideas of religious identity, turning the Catholic Church in these countries into a rallying point for resistance. The most potent modern-day challenge to Western economic and military power in Afghanistan, Iraq and Iran has been mobilised under the banner of Islam.

In the late seventeenth century, opposition to the power of the English Crown in Scotland merged with Presbyterianism. It kicked off with 350 ministers being expelled from their parishes for refusing to accept the new episcopal regime that had been imposed on the Church of Scotland. In defiance, they took to secluded fields and woodland glades where they kept alive the democratic spirit of Presbyterianism by preaching subversive open-air sermons against the church, parliament and crown. Thousands attended these illegal assemblies, known as conventicles.

This new wave of Presbyterian dissidents stressed the historical continuity of their struggle by defining themselves as Covenanters. But whereas the original Covenanters had been created and led by the nobility, this new movement had sprung from the grassroots, in opposition to the Scottish establishment. In the 1640s, the Highlands had risen up in rebellion to defend their culture, language, religion and way of life. Now it was the turn of the die-hard Presbyterians of the south-west to feel the blast of state repression. Nine thousand troops were drafted into the regions, mainly from the Highlands, ironically, to stamp out the embers of dissent.

But the new Covenanters, like the Palestinians of the West Bank and Gaza today, were prepared to die for their cause. They fought back against their oppressors in pitched battles across the uplands and lowlands of southern Scotland, opportunistically assassinating the hated figurehead of episcopacy,

Archbishop Sharp, while they were at it. The response of the authorities was brutal. At the Battle of Bothwell Bridge in Lanarkshire, on 22 June 1679, a 6,000-strong Covenanting army was routed by 5,000 regular government troops. Six hundred were killed and another 1,200 taken prisoner and incarcerated in Greyfriars Kirkyard in Edinburgh, still known today as the 'Covenanters' Prison'.

From there, those who were identified as dangerous radicals were taken to the Grassmarket and executed. Some were set free after swearing an oath of submission; others died of injuries and disease; the remaining 257 were manacled and herded on board a ship, docked at the Port of Leith, to await transportation to the English colonies in America, where they were to live virtually as slaves. The prisoners never reached their destination. The *Crown of London*, as the ship was fatefully named, ran into a storm off the Orkney mainland and was pulverised against the rocks. The captain and crew escaped to safety, leaving the prisoners for dead. Some 48 did manage to smash their way out of the locked hull but, for days on end, corpses were washed up on the shoreline and thrown into a mass grave now marked by a memorial pillar rising high above the cliffs.

The list of prisoners onboard the doomed ship reveals that the movement had support in towns and villages across the Lowlands, including West Lothian, Fife, Midlothian, Stirling, and the Borders. But by far the largest contingents hailed from the south-western counties of Ayr, Clydesdale, Galloway and Teviotdale, representing the lands that lie to the west of what is now the A74-M74 trunk road from Glasgow to the English border. In the late seventeenth century, it was the one region in Scotland where there lived large concentrations of peasant proprietors and small farm-owners, with little loyalty to feudalism.

The rebels who survived Bothwell Bridge reorganised into a guerrilla-style cell structure led by an 18-year-old student, theologian and poet called William Cleland. Calling themselves the United Societies – although they were to become better known as the Cameronians – they declared war on the state and called upon all Scots to 'stand against the ungodly arrogance of the King'. Given that they were mostly hiding out in the hills, with only guns and desperation for company, they were politically quite sophisticated, issuing a slew of proclamations, declarations and manifestos, including *The Queensferry*

Paper, published in 1680, described by historian Allan Armstrong as Scotland's first republican manifesto.

It stated: 'We shall no more commit of the government of ourselves, and the making of laws for us, to any one single person or lineal successor.' The crown and state responded by launching a war of extermination against the radicals, in a blighted period of Scottish history known as the Killing Times. The Cameronians were hunted down like deer on the hillsides and moorlands of Galloway, Ayrshire, Lanarkshire and Renfrewshire. Facing extinction, they nonetheless held fast to their beliefs. To speed the plough – or sickle, in this case – the crown introduced the Abjuration Oath, by which suspected dissenters were obliged to swear allegiance to the king, and sign an oath of repudiation of the Covenant. Or be shot on the spot.

Dozens of monuments and plaques commemorating their steadfastness in the face of tyranny survive to this day in old kirkyards, village squares and remote moors across south-west Scotland. None is more poignant than the Martyr's Stake on the edge of Wigtown Bay. According to oral history – which can, at times, waver between accuracy of sorts and outright romanticism – the monument commemorates the drowning of two radical women for resisting the Abjuration Oath. The story goes that Margaret McLachlan, who was in her 60s, and Margaret Wilson, in her early 20s, were tied to two stakes in the mudflats of the bay, and given the option to repent or drown. As far as they were concerned, there was no choice to be made. They sang psalms as the tide turned, before finally disappearing under the raging foam of the Solway Firth.

Given the nature of the era, such a story is not so very far-fetched, and the state atrocities of the Killing Times can arouse as much passion in Galloway and south-west Scotland as Glencoe or the Highland Clearances arouse in the north.

This was not a sectarian war between two separate denominations: it was a religious civil war conducted within the same tradition. This was Protestant versus Protestant. The fanaticism of the Presbyterian rebels may appear repugnant to modern observers, but religion represented, as Karl Marx commented two centuries later, 'the sigh of the oppressed creature, the heart of a heartless world, and the soul of soulless conditions'. An unshakeable belief in the righteousness and justice of their cause, combined with alienation from the values of the society they lived in, inspired total dedication to the cause.

Among the multitude of contradictions that have woven their way into the fabric of Scottish – and Irish – politics is the annual sight of marching bands, named in honour of the Cameronians, blasting out royalist anthems. There is no natural affinity between Presbyterianism, with its democratic, egalitarian overtones, and monarchism's ostentatious celebration of elitism and hierarchy. The tenuous connection between these two discordant worlds was, as it happens, forged by a random quirk of history.

7

THE HOUSE OF ORANGE

'An intensely conservative revolution'

When Charles II died, he left behind a horde of illegitimate children, but not a single legitimate heir to the throne. Which put his younger brother, James, squarely in line for succession.

This coronation, however, was not greeted with the customary fanfare.

James VII of Scotland – James II of England – wasn't to the taste of the English upper crust and its mille-feuille of hangers-ons. In their eyes, he committed a cardinal crime by converting to Catholicism after marrying his second wife, Mary, a devout Catholic from the Italian province of Modena.

Catholicism was the religion of England's enemies: the French and the Spanish, the rebellious Irish, and the mutinous clans of the West Highlands.

James's support for freedom of worship extended beyond his own faith, to include Protestant dissidents. But his tolerant liberalism outraged the Anglican establishment, who feared it would undermine the authority of the state church.

The new king's open-minded acceptance of religious dissent, however, stopped where the English border ended. In Scotland and in Ulster he pursued with a vengeance his father's merciless persecution of the radical Covenanters. Had he been more flexible and less messianic, his religious beliefs might even have been tolerated, grudgingly, as a kind of personal eccentricity, a temporary aberration that would be resolved by his death and the accession to the throne of one of his two Protestant daughters from his first marriage.

But this was a man who truly believed in the divine right of monarchs. His refusal to take advice; his drive to elevate his own hand-picked Catholic allies to key positions in the state; his warmth towards the regime of King Louis XIV of France, who was the supreme commander of medieval feudalism in Europe – all of this made James a threat to the stability of the English state.

The Anglican elite – the great landowners, the wealthiest merchants, the bishops, the military top brass, the legal establishment – now began to fear a revolt from below if they failed to curb the power of their out-of-control monarch. Still haunted by memories of the Cromwellian republic, these establishment figures, who should have been the king's natural allies, began to turn against him. It all came to a head when his son, Francis Edward Stewart, was born and baptised into the old faith. The arrival of the baby boy changed everything. Being male, the newborn prince automatically leapfrogged over his two grown-up, Protestant half-sisters to become first in line to the throne. A one-off deviation from Protestantism could be endured, but the prospect of a Catholic dynasty stretching generations into the future was untenable.

A solution had to be found, and found it was. When a group of English Protestant nobles invited William of Orange to come to England with an invasion force in tow, they probably hadn't anticipated how swiftly events would move. Without warning, James – who had managed to alienate his army, his navy, his parliament, his nobility and the Anglican Church – escaped across the English Channel to negotiate support from the French regime and ponder his next move. The Anglican nobility now seized the opportunity to rid themselves of their troublesome monarch without breaking any of the taboos of feudalism.

Hobbled as they were by a tradition of deep deference to hereditary titles, they could not countenance the removal of even a rogue sovereign; since the establishment of feudalism in 1066, only Charles I had been removed – and that had been the Devil's work of the upstart republican, Oliver Cromwell.

Today, we might struggle to understand that culture of servility that prevented the English ruling class from stripping a detested king of his crown – until we remember that even now, in the twenty-first century, we have convicted perjurers, arsonists and fraudsters sitting in the House of Lords because the law of the land decrees that they cannot be stripped of their peerages.

In a bid to skirt the rules, the English Parliament declared that James had voluntarily abdicated. As luck would have it, William's wife Mary was next in line to the throne, so to solve the problem of succession, someone came up with the novel idea of a dual monarchy. It was nonsense, of course. The new queen would never be more than a constitutional decoration, wielding about as much political power as her husband's great white steed – which, unlike Mary, is commemorated to this day in dozens of statues across Britain and Ireland, not to mention gable ends and banners paraded through cities and towns across Scotland and Northern Ireland.

This bloodless coup that elevated William of Orange to King William III in 1688 is hailed by British establishment historians as the Glorious Revolution. But it was neither glorious, nor a revolution. Revolutions bring about momentous change; they upturn the social order and remake the world. This 'revolution' maintained the status quo, in favour of the rich, the landed gentry, the military, and the established church. The people who brought us William of Orange were from the social groups who had cheered on the debauched throw-back, Charles II. The English Revolution was, according to Scottish historian William Ferguson, 'intensely conservative and largely concerned with property rights and privileges that had little or no radical content.'

North of the border, there was little enthusiasm for William and Mary, yet paradoxically, the revolution went significantly further. James had been no more popular in Scotland than in England, but he was considered the legitimate successor to the throne.

The English elite had not only engineered the removal of a king who ruled Scotland as well as England; they had also, unilaterally, without consulting the Scottish Parliament, changed the laws of succession to install a foreign king on the throne. The downfall of James II, moreover, spelled the end of the Stuart line, the old Scottish dynasty whose origins stretched back to Robert the Bruce and Bannockburn.

For Scotland, this was a humiliating kick in the teeth, and could have spelled the end of the Union of the Crowns. As an independent kingdom, Scotland was not obliged to accept the new ruler. Determined to reassert the sovereignty of the nation, a Convention of the Scottish Estates, comprised of nobles, bishops and representatives of the burghs, invited the two rivals for the throne to each write a letter presenting their case.

William responded, promising to bring about liberty, peace and stability so that the people, 'after so much trouble and great suffering, may live happily and in peace, and lay aside all animosities and factions that may impede so good a work.' Good answer.

James, in contrast, was both patronising and threatening. He demanded loyalty, stating that rejection of his fine self would bring 'infamy and disgrace... upon yourself in this world and the condemnation due to rebelliousness in the next.' Those who accepted his rule by the end of the month would be pardoned, but 'we will punish with the rigour of our laws all such as shall stand in rebellion against us or our authority.'

It was a major miscalculation by a ruler whose arrogance had always towered above his intellect. Instead of following London's lead by endorsing the fiction that James had abdicated, the Scottish Parliament took the more honest course of stripping him of the crown. He had 'by Advice from Evil and Wicked counsellors invaded the fundamental constitution of the Kingdom, and altered it from a legal, limited Monarchy to an Arbitrair and Despotic Power.'

In the eyes of England, James had resigned, but in Scotland there was no such pussy-footing: the king had been fired. From the Declaration of Arbroath onwards, the crown of Scotland had been treated as a contract rather than a one-sided *fait accomplit*, arranged by God over the heads of the people.

This more sceptical, hard-headed approach was then applied to James's replacement. Determined to drive a hard bargain before accepting the foreign usurper, the Scottish Parliament passed an act called the Claim of Right which, to this day, is one of the keystone documents in Scottish constitutional law.

It was also a statement of Protestant supremacy and anti-Catholic paranoia. This was in tune with the mood of the times across most of northern Europe, which associated 'popery' with tyranny, in much the same way that some Muslims today equate Judaism with oppression – understandable, perhaps, given the atrocities carried out by the Israeli state, but nevertheless wrong.

In other respects, the Scottish Bill of Rights was ahead of its time, curbing the power of the monarch, strengthening the power of parliament, outlawing the practice of torture without evidence, upholding the right to petition and protest, and clamping down on royal patronage. Not a bad piece of work, all told, and pretty advanced for its time.

A battle of two halves

Not everyone in Scotland was prepared to accept William of Orange as king. One such was John Graham of Claverhouse, the Viscount Dundee, subsequently immortalised in a famous song by Walter Scott, *Bonnie Dundee*.

A distant relative and disciple of the Marquis of Montrose, who had led the royalist forces in Scotland to a series of sensational victories almost half a century earlier, Dundee was cut from similar cloth. An Episcopalian Protestant, he was motivated not by religion, but by politics and power.

His portrait, made by David Paton between 1660 and 1695, and therefore drawn at least partly from real life, shows a man with a cool, direct gaze, suggesting someone with considerable personal charisma – a great asset in a time when many angry people felt rudderless, and in need of strong leadership. He had earned his stripes as a ruthless warlord when commanding state-controlled death squads against the radical Covenanters, for which he earned the less lovely nickname of 'Bluidy Clavers' in the Western Lowlands. By 1689, he was on his way north, marching in the footsteps of his illustrious forebear, to rally the clans once more around the battle-flag of the House of Stewart.

Jacobitism – the name derives from the Latin word for James – was born in the West Highlands and would remain a force to be reckoned with for the next seven decades, before it faded forever, a romantic lost cause harboured in the heart with sorrowful songs and melancholy verse. Its unifying ambition was to restore the Stuart line – and on this point, the movement had legal and constitutional legitimacy on its side.

As one of the foremost experts of the period, William Ferguson, points out: 'The Jacobites cannot be dismissed as mere divine right dotards at long last dispatched by "progress". In fact, most Jacobites had little truck with... moth-eaten iure divino [divine right] notions... Instead, the Jacobites came close to stealing the Revolutionist thunder by appealing to constitutional and legal arguments'.

In common with some Third World populist movements of the twentieth century, Jacobitism also drew on wider sentiments and deeper grievances. It mobilised national patriotism in support of a dynasty that, whatever its failings, had its roots in the historic struggle for Scottish independence. It provided an outlet for radical resistance against social and cultural persecution, and became the rallying point for the most downtrodden clans of the Highlands to unite in the face of their regional oppressors, notably the clan Campbell.

In the north-west, hatred for the House of Argyll had never subsided. No matter who was in power in London or Edinburgh, the Campbell chieftains had always displayed an impressive instinct for aligning themselves with the winning side. Even when they miscalculated, their diplomatic acrobatics would usually land them back on the side of power. This combination of what the Highland historian Jim Hunter calls 'political influence, legal machination and brute force' had turned the succession of Marquises, Earls and Dukes of Argyll into the supreme masters of vast tracts of the western seaboard of Scotland.

The Earl of Argyll had been a stalwart of Charles II, even while the Merrie Monarch waged a genocidal war against his Presbyterian kith and kin in the south west. But when James II took the throne, Argyll launched a failed coup against the Catholic king, after which the Campbell chief took to his heels, across the North Sea to the Netherlands. But now, with William on the rise, he was back in business as the Dutch king's man in the West Highlands.

The chief of the Clan Cameron, Locheil as he was known, soon assembled a confederation of rebel clans to destroy the House of Argyll, by tapping into popular support for the House of Stuart. When Claverhouse arrived from Dundee into the Cameron heartland of Lochaber to lead the alliance to war, it looked like history was about to repeat itself: another Graham, raising another Highland army, in the name of another Stuart monarch. As the late John Prebble comments in his brilliant analysis of the period, *Glencoe*: 'The cause he proposed was one easily understood by the clans. It was in defence of the Stuarts and therefore a Scottish king. It was, or seemed to be, in defence of Episcopacy and toleration of Catholics. It was, or seemed to be, in defence of their own way of life against Lowland authority.' And it was, above all, a war against the supremacy in the West Highlands of the hated Campbell clan, whose mini-empire now stretched from the Mull of Kintyre in the far south-west, just 11 miles from the coast of Ireland, to Glenlyon and Breadalbane in deepest Perthshire.

The Jacobite clans hailed from across the Highlands, though predominantly from the isles, peninsulas and glens of the west: Macleans and MacMillans from the Inner Hebrides; MacLeods and MacNeills from the Outer Hebrides; Stewarts from Appin; MacDonalds from Skye, Uist, Glencoe and Glengarry.

Three thousand strong, they marched south-east over the Monadhliath Mountains to the narrow pass of Killiecrankie in Highland Perthshire, where they launched an onslaught against a bigger force of Williamite forces from the Lowlands and the Netherlands. The Battle of Killiecrankie was a slaughter. When it was over, 2,500 corpses, most of them from the south, lay strewn across the beautiful wooded gorge that slopes steeply down to the River Tummel from the pass of Killiecrankie high above.

This swift and sensational victory might well have inspired a more widespread uprising across the Highlands, but for one thing: John Graham of Claverhouse, Bonnie Dundee, lay dead, struck down by a stray bullet in his moment of triumph.

Despite the loss of their great military leader, the rebellion pressed forward, but it was a runaway vehicle with no driver. Over the Perthshire hills and along the banks of the Tay the clans marched, until they reached the town of

Dunkeld to confront a hardline force of Cameronians – named in honour of a fallen hero of the Covenanting movement, Richard Cameron. These free radicals had little truck with the new king, or, indeed, any king imposed on them by external forces. Then again, the restoration of the Stuarts was unlikely to top their agenda either. They were outsiders, literally, given that they resided mainly in secret hide-outs in hillsides, and were regarded by mainstream Lowland society as fanatical extremists.

At one stage during the brief reign of James II and VII, the Presbyterian-led government in Edinburgh had raised a 6,000-strong Gaelic Highland army, commanded by Claverhouse, to occupy Galloway and Ayrshire in an attempt to smash the Cameronians into submission. The atrocities carried out by the Highlanders were never forgotten by the Cameronians. For this 'poor suffering bleeding remnant' as they described themselves, the prospect of a clan-based Jacobite Army taking power in Scotland was nothing short of a vision of hell. Yet neither had they any enthusiasm for King William.

Within their ranks, some had argued against taking any side in the struggle between Williamite and Jacobite. But at length, and by a majority, they decided to throw in their lot with the new king. At the same time, they preserved their independence from the regular army by forming their own militia, under the control of their own officers.

This bears comparison with the socialist Irish Citizens' Army during the Easter Rising of 1916, who were told by their leader James Connolly to have no trust in their nationalist allies: 'In the unlikely event of victory, hold on to your guns', he warned. The Cameronian militia was later co-opted into the regular state army, becoming the only regiment created from the grassroots.

Under the command of student-poet William Cleland, the zealous and disciplined little militia waited in Dunkeld Cathedral, and nearby Dunkeld House, for the Jacobite onslaught. Outnumbered four to one, and running out of ammunition, Cleland gave orders to march the short distance along the Tay to confront the rampant Highlanders in the centre of the town. Bonnie Dundee, a skilled military tactician, would never have contemplated leading these clansmen from the mountains and glens into a street battle.

In these narrow wynds and alleyways, their broadswords, dirks and bayonets were as much use as water pistols. When they tried to take refuge in the houses along the way, the cunning Cameronians turned the keys left in the locks and torched the buildings, burning most of the town to the ground. After 16 hours of street-to-street fighting, what had looked like a suicide mission had become a landslide victory for the underdogs. Yet there was an eerie twist to this tale. William Cleland lay dead in the smoking ruins of Dunkeld, just as Claverhouse had fallen one month earlier on another victorious battlefield. Both men became legends, while their causes were thrown to the four winds.

The Battle of Dunkeld could have changed the course of Scottish and British history. Had the Jacobites prevailed, they might have marched on to Edinburgh and reinstated King James VII to the throne of Scotland. Perhaps that would have provoked full-scale civil war, or possibly the opposition would have been too demoralised to fight on for a Dutch king. Certainly, a Jacobite victory would have meant the dissolution of the Union of the Crowns and for better or worse, set Scotland off on a separate journey.

This first Jacobite rising could have been a turning-point in Scotland's history, for good or ill, but the road ends here. For now, at any rate.

Orangeism against Presbyterianism

While the flames of Scottish Jacobitism had turned to ashes, things were beginning to hot up elsewhere. James had gone to Ireland in a reasonably successful bid to rouse the Catholic masses behind the Stuart banner. And William was on his tail.

The final clash came at the Battle of the Boyne, in County Louth, 25 miles north of Dublin. King William's army – 36,000 strong – was drawn from the four corners of Europe, and heavily outnumbered the predominantly Irish Catholic army bolstered by several regiments from France. William's great advantage was to be a central figure in the Grand Alliance that united most of Europe – Catholic as well as Protestant – against the ruthlessly autocratic regime of King Louis XIV of France. Hence his staggering manpower resources.

The scale of the battle was massive, involving 10 times the numbers that had fought either at Killiecrankie or Dunkeld. Yet only 2,000 died, barely 3 per cent of the total number of combatants. The victory of King William of Orange was toasted across the European continent – in Austria, Bavaria, the Dutch Republic, Sweden, Spain, Saxony, Austria, Portugal, England, Scotland. In one of the great ironies of history, it was also celebrated in Rome, at special mass conducted by Pope Alexander VIII.

It is one of the wonders of history that this obscure little man from the Dutch Republic, who could barely string a coherent sentence together in English, would become an enduring and influential legend in these islands. The date of his victory – July 12 1690 – remains engraved in the hearts of hundreds of thousands of Protestants in Ireland and Scotland to this day and is celebrated in parades tens of thousands strong each summer in Belfast and Glasgow. Few monarchs, anywhere in the world, are honoured three centuries after their death with such fervour, by people with so little in the way of wealth or status. For those born and bred in the west of Scotland or the north of Ireland, the image of the red-coated, sword-brandishing king, astride his rampant white horse, is as familiar as the McDonald's golden arches, or the red and white Coca-Cola cans. When it comes to historical celebrity, not even Robert the Bruce can hold a candle to King Billy.

According to the modern Orange Order, 'Our name comes from William, Prince of Orange and is kept because his victory over despotic power laid the foundation for the evolution of Constitutional Democracy in the British Isles.' Curiously, this assertion, that William represented revolution and progress while James stood for counter-revolution and tyranny, is accepted at face value, even by some who wrongly label the modern Orange Order as 'fascist'.

For the Gaels, the poorest and most marginalised people of the islands of Britain and Ireland, the Glorious Revolution was akin to being liberated from a prison into a concentration camp. In Ireland, Catholics – the vast majority of the population – were debarred from voting under the reign of King William III. They had special taxes imposed upon them; they were prohibited from teaching and excluded from all professions, other than medicine; they were banned from industries involved in publishing, printing or distributing books and newspapers. All Catholic orphans were to be raised as Protestants, while Protestants who married Catholics were disinherited. All bishops and archbishops were ordered to leave the country, under threat of execution for high treason, while only one priest per parish was permitted – and they were prohibited from setting foot outside their parish without special permission.

And it wasn't just Catholics who felt the whip of William of Orange. It seems hardly credible, yet the man sanctified on the banners carried through the streets of Belfast and Glasgow every twelfth day of July by diehard Protestants was actually more hostile to Presbyterianism than the Stuart king he deposed. King James had introduced laws for the religious toleration of non-Anglicans, including Catholics, Presbyterians and other dissenters. William reversed these laws, and ordered that the Anglican Church of Ireland, representing a tiny, privileged minority, become the only religious denomination recognised by law.

He was forced, for reasons of pragmatism, to recognise the authority of Presbyterianism in Scotland. But in Ireland, Presbyterian ministers became liable to three months' imprisonment for delivering a sermon, Presbyterian marriages were no longer recognised by law, and intermarriage between Presbyterians and Anglicans was prohibited. In 1704, under William's sister-in-law and successor, Queen Anne, repression against Irish Presbyterians was further ratcheted up. They were barred from holding office in the armed forces, the legal profession, customs and excise, or municipal government. In 1715, Presbyterian ministers were forbidden to teach children, under penalty of a three month prison sentence.

For James Connolly, the Edinburgh-born socialist who would later become the co-leader of the Easter Rising in Dublin, the Jacobite-Williamite conflict was a war between alligators and crocodiles:

> 'Never in all the history of Ireland has there been a war in which the people of Ireland had less reason to be interested either in one side or the other. Irish Catholics shed their blood like water and wasted their wealth like dirt in support of one of the most worthless representatives of a race that ever sat upon the throne.'

He described William as a 'mere adventurer fighting for his own hand', with an army that 'cared as little for Protestantism as they did for human life'. This was 'a war between one set of usurpers who wished to retain, and another set of usurpers who wished to obtain, the mastery of lands stolen from the people'.

Connolly's words could equally be applied to Scotland. The Highland clans and radical Covenanters represented different cultures, different philosophies, different religions, different lifestyles; yet both were in the business of resisting oppression. The Covenanters, and their Presbyterian faith, were feared by the Anglo-Protestant ruling-classes as the devil fears holy water. They had been driven underground, and persecuted brutally by Bonnie Dundee. The Highlanders too had suffered prolonged persecution by the ruling powers in Edinburgh and London. The notorious Statutes of Iona, passed by the Scottish Parliament in the early seventeenth century, had ordered clan chiefs to educate their heirs in English-speaking Protestant schools in the Lowlands, prohibited traditional hospitality and strong drink, and outlawed bards and other bearers of Gaelic culture.

Much of this legislation remained unenforceable. For King William III, however, there was no such word as 'unenforceable'. He resolved to sort out the Highlands once and for all.

Slaughter in the snow

At the head of Loch Linnhe, in the heart of the rebel West Highlands, King William built a mighty military fortress and modestly named it Fort William. He then compelled each and every clan chief to sign an oath of allegiance to the crown. By this time, there was little stomach for resistance in the war-weary Highlands. Not least in Glencoe, a narrow, glacial valley walled steeply by almost menacing, volcanic peaks. Even today, its stunning beauty is shot through with an eerie sense of the events that passed here.

Back in 1692, the tiny settlements at the head of Glencoe, near the modern-day Glencoe village, were inhabited by a peaceable tribe of MacDonalds. They were the smallest of all the sects of Clan Donald, and supporters of the Jacobite cause, though never fanatically so. Because of their habitual cattle rustling they we regarded as a nuisance by the authorities and by some neighbouring clans. But they were also renowned for their generosity and hospitality, admirable even by Highland standards. This was a peaceable community whose easy-going tolerance extended to offering food, drink and shelter to a band of Campbells from Glenlyon, in Perthshire, despite their historic political and religious animosity.

It was a terrible mistake. They should have drawn swords on their guests, and driven them from the hillsides. But how were they to know these friendly strangers would, within a matter of days, attempt to liquidate their community?

A month or so earlier, MacIain, the elderly chief of the Glencoe MacDonalds, had signed the oath of allegiance to King William. He had been naturally reluctant to submit, and had left it to the last day of 1691, the final deadline, going right to the wire as a matter of pride. This was about as much fight as any Highlander had left in him. MacIain had ridden on horseback, at the eleventh hour, to the garrison in Fort William to sign the papers, only to discover he was in the wrong place. The signing, he was told, must be conducted in the presence of his local sheriff – based at the courthouse in the Clan Campbell stronghold of Inverary, 32 miles to the south, as the crow flies. It took him three days to make the journey, partly because of deep snow and partly because, *en route*, he was detained for questioning about the purpose of his journey by a gang of redcoats from the Earl of Argyll's foot regiment.

When his signature was refused, the old man broke down in tears. Fearful of the consequence for his tribe, he begged forgiveness for his lateness. The sheriff informed MacIain that it would be up to the Privy Council, the king's group of official advisers in Scotland, to decide whether the signature was valid. With a sense of relief, the Glencoe chief turned homewards. There he called the men and women of the clan together, telling the assembly that he had signed the oath of allegiance and that they should all now make their peace with King William's government.

Weeks went by.

Then 120 men arrived at the head of the glen, where it opens out onto Loch Leven. They had come from Fort William, across the Ballachulish ferry. They were here, they insisted, not as enemies but as friends and were seeking accommodation locally, because Fort William was full up.

The man in charge, Captain Robert Campbell of Glenlyon, may well have been deliberately set up. Sixty years of age, and an alcoholic shambles by all accounts, he was expendable – a useful fall guy, and unlikely to refuse orders from the king. In a nasty twist, he was also related by marriage to the Glencoe MacDonalds, making it easier for him to ingratiate himself into the community.

Relieved that this was not the feared garrison come to wreak reprisal for the missed deadline, MacIain bid them welcome. And for 11 days, the soldiers stayed, four or five to a cottage, in the tiny hamlets strung along the eight-mile glen. During the day, they played sports with the men of Glencoe: shinty, archery, wrestling, throwing the stone, tossing the caber. It was so cold that they even played curling on Loch Leven. And in the evenings, they gathered around the peat firesides with their hosts to eat and drink, to sing and tell stories, to perform sword dances and play cards.

But on the 12th of February, Robert Campbell's superior officer, a shadowy figure by the name of Captain Thomas Drummond, arrived in the glen to hand him a letter from Major Robert Duncanson, the commander-in-chief of the Argyll Foot Regiment. 'You are hereby ordered to fall upon the rebels, the MacDonalds of Glencoe, and to put all to the sword under seventy. You are to have a special care that the old fox and his sons upon no account escape. This you are to put into execution at five of the clock precisely…' This was, the letter stated, 'by the King's special command'. Failure to comply with the instructions would result in Campbell himself being regarded as a traitor.

That night, snow began to fall gently across the glen. By five o'clock on the morning of the 13th it had turned into a blinding, swirling blizzard, and the killing began. Not all the soldiers participated; some gave warning to their hosts, two others broke their swords in protest. But by sunrise, 38 innocent men were murdered, some in their beds, others as they tried to escape. Forty women and children perished in the freezing snowstorm, after fleeing from their burning homes. Old MacIain had been shot in the back of the head. His wife froze to death after being stripped naked and forced out of her home.

The weather also spared lives. With their intimate knowledge of this landscape, many were able to find their way to safety through the white-out, including the two sons of MacIain, who had been singled out as targets for execution.

Glencoe was a shameful war crime. The numbers who died were small compared to the death tolls tallied up on Scotland's battlefields during that violent century. But this was no battlefield. This was a community of families, unarmed, unsuspecting, and having made their peace with the enemy.

News of the massacre aroused revulsion the length and breadth of Scotland. Hastily, the Scottish Government ordered a Commission of Inquiry, and when they received the report, condemned the slaughter as 'Murder under Trust' – a Scots Law category more heinous than simple murder. They also identified the man responsible – the Secretary of State for Scotland, John Dalrymple, Master of Stair. He had, said the report, urged the destruction of the MacDonalds of Glencoe 'with a great deal of zeal as a thing acceptable, and of public use'.

It was a sensational result. Dalrymple, a wealthy landowner who could trace his lineage back to the fourteenth century, was the crown's supreme ruler in Scotland. He was also a fanatical unionist, whose conviction that Scotland and England would be better together drove him to order the extirpation of the Glencoe clan. In his authoritative 1966 account, *Glencoe*, historian John Prebble notes: 'Dalrymple knew that the English would never accept the Scots as civilized equals until their warring mountain tribes had been crushed.' He hoped to make an example of the clan in the expectation that this would cow the rest of the restless Highlands, thus making England more amenable to union, and allowing a smooth progression towards the formation of a British state.

In the aftermath of the slaughter, Dalrymple was remorseless. 'Tis strange to me that there is so much regret for such a sept of thieves', he said, in response to criticism of the atrocity. Under orders from King William, Dalrymple continued to hunt down the remnants of the Glencoe MacDonalds, and saw to their deportation to the colonies on the grounds that they were enemies within. But when the Scottish Parliament named him as the guilty man, his career was shattered. He had no option but to resign his post as Secretary of State for Scotland, and keep his head down for the next few years.

Meanwhile, William denied all knowledge of the plan, claiming that he 'knew little about it until eighteen months after'. Few people in Scotland believed him, but Dalrymple, staunchly loyal to his royal master, and probably knowing full well there was something in it for him, said nothing. In return, William treated the naming and shaming of his servant with open contempt. In a kick in the teeth to the Scottish Parliament, he publicly exonerated Dalrymple, insisting that 'he could have had no knowledge nor accession to the method of that execution… he had no hand in the barbarous manner of execution.' Instead, he laid the blame squarely on the soldiers and officers on the ground. Yet no-one was punished; not Captain Robert Duncanson, whose signature was on the letter ordering the massacre, nor Captain Robert Campbell, who carried out those orders. Instead all those responsible for the massacre were promoted. One became a colonel, another a knight, a third a peer, and a fourth an earl.

Glencoe was not a turning-point in history. It didn't alter the course of events, nor even the course of careers. But in the Highlands those responsible would never be forgotten nor forgiven.

8

THE END OF A WRETCHED CENTURY

Poured down the Panama

The 70 years from around 1645 to 1715 are today known by scientists as the Little Ice Age. These were decades of ferocious storms and vicious frosts, when great tidal waves flooded fertile coastal plains and a seemingly permanent blanket of snow smothered the mountains, even in midsummer. During this series of long, bitter winters, the Thames froze over, sports such as curling and skating became popular in Scotland, and Inuit people arrived in Orkney in canoes as the Arctic ice sheet expanded southwards.

The climate crisis reached its climax between 1695 and 1698 when the harvest failed for three years out of four. Grain prices soared, cattle perished, and human hordes roamed the countryside desperately seeking scraps of food. An estimated 5 per cent of the population starved to death, though in some regions – Aberdeenshire, for instance – as many as 20 per cent, or one in five, are believed to have perished. 'Everyone may see Death in the face of the poor that abound everywhere; the thinness of their visage, their ghostly looks, their feebleness, their agues and their fluxes', wrote the eminent physician, Sir Robert Sibbald, in 1699.

According to historian Tom Devine, in *Scotland's Empire*, the death toll pro rata to the population puts it on a par with the great Irish Famine 150 years later. In total, Scotland lost up to 160,000 people, half from hunger and disease, and the rest from a combination of mass emigration and a plummeting birth rate. Of the tens of thousands who fled the country, the vast majority went to Ulster. These were not swaggering colonisers but impoverished refugees, some of whose descendants would, a century later, play an active part in Ireland's first revolutionary republican movement, the United Irishmen.

The primeval force of nature was more powerful than any monarch – and in those religious times, the winter of desolation must have felt like a punishment sent by God himself.

The second catastrophe in the twilight years of the seventeenth century can be blamed neither on divine intervention nor on nature. It was a man-made disaster, borne of overarching ambition and greed. The Darien Affair – a bid to establish a Scottish colony on a narrow isthmus in the Bay of Panama in Central America – was an audacious attempt to buck the trend and bring in the riches that other, more aggressively imperialist nations had enjoyed. It was also, according to John Prebble, an attempt to take a step away from centuries of violence and bloodshed towards a brighter future of trade and commerce.

By this time England, with its larger population, greater wealth and royal sponsorship, had built the strongest navy in the world and was busy carving out an empire stretching almost 10,000 miles around the globe, from the eastern seaboard of North America to the Bay of Bengal. Its warships also patrolled Scottish waters, watching out for Jacobite activity and clamping down on clandestine trade between Scotland and the English colonies.

Desperate to break free of this stranglehold, the Scottish Parliament passed an Act in 1695 setting up the Company of Scotland, which authorised its directors to establish Scottish colonies in areas where there was no existing European presence. When they went to London to drum up investment for the first expedition, to Panama, both houses of the Westminster Parliament piled pressure on the king to scupper the project, which was deemed a threat to England's interests. William himself expressed outrage at the brazenness of the Scots in trying to rise above their station. 'I have been ill served in Scotland', he thundered. English investors pulled out and the nation was left to fund the venture alone.

According to Tom Devine, the total capital tied up in Darien amounted to two and half times the total value of Scottish exports – and this at a time of famine. It was a monumental gamble of the same order as the bank lending spree that would bring the global financial system crashing to its knees four centuries later. In July 1698, a fleet of four ships carrying 1,200 settlers arrived in Darien, an area roughly the size of the Highlands north of the Great Glen. With no means of communication, their fate was unknown until a second expedition arrived a year later to find a ruined, deserted settlement. The following year, the final remnants of the colony returned to Scotland. Out of 13 ships, only two returned.

The Darien failure was so calamitous that it almost eclipsed even the famine ravaging the Scottish countryside. Almost a quarter of the country's liquid assets had been swallowed up in its ruinous vortex. Some 2,000 men and women had sailed from the Port of Leith, never to return. Scarcely a family in the Lowlands was unaffected by this tragic misadventure.

What went so wrong with Darien? In fact, almost nothing went right. First, there was the tropical fever that wiped out scores of colonists. Then there was the aggression of the Spanish, who regarded this entire region of Panama as their own. Perhaps most decisive of all was the hostility of King William, who ordered all English colonies in the Americas to resist and destroy the colony. In the late 1690s, Spain was a key ally of England in the marathon war in Europe against Louis XIV of France – and the last thing King William needed was a bunch of upstart Scots jeopardising that military coalition. As Tom Devine comments, 'Darien proved conclusively that when the vital interests of Scotland and England were in conflict, the monarchy would always opt to support the position of the more powerful kingdom.' The Union of the Crowns had lasted almost a century, but now the writing was on the wall. King William was despised across most of Scotland; for Glencoe, for Darien, and for the exploitation of Scotland to fund foreign wars on behalf of what was essentially an English empire.

By the end of the wretched century, Scotland was on its knees. The country had been torn apart by a series of destructive conflicts. The old cultural divergence between Highland and Lowland had mutated into an ugly, gaping chasm through which had poured torrents of blood. And the economy of the nation was now slowly suffocating following the removal of foreign policy from Edinburgh to London. Scotland was not only cut off from its important French markets as a result of England's ongoing wars with that nation, it was also crippled by the tax burden imposed by King William to finance these very conflicts. Instead of prosperity, the Union of the Crowns had dragged Scotland into a cesspit of war, starvation and bankruptcy. Andrew Fletcher of Saltoun, who would become the foremost opponent of the Union of 1707, was moved to comment: 'Notwithstanding the great and disproportionate numbers of sea and land soldiers that we were obliged to furnish for the support of the war, yet not one tittle of advantage was procured to us by the peace.'

The dying dynasty

Tensions came to a head in 1701 when the ancient royal family of Scotland, which had been central to the Union of the Crowns, began to hurtle towards oblivion. The Stuart line was the fragile thread that had held the two countries together for a hundred years. It had even survived the overthrow of James VII in favour of William of Orange, who had inherited a few drops of Stuart blood through his maternal line, and had then wed the King's estranged Protestant daughter. It was a piece of constitutional trickery, the genealogical equivalent of cooking the books, but it helped keep the Union of the Crowns intact.

King William, however, had an Achilles heel. He failed to produce an heir. Perhaps he was infertile, or perhaps, as some historians claim, he was gay, and his marriage was a sham. Either way, the problem could have been sorted had only his sister-in-law and successor, Queen Anne, delivered the goods. She did try, heroically. No fewer than 17 times she became pregnant by her Danish husband. But she suffered a dozen miscarriages and stillbirths, and four other children died in infancy. When her last surviving child died at the age of 11 in 1700, the Protestant strand of the Stuart family was set to snap.

Queen Anne had dozens of cousins and second cousins scattered across Europe. Inconveniently, they were of the wrong religion. In the paranoid anti-Catholic atmosphere of the times, this amounted to a constitutional time-bomb, and it was set to detonate on the day of the ailing Queen's death. To defuse the crisis, the English Parliament passed the notorious Act of Settlement of 1701, which remains on the statute books to this day. This legislation to ban Catholics from the throne might have been expected to go down well in Presbyterian Scotland. Instead it caused uproar.

First, because it effectively served notice on the the ancient bloodline of Scotland, the House of Stuart, in favour of the German House of Hanover. Second, Jacobite sympathies remained strong in the Highlands and north-east of the country, and this provocation could rekindle the violent divisions of just a few decades earlier. Third – and perhaps most seriously of all – the Scottish Parliament had never been consulted over the inflammatory legislation. Coming on top of the Darien debacle, this casual assumption of superiority by Westminster looked like a calculated insult to the Scottish nation. It was the most blatant assault yet on Scotland's sovereignty.

The Scottish Parliament retaliated by insisting that it alone would decide upon Queen Anne's successor for the crown of Scotland. It further warned that, unless Scotland was granted free trade and access to the colonies, the Union of the Crowns itself would be dissolved. And while they were about it, the parliament decided that from now on, Scotland would have the right to declare war and peace, independently of England and its monarch.

Enraged by this bare-faced defiance, Westminster hit back with the Aliens

Act, passed in February 1705. The legislation ordered that Scottish nationals in England were to be treated as aliens, and estates held south of the border by Scots regarded as foreign-owned property, leaving it open to confiscation. It then demanded that Scotland enter negotiations for an incorporating union by Christmas Day, 1705, or face the consequences: a blanket ban an all exports of coal, linen and cattle to England and the English colonies, which would effectively shut down half of all Scottish trade. It was, says Tom Devine, 'a naked piece of economic blackmail designed to bring the Scottish Parliament to heel.'

It sparked a fever of anti-English rage with tragic consequences for three innocent sailors whose ship was intercepted on the Firth of Forth. When word spread that some English pirates had been captured, mobs many thousands strong rampaged down the Royal Mile, hell-bent on revenge. Such was the intensity of anti-English hysteria in the weeks following the Aliens Act that everyone wanted to believe they were guilty of heinous crimes. It was an ugly display of ethnic hatred; some had walked for 50 miles, armed with clubs and swords, to wreak revenge on these unfortunate wretches, who were almost certainly innocent of any crime other than their assumed nationality. As it happens, one of the three men was actually Scottish, so he was branded a traitor and enemy collaborator. The trial was a travesty of justice, with no credible evidence brought forward to support a conviction. But swept along by public outrage, like a flotilla of canoes caught up in a hurricane, the crown's legal representatives in Scotland pronounced the three men guilty and sentenced them to death. On 11 April, they were taken to Leith Sands and hanged.

The two nations were now diverging rapidly. Among the mass of the Scottish population, England was viewed in much the same way as the state of Israel is viewed in Gaza and the West Bank today. Scotland felt itself imprisoned in a bitter and at times violent relationship, which over the centuries had deteriorated from mutual suspicion to outright hatred. So what was to be done? 'Let's publish the banns!' was the cry of the ruling elites, on both sides of the border.

9

SURRENDER

A monarchist mission

The struggle for the soul of Scotland began in earnest on the first day of September 1705. On that day, under pressure from Westminster and the crown, Scottish MPs voted to set a up a commission to negotiate a treaty with England, to try to resolve the bitter conflict between the two countries.

At that stage, Scotland was overwhelmingly opposed to the idea of an incorporating union, or an 'obliterating union' as it was described by opponents. Among the broad mass of the population, opposition ran at a level of around 99 to 1 – and that was according to a prominent unionist, Sir John Clerk of Penicuik. Even among the elected MPs, there was an outright majority opposed to the liquidation of the Scottish Parliament.

So what happened over the next 16 months to deliver the Act of Union that would spell the end of centuries of political independence? Who drove the pro-union agenda? And why did Scotland finally capitulate? Many historians to this day portray the union as a goal that was driven by the rising merchant classes desperate to get access to England's colonial markets. In this version of events, it was a pragmatic case of sacrificing national sovereignty in exchange for a share of the spoils of a burgeoning empire. The battle for Scotland's independence was, in essence, a confrontation between insular conservatives clinging to the past, and progressives facing the direction of travel. Neat, but the opposite of the truth.

From the start, the idea of union was a monarchist mission driven by the crown. King William had set the ball rolling – fittingly perhaps, given his later canonisation, so to speak, by Irish and Scottish unionists. In his final message to the House of Commons, just eight days before his death in 1702, he urged closer union. His successor, Queen Anne, had scant knowledge of Scotland beyond a brief sojourn north of the border at the age of 16, which wasn't yesterday. Anne regarded the Scots with cold contempt. They were repellent, unreasonable, strange people. Their only saving grace was that they were not as bad as the Irish.

Nevertheless, she advocated 'indissoluble union between the two nations as the most likely means under heaven to establish the monarchy, secure the peace and increase the trade, wealth and happiness of both nations'. Her Scottish accomplices were mostly to be found amongst the feudal aristocracy, while Scotland's burghs, ports and traders were overwhelmingly against union, including even the Glasgow tobacco barons, who would eventually gain most from access to England's transatlantic markets.

The Scottish Parliament was a unicameral, or single chamber, body made up of three estates: a contingent of elected commissioners from the burghs; a further group of commissioners elected from the shires; and 62 unelected nobles, around a third of the total number of parliamentarians.

By the early eighteenth century, the chamber was roughly divided into four political blocs, the biggest being the Court Party, which had run Scotland since 1689. During the revolution, it had supported King William against King James, but had since had become the most conservative political force in the land, resisting every attempt at further reform and defending the status quo against all-comers. It was, in essence, an alliance of feudal magnates and pro-Whig members of the legal establishment.

The Court Party's key leaders were the Duke of Queensberry, an ancestor of the Duke of Buccleuch who owned vast estates in the south of Scotland; John Campbell, the second Duke of Argyll, who was notoriously driven by insatiable greed for wealth and status; the Earl of Stair, who had orchestrated the Glencoe Massacre; and the Earls of Cromartie and Seafield, two slippery nobles who had supported the Stuart dynasty before switching to the winning side. As its name suggests, the Court Party was loyal through and through to the crown. And the monarch was now demanding union.

The anti-union forces were bigger, but less cohesive. They included a band of Jacobites, who wanted to restore James VII to the throne of an independent Scotland. Another small group, the Squadron Volante, or Flying Squad, was a loose association of nobles from the south of Scotland with around two dozen votes in parliament. They began by opposing union, but then switched sides when the bribes began to flow. The biggest anti-union force by far was the Country Party, a loose coalition of dissidents united in opposition to the corruption and conservatism of the crown's satellite government in Edinburgh. In common with the modern SNP, it was an ideological and social hodgepodge, an amorphous national movement capable of appealing to a broad cross-section of the population in the name of patriotism. Initially it stood for an equal, federal union; but as it became clear that such an arrangement would never be countenanced by the English state, the Country Party's attitude hardened into support for independence.

Its parliamentarians included some discontented nobles who had been bypassed for key positions. But it also contained a radical nucleus around Andrew Fletcher of Saltoun, one of the most outstanding political thinkers in Scottish history, respected even by opponents for his intellectual rigour and vision. For years, Fletcher had been scathing of the Union of the Crowns: 'Since that time we have had neither spirit, nor liberty, nor trade, nor money among us.' In his view, it had bred corruption and subservience. His absolute honesty and integrity impressed even those who did not share his political views. One English secret service spy described him thus: 'A gentleman steady in his principles, of nice honour, with abundance of learning, brave as the sword he wears and bold as a lion. He would lose his life readily to save his country, and would not do a base thing to save it.'

Fletcher was immensely popular outside parliament for his implacable opposition to corruption – 'the blackest of all crimes; when I name any guilty of it, I name an odious criminal'. While avoiding personal rancour, he was scathing of the greed and ambition of the Court Party, which had been 'bought off with positions and profit by the crown' and was now 'nothing but an English interest in this House'. He opposed union on radical grounds. It had no shred of progressive political or social content; it would make honest, enlightened government more difficult; it pandered to the aristocracy by guaranteeing the preservation of feudalism; it would lead to a political system even more corrupt than the current arrangement.

His faction developed a twelve point programme of advanced constitutional reform that included annual parliamentary elections; an end to the royal veto over legislation; parliament rather than the monarch to have the sole right to declare war or to sign peace; a people's militia for national defence; and the monarch to forfeit the crown if he or she defied parliament. Fletcher stopped short of outright republicanism, but his programme would have reduced the monarch to a mere decoration and, had it ever been implemented even in part, could well have set Scotland on course for republicanism.

The idea of universal suffrage was unthinkable at that point in history. The Chartist movement was still more than a century away, and the Suffragettes, two centuries. Yet Fletcher was more than 50 years ahead of his time, anticipating some of the central ideas that would propel the American and French Revolutions. His radicalism extended to economic matters and international affairs. Himself a laird – a non-aristocratic small-scale landowner – he attacked the vicious oppression of poor tenants under the feudal agrarian system. He supported the idea of a rudimentary welfare state, in which the government would take responsibility for the sick and the elderly. He called for society to be 'attended with a more equal distribution of riches than trade and commerce will allow', and supported reform of the educational system to make it practical and relevant to those from the lower social classes.

Fletcher was no insular nationalist, but an internationalist critical of the crown's colonial policy. He condemned England's tyrannical rule over Ireland and its ill-treatment of Wales and the American colonies. He believed the 'great and overgrown powers' of Europe had become too big for their boots; their sheer size encouraged corruption at home and provoked conflict with neighbours. He advocated the sub-division of Europe into smaller states, which would be free to enter into voluntary federations. Within national states, he argued for maximum decentralisation. Too much wealth and power was concentrated in capital cities, sucking the lifeblood out of the provinces. The solution, he suggested, would be to develop regional centres of government in fledgling cities such as Bristol, Exeter, Chester, Norwich, York, Stirling, Inverness, Dublin, Cork, Galway and Derry.

Fletcher displayed no trace of anti-English sentiment, believing that relations between the two countries would improve if Scotland moved towards real independence. The alternative to union, he argued, was not the status quo, but political and social reform, which in turn would help push England in a more progressive direction. Many of his ideas were generations ahead of his time, but although some of his solutions were too radical to be taken seriously in the early eighteenth century, his programme to curb the powers of the crown and the nobility resonated strongly with the wider population outside parliament.

Unfortunately, the recognised leader of the Country Party was made of different material. Unlike Fletcher, the Duke of Hamilton was a powerful aristocrat, with great landed estates on both sides of the Scotland-England border and a clutch of grand titles to his name, including the Premier Peer of Scotland, the Keeper of the Palace of Holyroodhouse, the Master of the Great Wardrobe and the Master-General of the Ordnance. He was, says historian William Ferguson, 'a haughty aristocrat who could not really endorse the radical schemes proposed by Fletcher of Saltoun'. His support for reform was shallow and insipid, a reluctant but necessary concession to Fletcher and his allies.

With such a pedigree, Hamilton would have fitted cosily into the leadership of the governing Court Party; but despite his illustrious genealogy, he was viewed as something of a maverick within Scotland's ruling elite. Although a Presbyterian, he had supported James against the Prince of Orange, and had refused to cross over to the Williamite camp even after the Glorious Revolution. He had even spent a few short spells imprisoned in the Tower of London for suspected intrigue against the state. As a descendant on his mother's side of the House of Stuart, he almost certainly harboured ambitions to become king of an independent Scotland. He also nursed a personal enmity towards the leader of the Court Party, Lord Queensberry.

As the debate over the union intensified, Hamilton's erratic behaviour left his own anti-union side disoriented and demoralised. His bizarre zig-zags and mysterious U-turns have even baffled generations of historians. On 1 September 1705, the day when parliament discussed the proposal to set up a commission to negotiate a treaty with England, Hamilton unexpectedly endorsed the plan. Perhaps he thought it could lead to some kind of federal union with England, in which Scotland's parliament and sovereignty would be safeguarded? But to the shock of his own party, and the amazement of his opponents, Hamilton then stood up and proposed that Queen Anne should be invited to appoint Scotland's team of commissioners. His motion was carried by just four votes, and would almost certainly have been defeated had the forces of the Country Party not been depleted. 'From this day, may we date Scotland's ruin,' wrote Jacobite MP George Lockhart in his Memoirs.

No fewer than 29 Scottish commissioners out of 31 Scottish hand-picked by Queen Anne were landowners and bankers connected with the pro-union Court Party, which made up less than half the membership of the Scottish Parliament. To give pretence of balance, the numbers were made up with a token Jacobite, George Lockhart, and a member of the Squadron Volante.

Negotiations began on 16 April 1706, in the Cockpit Theatre in London, now part of the Cabinet Office in Whitehall. The first hurdles were overcome within days when the Scots accepted that the German House of Hanover would take over the throne after Queen Anne's death, and the English agreed that Scotland would gain open access to its colonial markets.

Thereafter, Scotland's commissioners did indulge in the occasional bout of posturing as a PR exercise to persuade the Scottish public that they were driving a hard bargain, but they gained nothing more. After three months, the discussions were complete – and Scotland's team of commissioners voted by 30 to 1 to ratify the Treaty, with only George Lockhart dissenting.

Cash, titles and riots

For a further three months, the Treaty was kept under lock and key. Meanwhile, behind the scenes, the real negotiations began – for the spoils of the future union. The full extent of the financial bribery would only be uncovered by later historians. The Earl of Glasgow, for example, secretly received and disbursed a slush fund of £20,000 sterling, with no receipts or vouchers – the equivalent of £350 million in today's money. Queensberry himself managed to negotiate £12,000, equivalent to £200 million (as measured by relative value).

Money didn't do all the talking. There were peerages and offices of state too. John Campbell, the Duke of Argyll, demanded a seat in the House of Lords and a major-generalship within the British Army. He also negotiated a peerage for his younger brother, Archibald, who chose the title Earl of Islay after first causing fury among the Graham clan when he tried to declare himself Earl of Dundee.

Perhaps the biggest coup of all was the perfectly targeted bribe bestowed on the Earl of Roxburghe, leader of Squadron Volante, the flabbily anti-union party that held the balance of power in the parliament. At a crucial stage in the debate, he persuaded his party to execute a dramatic U-turn, transforming the fortunes of the pro-union camp. It was well known that he was desperate for a dukedom. Lo and behold, after his party secured the union, Queen Anne elevated him to the position of Duke of Roxburghe. To celebrate his promotion, the grateful noble built the magnificent Floors Castle, just outside Selkirk in the Scottish Borders.

Bitterness over the skulduggery of the Scottish nobility has festered ever since, the sordid goings-on summed up contemptuously by Robert Burns in *Such a Parcel of Rogues in a Nation*:

'What force or guile could not subdue,
Thro' many warlike ages,
Is wrought now by a coward few,
For hireling traitor's wages.
The English steel we could disdain,
Secure in valour's station;
But English gold has been our bane,
Such a parcel of rogues in a nation!'

The 25 articles of the Treaty of Union were finally published on October 1706, and for the next three months, parliamentarians wrangled over it, clause by knotty clause. But it was a phoney war. The battle had already been won and lost, not in the debating chamber but in the backrooms of Edinburgh's salons and cafes, where the weapons were neither words nor swords, but cash and titles. According to historian Tom Devine, when the crunch came, only 12 MPs supported the union without financial inducement or promise of high office. While the charade rumbled on inside the parliament, the rest of Scotland went into meltdown. For three weeks in late November and early December 1706, Glasgow was convulsed by riots, provoked by the refusal of the city's magistrates to sign an anti-union petition. James Clark, a Presbyterian minister at the city's Tron Church, called on his congregation to put no trust in petitions or pleas to 'parliaments or princes' but to take to the streets. One old soldier of Jacobite sympathies, known only as Finlay, emerged as the key leader of anti-union resistance in the city, and was arrested for trying to turn the disorder into an armed insurrection. Amid this chaos, the city's Lord Provost attempted to flee to Edinburgh, while the town council was forced by mass pressure to deliver an anti-union address.

On 21 November 2006, a group of 300 armed Cameronians, the remnants of the militant Covenanters, took over Dumfries town centre and, before a cheering crowd of thousands, burned the Articles of Union, after pronouncing them 'utterly destructive of the nation's independency, crown rights and constitutional laws, both civil and sacred'.

Traditional divisions of religion, culture and geography were cast aside as historical enemies began to make common cause in the movement to stop the destruction of Scotland's independence. In November, secret discussions were held between Cameronians in the south-west and the Earl of Atholl in Perthshire, with the aim of raising a Jacobite-Covenanter army, 8,000-strong, to march on Edinburgh and halt any further discussion of the Treaty. A force of that size would have easily overwhelmed the 1,500-strong Scottish standing army which had been mobilised to protect the capital, but at the last minute, the wavering Duke of Hamilton intervened to call off the uprising.

In Edinburgh itself, pro-union politicians were pelted daily with improvised missiles as they made their way up the Royal Mile to Parliament House to discuss the details of the Treaty, while the arch-unionist Duke of Queensbury required a daily military escort to protect him on the half-mile journey from his home in the Canongate. In one incident an angry mob laid siege to the home of the capital's Lord Provost, Sir Patrick Johnstone. Daniel Defoe, the future author of *Robinson Crusoe*, who was then employed as an English Government spy and propagandist in the city, captured the sense of mutiny in the city in one vivid description:

> 'I heard a great noise and looking out saw a terrible multitude come up the High Street with a drum at the head of them shouting and swearing and crying out, all Scotland would stand together, No Union, No Union, English dogs and the like.'

Fortunately for the crown, fierce storms raged across the nation during these dark winter months, rendering the primitive roads impassable and isolating Edinburgh from the rest of the country. In those devoutly religious times, it must have seemed that God was a unionist.

The ruling elites of both Scotland and England knew that they had unleashed a force that could escalate out of control. The status quo was no longer an option. If the Scottish Parliament failed to liquidate itself, the Union of the Crowns would almost certainly topple, given the zealous role of Queen Anne and the passions that had been aroused. The stakes were sky-high. So they pulled out all the stops to divide the opposition and deliver victory. In November, the crown guaranteed that the Church of Scotland would retain its status as the national church. The General Assembly was placated, which helped partially defuse resistance at a local level; however, many ministers continued to denounce the Treaty from their pulpits.

There were sticks as well as carrots. Forever lurking in the background during several years of negotiations was the threat of invasion. During the 1706-1707 winter of discontent, English troops began to mass in the north of Ireland, ready to invade south-west Scotland, while further contingents marched northwards through England to the border, within striking distance of Edinburgh. Some historians suggest that this mobilisation was merely to maintain law and order, and to prevent mob rule. Others insist that the threat of military occupation was designed to intimidate the parliamentarians, turning the union into the kind of offer you can't refuse. Whatever the purpose of these military machinations, the parliament was soon sewn up, certainly by bribery, and probably also through fear.

The only way forward for the anti-union forces inside the parliament was to carry the struggle outside to the people. It was agreed to stage a walkout in January 1707, before the bill was voted upon, then boycott the rest of the proceedings. Such a dramatic gesture might well have detonated a movement of such magnitude that that the union, even at that late stage, would have been halted in its tracks. But just as the anti-union parliamentarians were ready to walk out and set Scotland alight, the recognised leader of the anti-union forces, the Duke of Hamilton, failed to appear. His excuse? Toothache.

It may have been described by Burns, in a moment of torment, as 'the hell of all diseases', but it was a hell of a lame excuse for stumbling at the gate of history – like Robert the Bruce putting in his apologies for Bannockburn because he had a bit of a sniffle. Historians debate to this day whether Hamilton was bribed or blackmailed – or whether he simply took fright at the prospect of spearheading a full-scale rebellion against the crown and the English Parliament. It is now known that he was heavily in debt, and that he had, through marriage, acquired substantial landed estates in the north of England which he would forfeit if the union failed to materialise. Some believe he may also have been threatened with a charge of treason, carrying the death penalty, because of dealings he had had with King Louis XIV in France. Either way, it was yet another inglorious episode in the sorry history of the Scottish aristocracy.

Bribery, blackmail and bullying had won the day. On 16 January 1707, against all the odds and in defiance of an enraged nation, the Scottish Parliament voted itself into oblivion by 110 votes to 67. When the deed was done, 'there was nothing save discontent and lamentation to be heard throughout

Scotland', and that was according to the Tory Unionist, Sir Walter Scott. England celebrated with joyous bell-ringing across the land. The hero of the hour, the Duke of Queensberry, the man who had delivered Scotland, was invited to a celebration service in April in St Paul's Cathedral, alongside Queen Anne and her ministers. As he made his way through the streets of London he was greeted like an Olympic gold medallist.

In Scotland, there was no flag-waving or cheering – only the mournful cry of the wind and the rain.

Better together?

There was one grisly postscript to the sorry saga. On the day the Treaty of Union came into effect, May Day 1707, the Scottish elite celebrated in Parliament House while angry crowds protested outside. While this commotion was in full throttle, the Duke of Queensberry's mentally ill young son, the Earl of Drumlanrig, escaped from his room, seized a servant boy in the kitchen, roasted him on the spit and began eating his flesh. For opponents of the union, this was an act of God, a punishment for Queensberry's role in the Act of Union. The former kitchen of Queensberry House, now the Allowances Office of the Scottish Parliament, is said to be haunted.

For the English ruling class, the Act of Union had been a masterfully engineered takeover. Their long-held ambition to rule the entire island had at last been achieved, at a bargain-basement price. England had secured its vulnerable northern border, opened up a sizeable new market for its fledgling manufacturing industries and increased the landmass under its control by an extra 50 per cent. Further, it had enlarged its tax and revenue base by an additional 20 per cent and secured a generous supply of well-educated recruits to help staff its expanding overseas empire. All of these gains were achieved without any legal or constitutional upheaval, because the new United Kingdom of Great Britain was essentially an enlarged version of England. Over the centuries, the terms Britain, England and the United Kingdom would become interchangeable south of the Tweed and east of the Severn.

But what if Scotland had refused the road to union? What if, after all, we had remained apart? Some historians insist that a stubbornly single Scotland would have been invaded and crushed by England – that union was simply a polite version of the inevitable. In *Scotland: Shaping of a Nation*, Gordon Donaldson argues that 'England was not going to permit a disruption of the existing [regal] union, and the scanty and ill-trained Scottish regiments could not have resisted Marlborough's veterans'. Michael Lynch, author of *Scotland: A New History*, argues that 'the need to make a decision at all depended on the threat of English invasion'. Paul Scott, a strongly anti-union historian, is adamant that the military threat was real, and decisive in securing the vote.

Yet despite the threat of invasion, and despite the bribery, and despite the blackmail, over a third of Scotland's politicians voted to defy the crown. Whether England would have gone the full hog and invaded Scotland is an open question. It is, after all, one thing to threaten an invasion, and quite another to carry it out. England was already embroiled in a major war on the continent in 1707. A full-scale occupation of Scotland would have been a massive drain on the country's already stretched military and financial reserves.

So what if Scotland's parliamentarians had faced down the threat of invasion, spurned the bribery, and ignored the blackmail? Would that have led, as some pro-union historians claim, to the restoration of the Stuart monarchy north of the border and an alliance with the royal dictatorship of Louis XIV of France? Given the political balance of forces in Scotland, that seems unlikely. The main strut of feudalism – the aristocracy – was overwhelmingly on the side of the crown and the union. The anti-union currents that had most influence among the people were closer to Dutch-style republicanism than to French absolutism. A defeat for the union of 1707 would more likely have shifted the balance of power in Scotland away from the feudal lords towards the emerging middle classes.

Jacobitism, at this stage, was a flame that flickered rather than roared. In any case, by 1707, the Jacobite movement was less a coherent ideology and more a resistance force against religious and cultural oppression. Within a progressive, independent Scotland, free from religious discrimination and cultural imperialism, Jacobitism could potentially have faded away altogether.

Andrew Fletcher, we know, was trusted by the Jacobite minority; although a Presbyterian who had participated in William's coup against James VII, he had later turned against the Dutch-born king with a vengeance, increasingly so in the wake of Glencoe, when he accused the Earl of Stair of murder, thundering: 'I once believed William of Orange to be an honourable man even though, like other men, he can act mistakenly. But this, this is beyond all bearing. Execution without trial, without legal sanction, of a number of the King's subjects, in time of peace, of Scottish subjects on the orders of a man who has never so much as set foot in Scotland.'

Jacobitism would later lead the struggle to dissolve the union only because, as historian Bruce Lenman explains, 'After 1707, only force could reverse the decision and only Jacobites were prepared to give a lead in resorting to force to break the Union. They had nothing to lose.' By that time, Fletcher was dying. From his death bed, he left £200 in his will to assist Jacobite prisoners, while lamenting that 'there wasn't too much to be said for either side'.

From the outset, it was perhaps inevitable that Scotland would be swallowed alive. England, as well as being richer by 10 to 1, was also five times more populous. Some concessions were granted to sweeten the bitter pill. To keep the law and judiciary on board, Westminster had permitted Scotland to keep its own legal system. To silence the Kirk, they had allowed the Church of Scotland to retain its status as a national institution. To defuse discontent in the universities, and across the influential teaching profession, they had backed off from imposing an alien education system. But all of this was small beer compared to what went south – which was pretty much everything else.

Scotland's commissioners had consented to 45 seats in the House of Commons and 16 in the House of Lords. With just one-twelfth of the total representation in Westminster, Scotland's influence would be marginal.

This gross power imbalance is accepted by historians as unavoidable in a union between two numerically unequal states. Yet consider the creation of another historic union several centuries later. The much maligned Union of Soviet Socialist Republics was formally established in 1922, as a consequence of the 1917 October Revolution. In the early days, when it was still based on ideals of justice and egalitarianism, the Soviet Union was a model of national equality, diversity and autonomy. Under the ultra-centralised Tsarist state, only the Russian ethnic group had been officially recognised as a nationality within the great empire that stretched from the Arctic Circle to the Black Sea, embracing scores of languages and cultures. But within five years of the revolution, small nations that wished to secede were set free, and new democratic republics were founded in territories which had previously known only vicious persecution. All ethnic minorities, no matter how small, were granted their own national territories and awarded a high degree of autonomy. In some of these territories, new written national languages were created from scratch. New alphabets were even invented to facilitate the development of national culture. And most strikingly relevant to the Act of Union, each of the republics which made up the Soviet Union was granted equal representation in the government, irrespective of their size or population.

That process of encouraging democracy, equality and decentralisation would eventually be halted, then crudely reversed by Josef Stalin, the Georgian-born dictator whom Lenin denounced from his death-bed as a 'Great Russian bully'. But from 1917 until well into the 1920s, Soviet socialism was a colourful mosaic of flourishing cultures, rather than the grey monolith of its later decades. By contrast, the new British state was based on the same philosophy of centralism, regimentation and uniformity that motivated the Russian Tsars and Stalin.

Many mainstream historians – on both sides of the border, and on both sides of the current debate over Scotland's constitutional future – insist that the Act of Union was a great leap forward in human civilisation. The skulduggery that achieved it may have been distasteful, but ultimately it saved Scotland from itself. Without Britain, this small northern country would have slid into a Celtic twilight of eternal destitution and backwardness. Instead it powered its way into the industrial age and beyond, to become a peaceful, prosperous successful nation, thanks to those 110 men who decided that Scotland should cease to exist as an independent sovereign state.

There is, however, an alternative view, which suggests that far from being better together, Scotland's long term confinement within a political union moulded and shaped by external power structures would ultimately be detrimental to the political, social, cultural, economic, ecological and psychological health of the nation.

10

UNDER THE UNION FLAG

'The Grand Masters of corruption'

Under the union, things surely could only get better? Actually, they got worse. Much worse.

Before 1707, Scotland's political classes could not entirely disregard the mood of the people. During the debates over the fateful Treaty, members of the pro-union Court Party had to be smuggled into the parliament via underground tunnels to protect them from the wrath of the masses. But with the politicians now living in a distant city, one month's journey from Edinburgh by stagecoach, there was no trace of public accountability. Marginalised in Westminster, and shorn of responsibility for deciding anything of any significance, Scottish politicians now concentrated their efforts on self-enrichment. Bribery, fraud, corruption and nepotism in public life began to spiral out of control. As labour historian Tom Johnston put it: 'Politics was simply the high road to plunder for the landed interest.'

One key clause in the Treaty sums up the essence of the anti-progressive character of the union: 'That all heritable Offices, Superiorities, heritable Jurisdictions, Offices for life, and Jurisdictions for life, be reserved to the owners thereof, as Rights of Property, in the same manner as they are now enjoyed by the Laws of Scotland, notwithstanding this treaty.' Far from liberating Scotland from the middle ages, the union created a stalemate state which centuries later still has one foot mired in the fusty clay of feudalism. Even today, for a mere four hundred quid on Amazon, you can peruse 4,500 pages of *Burke's Peerage*, which describes itself as 'the definitive guide to the genealogy and heraldry of the Peerage and Landed Gentry of the United Kingdom', including 'knights, Scottish and Irish chiefs, and Scottish Feudal barons'. If you thought such types only existed at Historic Scotland special events, dressed in clanking armour or swinging plaids for the entertainment of children, think again. Over 120,000 people are listed, each assigned a specific number to show their precise ranking in the social hierarchy of Britain. And if you're not at least 4,500th in line to the throne, consider yourself a nobody.

Without the union, Scotland would almost certainly have faced decades of austerity. Within the union, Scotland faced, well... decades of austerity. The age of prosperity promised by supporters of the union failed to dawn for several generations. In the meantime, the country slid into a deep depression. Scotland's embryonic manufacturing sector, which had been poised for bonanza as a result of the opening of cross-border trade, was all but crushed by stronger, more established, and better financed rivals from the south. Instead of creating an equal playing field, the opening of the new single market was akin to throwing the lions in with the zebras.

At the same time, Scotland was engulfed by an avalanche of new taxes. In Westminster's eyes, Scotland was a subsidy junkie. And Britain had a growing military monster to feed. State borrowing was a new concept back then, only made possible by the formation of the Bank of England in 1694. In 1700, England had zero national debt. The following year, it became involved in a major conflict in Europe, the War of Spanish Succession. It raged on for 13 years, ultimately saddling the new British state with a national debt of 60 per cent of GDP. At the time this was terrifying – although in mid-2013, it stood at 90 per cent, which just goes to show that you can get used to anything. Financial panic gripped London, and Scotland became a scapegoat. Instead of generating new revenues, the northern appendage was regarded as having failed to pay its way. It was a drain on England's resources, and Something Had to be Done.

Smuggling had long been rife north of the border. Every day, vast quantities of salt, sea salt, tea and tobacco were illegally brought into the country from the continent. When it realised the scale of the operations, the British state attempted a full-scale clampdown, but it was, and is, impossible to patrol and police all 7,000 miles of Scotland's coastline, much of it rugged, remote and treacherous. To compensate for its excise losses, Westminster imposed a whole raft of new taxes on Scotland, at the point of sale, on a wide range of commodities. The salt tax, the beer tax, the linen tax and the soap tax were the early eighteenth century equivalents of the Poll Tax and Bedroom Tax – and even more politically explosive. These were staple necessities of everyday life. In 1713, the price of salt – used to preserve meat and fish for the long winter months ahead – doubled overnight.

In this climate of corruption and decay, resistance flourished like fireweed. Warehouses and ships were looted by starving mobs. In several towns, armed guards were brought in to protect tax officials as they carried out their duties. It all came to a head in 1713, when the House of Commons voted to levy a malt tax on Scotland, a move which threatened to ratchet up the price of ale to unaffordable levels. The uproar that ripped across Scotland forced its 45 MPs and peers to come together to demand the repeal of the tax – or repeal of the union. Faced with a political revolt of this magnitude, the government backed down. But the future of the six-year-old British state suddenly looked precarious, as deep-rooted discontent with the government began to rumble, not just in Scotland, but across England and Wales too.

The House of Commons was under the control of the Whigs, a strange, eclectic political faction which preached enlightened liberalism and practised conservative reaction. Karl Marx later mocked the Whigs in the customary withering prose he reserved for plastic radicals:

> 'The oldest, richest and most arrogant portion of English landed property... a distastefully heterogeneous mixture of money-mongers with feudal prejudices, aristocrats without point of honour, bourgeois without industrial activity, men with progressive phrases, progressives with fanatical Conservatism, traffickers in homeopathical fractions of reforms, fosterers of family-nepotism, Grand Masters of corruption, hypocrites of religion.'

And that was the progressive wing of the British ruling class. With the Whigs detested as incompetent, corrupt and autocratic, their old Jacobite enemy was resurgent, and it was no longer marginalised on the Celtic fringes. On both sides of the Tweed, it became the focal point of opposition to the ruling elite in London. North of the Tay, where half the population of Scotland lived, Jacobitism now enjoyed majority support, not just among the Highland clans, but also in Lowland burghs along the east coast from Inverness down to Perth.

Just as important as the strident confidence of Jacobitism was the demoralisation of those who had once supported King William, the Glorious Revolution and the Treaty of Union. Even the accession in 1714 of George I, the first British monarch of the Protestant House of Hanover, failed to convince many former Williamites in Scotland to stand loyal to the union.

In early 1715, the Duke of Atholl, on behalf of a group of Scottish nobles who had welcomed the Protestant succession guaranteed by the House of Hanover, presented a petition for the dissolution of the union. It had, they said, failed to live up to its promises. The proclaimed advantages had proved imaginary, while the disadvantages were all too real, and multiplying by the day. The petition pleaded with the new king to restore the Scottish state. It was laughed off by the London establishment, but as historian Bruce Lenman points out: 'Those who find that the force of their argument is ignored are liable to resort to the argument of force.'

An unlikely William Wallace

By the end of the year, a great rebellion would light up the skies over Scotland, and the future of the union hung in the balance. Bizarrely, it all began over a personal slight to the Earl of Mar by the new king.

In 1707, Mar had been one of the hand-picked commissioners who negotiated the Treaty of Union. He had then gone on to become one of the select band of Scottish MPs at Westminster, rising to the heady heights of Third Secretary of State in the British Government in 1714, with special responsibility for Scotland. He had never been the most consistent political operator – his constant flitting between the Tory and Whig parties at Westminster, and his shifting loyalties from the Jacobite to the Hanoverian cause, had earned him the nickname 'Bobbing John'. It was no great shock when he felt out of favour with the new British monarch, George I, who kicked him out of office because he didn't trust him to stay loyal to the House of Hanover. What was shocking was that, in a fit of personal rage, the Earl raised the banner of open revolt against the state. An armed uprising is never something to be taken up lightly, but in 1715, it was tantamount to suicide.

Six years earlier, Westminster had scrapped Scotland's relatively humane treason laws in favour of new legislation designed to bring Scotland down to England's level. Those found guilty of treason would first be dragged – 'drawn' – on a species of sledge, known as a hurdle, to a place of execution, where they would be hung for a few minutes before being cut down alive, in order to be castrated and disembowelled. Every effort was made to keep the wretched prisoner conscious while their entrails were burnt before their eyes. Finally their bodies would be hacked into four quarters and put on public display as a warning to anyone else who might be considering a bit of seditious behaviour. Even beyond the grave, they were punished by proxy, their families penalised for the sin of 'corruption of the blood' with the forfeiture of all property and titles. If this all sounds a little familiar, that's because the grisly procedure had been used back in early medieval times to see off William Wallace.

The sadistic Act of Treason was railroaded through Westminster in the teeth of opposition from every Scottish MP and member of the House of Lords. Its purpose was to secure the survival of the British state by cold-blooded terror. The Earl of Mar was an unlikely William Wallace. As Bruce Lenman drily notes, 'he loved office, revelled in the deference that a minister of the king could attract among his contemporaries, and appreciated the salary'. But such was the state of unrest in Scotland in 1715, Mar clearly calculated he would win.

Before 1707, opposition to the union had pulled together a broad coalition of competing and even conflicting currents. These included Jacobites, who feared the Treaty would sound the death knell of the ancient Scottish bloodline; Presbyterians, who feared the national church would be forced to compromise with Anglicanism; and radicals, who feared any potential for progressive reform in Scotland would be blocked by a British parliament. The removal of the parliament from Scotland had closed down the forum in which the different versions of independence could be debated. Thus, the future of Scotland could no longer be directed by argument and polemic. And only Jacobitism, with its links to the Highland clans, possessed the military capacity to stage armed rebellion.

The Jacobites had opposed the union in 1707, not as matter of principle but as a means to an end. Their goal was the full restoration of the Stuart dynasty, and the Union of Parliaments was merely an obstacle to realising that ambition. By 1715, this ambition was still alive in the hearts of some of Scotland's Episcopalian noble families. Their brand of Protestantism had been consolidated when Charles II restored bishops to the Church of Scotland, following the restoration of the monarchy in 1660. That had led ultimately to a split in the Church of Scotland, with Presbyterianism triumphant in the south and Episcopalianism dominating the north. With its flamboyant rituals and hierarchical structure, the Scottish Episcopal Church was much closer to the Church of England than to the Church of Scotland. Yet paradoxically, its enduring loyalty to the now redundant Stuart dynasty had driven Episcopalianism into the anti-union camp, while Presbyterianism, with its distinctly Scottish accent, tended to oppose independence for quite the opposite reason.

By 1715, some Episcopalian noble families still dreamed that the Stuart kings might return and restore their church to its rightful place at the heart of Scottish religious life. But for many more, the ultimate goal was an independent Scotland, and the Jacobite banner was the vehicle through which it could be delivered. The cause of the Stuarts was now subordinate to the cause of independence. Mar even failed to inform the exiled James Francis Edward Stuart of his plans until after he had raised the Jacobite standard at Braemar on 6 September 1715, accompanied by 600 supporters. Yet by October, he had under his command a mighty force of anything between 12,000 and 20,000 – three to five times the size of the entire Hanoverian army in Scotland – and had effective control of the whole of Scotland north of the Forth, with the exception of the Stirling.

This was a much bigger and broader movement than the first Jacobite rebellion, led by Viscount Dundee in support of James VII against King William back in 1689. Then, most of Scotland's powerful landowners had backed William, while the Jacobite forces had been drawn almost entirely from the Gaelic clans of the West Highlands. The 1715 rebellion was of a different calibre altogether. It was supported by the more prosperous and influential clans of the East Highlands, and the more or less all-powerful aristocratic families of the north-east Lowlands. Its stronghold was the Grampian Mountains, the vast wild terrain that sweeps southwards from the Great Glen, down through the Cairngorms and the Monadhliaths, to Highland Perthshire. So deep-rooted and widespread was hatred of the union, and so bitter the contempt for the British Government, that even traditional enemies of the Jacobite cause joined the rising, from Presbyterian ministers to members of the Faculty of Advocates in Edinburgh, and even a detachment of the Glenlyon Campbells, who had carried out the Massacre of Glencoe on behalf of King William.

Across the Lowlands there was little stomach for a fight, prompting John Campbell, the second Duke of Argyll and general of the Hanoverian forces in Scotland, to express his disgust at the calibre of the men under his command: 'A lamb is no more afraid of a lion than these Low Country people are of the Highlanders.'

Alas, like Ally's Tartan Army, the 1978 World Cup Scotland football squad, it began with an upsurge of rampant euphoria and ended with wretched humiliation. Marching south to what seemed like certain victory, Mar's all-conquering Jacobites confronted a Hanoverian army at Sheriffmuir in Stirlingshire on Sunday 13 November. The chaotic muddle that ensued was described by one historian as 'a comedy of errors'. Initially the Jacobites, with four times as many troops on the battlefield, overran their opponents. Had they been ordered to press ahead and march on Edinburgh, Lowland resistance would in all likelihood have given way. Instead, the Earl of Mar, in the words of Scottish historian Murray Pittock, 'waited and waited: he waited for French help, he waited for the Duke of Berwick, he waited for the king, he waited for more recruits to make his position impregnable'.

French help never came. The king, the would-be James VIII of Scotland, did come – but not for another month, by which time it was all over bar the shouting. Reinforcements failed to materialise either, and so the Jacobites dwindled to nothing as a result of the inglorious failure of Sheriffmuir. Mar had effectively snatched, not defeat, but a draw from the jaws of victory – and a draw was just not good enough. The momentum was gone, and his Highland troops, baffled and dispirited by the indecision and incompetence of their commander, drifted home. He may have been an efficient administrator, a competent but uninspiring bureaucrat, but the Earl of Mar was never cut out to carry the weight of Scotland's future on his shoulders. His rebellion had been motivated not by any grand vision, but by bitterness towards a king who had deprived him of royal patronage. Consequently, he often appeared ambivalent and apprehensive about where the whole project was leading.

In one strange incident, at the height of the rebellion, Mar wrote to the Duke of Argyll asking him to ensure his government troops didn't damage his (Mar's) gardens at Alloa. He might as well have asked Campbell to feed the cat and give the furniture a polish while he was at it. It was the behaviour of a man out of his depth, naïve as to the seriousness of the rising he had recklessly launched, and anxious to stay on amicable terms with his enemies. As Bruce Lenman notes, the British system in 1715 was 'so deeply corrupt and obnoxious that it was ripe for a fall, but it was saved by the fact that the challenge to it was led by one of its own… a self-centred, monstrously incompetent poltroon'.

After it was all over, retribution was milder than might have been expected, given the recent amendments to the treason laws. Fourteen peers were stripped of their titles. Many were imprisoned, but there were only two executions. Some went into exile, by arrangement with the British Government, and one of these was the Earl of Mar.

The spectre haunting Britain

The lack of brutality meted out to the 1715 rebels was partly due to the government's deep unpopularity. Greatly relieved that it had all come to nothing, Westminster sensibly realised that fearsome revenge would only trigger further backlash. More important than this, however, was the recognition that the rebels had friends in high places. As was pointed out by Duncan Forbes, a rising star in the legal profession and a future Lord Advocate of Scotland: 'There are not 200 gentlemen in the whole kingdom who are not very nearly related to someone or other of the rebels.'

Instead, the government exploited the failed rising to whip up fear of a foreign tyranny, in this instance a French one, thereby boosting its own hold on the nation. The politics of fear have been used time and again, by operators from Adolf Hitler to George W Bush to, closer to home, the Tory governments of the twentieth century. Faced with a general strike, or social disorder, or even a march in favour of nuclear disarmament, Conservative governments have shamelessly raised the spectre of Communist Russia to deflect public attention from the failings of those in power, and keep the people at heel.

For decades to come, even though Jacobitism looked like an exploded shell, any protest against any injustice in any part of Britain was blamed on the Jacobites and their 'friends' across the English Channel. And there were injustices aplenty – and protests and riots to match. One of the great paradoxes of the time is that French absolutism operated a less regressive tax regime than the supposedly enlightened British state, run by those self-proclaimed progressives, the Whigs, under Prime Minister Robert Walpole. 'His central political principle when in office was to make sure that the fat cats of early Hanoverian Britain had plenty of cream', comments Bruce Lenman. 'Taxation policies were consciously geared to this end.'

During the first decade of the eighteenth century, including the few years following the Act of Union, direct taxation – mainly on landed wealth – accounted for 35 per cent of total government revenues. This was relentlessly reduced by Walpole, the Margaret Thatcher of his day, to just 17 per cent by

1735. The state made up its considerable financial shortfall through savage indirect taxes on basic commodities such as soap, salt, candles, tobacco and ale, all of which bore down heavily on the poor. Then, as now, Britain led Europe in implementing regressive fiscal policies that pampered the rich and punished the poor. Across the English Channel, meanwhile, the reactionary conservatives in charge of France continued to raise at least 50 per cent of their revenues from taxes on wealthy landowners, right up until the 1740s. And the beauty of it all was that the blatantly corrupt Whig government still managed to terrify the public with warnings of an imminent French invasion that would drown the ordinary people of Britain under a Niagara of draconian taxes.

After the 1715 debacle, the Jacobites were on the ropes and would remain there for three decades. But like Tony Blair and David Cameron in the decade or so after 9/11, the government of the day pursued the power of nightmares, enforcing repression in the name of protecting the people from an invisible enemy that lurked (largely) in the dark wynds of their own imaginations. Without the fear of a Jacobite takeover to bind it together, Britain may well have broken apart into three or four separate states during the first half of the eighteenth century, or become engulfed in another Cromwellian-style civil war. Because it suffered disproportionately, and was treated with utter contempt by the Whig government in London, Scotland smouldered like a wounded wolf – and occasionally flashed back like an angry wildcat.

In 1714, Westminster had gingerly retreated after testing the water with the malt tax. The public backlash was fearsome. In Glasgow, the natives were restless. Duncan Forbes reported to Westminster that such was the disorder in the city, tax officers were unable to safely perform their duties. Another official complained that excise officers were in fear of their lives; some, who had been brought in from England, had fled back across the border, such was the scale of anti-English sentiment. In the Glasgow heartland of Presbyterianism, Jacobite slogans were painted on walls and chanted – partly, no doubt, to wind up the authorities, but partly also to express national resentment.

When several companies of the British Army arrived from Edinburgh to quell rising disorder, a mutinous crowd gathered outside the city's military watchtower in Candleriggs, blocking their entrance to the building. The stalemate ended only when the crowd secured the keys, and ran off with them. While the army tried, and failed, to persuade the city's Lord Provost to smash down the doors, the protesters invaded and occupied Shawfield House, a mansion on the southern outskirts of the city belonging to Daniel Campbell, a wealthy merchant and MP who had strongly supported the malt tax. Naturally, the protesters helped themselves to the honourable gentleman's fine bottles of Bordeaux, it being thirsty work, the pillaging of mansions. When two men, still the worse for drink, were arrested on the street in the vicinity of the ransacked house, crowds appeared on the street and liberated them forthwith. In panic and anger, soldiers fired into the crowd, killing several people. Instead of dispersing, the protesters turned on the troops, chasing them a full six miles out of town. Taking no chances, the retreating soldiers finally locked themselves up in Dumbarton Castle.

For decades, the British state forces in Scotland encountered violent resistance from 'the mob' – as the common people were disparagingly referred to by those who considered themselves socially superior. In 1736, Edinburgh became the scene of a brutal confrontation – the Porteous Riots, made famous in Walter Scott's novel *The Heart of Midlothian*, the title referring to the old Tolbooth Prison on the Royal Mile. It was triggered when three smugglers – Andrew Wilson, William Hall and George Robertson – were convicted of burgling the Customs House at Pittenweem, in Fife, and stealing £200. Hall was ordered to be transported to Australia, while Wilson and Robertson were given the death sentence.

At a service in St Giles Kirk, to which condemned prisoners were taken on the Sunday before their execution, the powerfully-built Wilson helped his comrade to escape by holding two guards in each arm, and pinioning a third using his teeth. Wilson's audacious and selfless act captured the hearts of the huddled masses of the Old Town. He had humiliated the detested authorities and was now a local hero. When he was brought to the scaffold six months later, scores of people gathered as usual to witness the grisly ritual. In this case, however, they were not here to cheer the executioner, but to liberate the condemned man. Surging forward, they managed to break through the guard and cut down Wilson, but he had already gasped his final breath.

In a state of rage, Captain John Porteous ordered his soldiers to open fire on the crowd. Six members of the public were killed and dozens more were wounded. The public outrage was such that the authorities were forced to arrest Captain Porteous and convict him of murder. General George Wade, however, was having none of it. The Irish-born British Army officer had been sent by George I to sort out Scotland in the wake of the 1715 Jacobite Rising. His official title was 'Chief of His Majesty's Forces, Castles, Forts and Barracks in North Britain'. To this day, the Highlands are criss-crossed by hundreds of roads, tracks and bridges built under the direction of Wade to enable the British Army to subdue the pockets of Jacobite resistance.

Now he turned his gaze southwards to Edinburgh and used his influence to bring about a six-week stay of execution for Captain Porteous. It was a softening-up exercise, the prelude to a full reprieve.

The Old Town was incandescent. To quote Scott's novel: 'The mob of Edinburgh, when thoroughly excited, had been at all times one of the fiercest which could be found in Europe; and of late years they had risen repeatedly against the Government.' At ten o'clock on the evening of Tuesday 7 September, a huge, well-disciplined crowd marched on Tolbooth Prison, to the steady beat of a drum. On reaching the gates, they overpowered the guards, entered the jail and seized Captain Porteous. By midnight, he was dangling from a dyers pole in the Grassmarket. The British Government, writes Bruce Lenman, 'was beside itself with rage at the flouting of both its dignity and its authority'. General Wade, the Lord Advocate, and the Solicitor General were dispatched to Edinburgh to identify and prosecute all those involved.

After running into a wall of silence, Westminster in its rage brought in a Bill of Pains and Penalties to punish the entire city of Edinburgh. The city was fined £2,000 for its complicity in this act of rough justice. The Lord Provost was thrown out of his post and banned for life from holding public office. In a blatant attempt to turn the Church of Scotland into a clerical police force, ministers were ordered to preach a sermon on the first Sunday of every month, for an entire year, demanding that those responsible for the Porteous lynching hand themselves in, on pain of incurring the wrath of God.

This heavy-handed and oppressive treatment of Scotland in the first decades of the new British state generated an upsurge of resentment that cut across boundaries of geography, religion and even social class. In such a climate of disaffection, the Jacobite movement rose up from its death bed. The spectre had turned back into flesh and blood.

11

THE POPULIST REBELLION

Flamboyant messiah

At the head of Loch Sheil, a towering monument stands like a sentinel gazing up towards the 21-arch railway viaduct known to millions worldwide after making an appearance in three Harry Potter movies. Back in the eighteenth century, it was another glamorous character who gave Glenfinnan its gilt of fame. At this spot one Monday morning in August 1745, the 24-year old son of the exiled King James raised the Jacobite Standard, kicking off the last war to be fought on British soil.

Bonnie Prince Charlie – or Charles Edward Stuart to give him his proper name – is one of the most flamboyant figures of Scottish history, immortalised in songs, poems, novels and paintings. He was good-looking, charming, persuasive, and in the right place at the right time. He truly was a man of his moment. His largely unheralded arrival in Glenfinnan marked the beginning of what would become a sensational rebellion, conquering – within a year – the whole of Scotland, and advancing within 150 miles of London. In military terms, it was the equivalent of the Apache, under Geronimo, seizing half the United States before marching on Washington DC.

For centuries afterwards, as Scotland powered into the industrial age, the 1745 rebellion was treated on one side with starry-eyed romanticism as the last stand of a noble society doomed to extinction, and on the other side with scornful contempt as a revolt of primitive neanderthals, ill-fed and ill-armed, manipulated by a charismatic charlatan. Either of these caricatures chimed with the climate of British capitalist triumphalism that would reign for many generations to come. Romantic or rueful, by the nineteenth century the Jacobites were a busted flush.

From a British perspective, a stark, black-and-white version of the 1745 rebellion has been widely accepted across the political spectrum. In the recent past, the Orange Order has considered holding an annual ceremony at the Culloden battlefield to commemorate Scotland's own version of the Battle of the Boyne; another 'glorious' victory for the forces of light and liberty over the hordes of darkness and tyranny. The British left steer well clear of the murky waters of the

Boyne, yet seem content to endorse the Duke of Cumberland's redcoats. In that version of history, the Jacobites represented feudal counter-revolution, and their defeat was a necessary pre-condition for the Scottish enlightenment, the rise of British capitalism, and the emergence of an industrial working class.

Yet the truth is more complex, as some of the most recent research has revealed. In the first place, Jacobitism was never quite as backward-looking as it has been portrayed through the centuries by Whig historians. The 1745 rising took place against a background of mass discontent with the British state, not just in Scotland, but in the marginalised north of England, Wales and Ireland. There was always a reactionary current within the Jacobite movement, but in the absence of any other coherent opposition to the British government and crown, Jacobitism evolved into a heterogeneous alliance of the disaffected and marginalised, be they royalists or radicals.

Charles Edward Stuart was driven, not by political or theological zeal, but by a sense of destiny and a raging personal ambition. That was both his strength and his weakness. It allowed him to appeal to a broad swathe of the population by promising religious liberty for Catholics and Episcopalians; commercial regulation in place of the free market which was destroying Scottish agriculture and industry; annual parliamentary elections to hold politicians to account; lower taxes; and the restoration of the Scottish Parliament. Charles had inherited the Stuart flair for populism; if anything, it was the Jacobites who gave the impression that they stood at the vanguard of radical change in Scotland and across Britain, while the House of Hanover represented the bleak and dismal status quo.

The heartland of the rebellion was the great stretch of land north of the Tay and south of the Great Glen, encompassing the West Highlands, the Central Highlands, and the fertile coastal plain that runs south from the Cairngorm Mountains to the North Sea. Of the major Highland clans who took one side or the other, 22 joined the rebellion, while 10 remained loyal to the British state. Those who opposed the Jacobites were generally the most prosperous, such as the Campbells of Argyll, and the Mackays and Munros in the far north. Most of those who joined the rebellion were even poorer than the Native Americans of the Great Plains, with whole families living on the edge of starvation in one-room bothies made of mud and stone. Even the chiefs were impoverished compared to the Lowland nobility: the total annual income of all the clans which marched with Prince Charlie was estimated at under £1,500 a year – or less than one-tenth the sum that Lord Queensbury had been given by the British Government in reward for driving through the Act of Union forty years earlier.

Such was the nature of clan society that many men were forced to enlist under threat of punishment by their clan chieftains. Some of those put on trial after Culloden certainly denied they had voluntarily joined the rising, but given the penalties for disloyalty to the British crown, not all of these pleas for leniency can be taken at face value.

Overall, there is no doubt that, of the two armies, there were many more on the Jacobite side than the Hanoverian side fighting from conviction rather than compulsion. Ludicrous as it may seem from the vantage point of the twenty-first century, Bonnie Prince Charlie cut something of a messianic figure across much of the famished west and central Highlands. Twenty-four years earlier, to commemorate the birth of Charles Stuart, the Argyllshire poet John MacLachlan put into words the popular fantasy that the return of the House of Stuart would magically transform mud into gold:

> 'The woods will put leaves over our heads; the earth will yield crops without strife; the sea's fruit will fill every net; herds will give milk everywhere; and honey on straw-tops will be found; without want, unstinted forever; without storms, but every wind warm.'

Charlie was their Golem, their avenging angel, the supernatural creature who would lead them to salvation. They needed him almost as much as he needed them. Many of these desperate Highlanders were the direct descendants of those who had fought the Scottish government and the British crown the previous century, to preserve their way of life. But in 1745, they were fighting for change, for an escape from the miserable drudgery of everyday life, and the promise of a better future.

For honour, liberty and independence

The Jacobite army was not drawn solely from the desolate glens of the Highlands. A list of several thousand prisoners captured after Culloden reveals that less than half had Highland clan surnames. Almost 500 were from the city of Dundee. Hundreds more hailed from Edinburgh, Aberdeen, and the fishing villages of the Buchan coast. One man in the north-east, however, remained staunchly Hanoverian – Cosmo, the Duke of Gordon, and the most powerful landowner in this part of Scotland. After the rising was over, his loyalty was rewarded when the Peerage of Scotland – the old feudal aristocracy – elected him to sit in the House of Lords.

By contrast, the list of occupations of rebel prisoners reveals the rank and file of the Jacobite army to be something of a cross-section of the common people of Scotland. There were labourers, stonemasons, blacksmiths, farmers, boatmen, printers, dyers, weavers, ploughmen, servants, barbers, brewers, distillers, gunsmiths, glaziers, merchants, carpenters, coal hewers, fishermen, skinners, tailors, carters, bakers, bricklayers, gardeners, alehouse keepers, wigmakers, watchmakers. There were even surgeons, writers, drummers, fiddlers, priests, ministers, vagabonds and tinkers. Seventy were women.

According to historian Tom Devine, 'throughout the entire rebellion only a tiny minority of the landed classes came out for the Stuarts,' while Frank McLynn, the leading historical expert on Jacobitism, says that even covert republicans gave support to the cause. In their eyes, Charles Edward Stuart could be the Trojan horse that would throw open the gates of power to more radical dissidents. The most prominent of these was George Keith, the 10th Earl Marischal of Scotland, who had fought in the 1715 rising, and was now working flat out in France to rally support for the '45. A friend of Jean-Jacques Rousseau, he tried to persuade the French revolutionary philosopher to write a biography of Andrew Fletcher of Saltoun. He may also have influenced another French radical philosopher, François-Marie Arouet – better known by his *nom de plume*, Voltaire – who was famous for his advocacy of freedom of religion, freedom of speech, and separation of church and state. Voltaire also had Jacobite family and friends and is believed to have penned an anonymous manifesto in support of the 1745 rebellion. Other great figures from the Enlightenment, such as David Hume, opposed the rising – but from a conservative and sectarian standpoint. The substance of his argument in support of the Hanoverian government was that it's always dangerous to allow Catholics near the throne.

At the heart of the rising was the popular demand for independence. The Jacobite Manifesto, proclaimed at Glenfinnan, thunders against 'the hardships and impositions which have been the consequence of the pretended union', and promises that the nation of Scotland will be 'restored to that honour, liberty and independency it formerly enjoyed'. Significantly, it also advanced economic demands, including the repeal of the Malt Tax and protection of the fisheries and linen industry. And it pledged religious freedom: 'We likewise promise our royal word to protect, secure and maintain all our Protestant subjects in the free exercise of their religion, in the full enjoyment of all their rights, privileges, immunities.'

As a result, even in the Presbyterian Lowlands, there was ambivalence and even a strain of sympathy for the rising, especially amongst the working people, the poor and the most radical. As Bruce Lenman notes, 'The union was profoundly unpopular in Scotland... What shook the union to its foundations was the willingness of laymen touched by the Fletcher of Saltoun tradition to use Jacobitism as the tool for their nationalist aspirations.'

One entire Jacobite regiment, commanded by the Badenoch poet John Roy Stewart, was recruited from the slums of Edinburgh. In the same city, a young anti-Jacobite zealot, Sandy Carlyle, described how he and his pro-government battalion, comprising of rather upper-class and well-to-do students, professors, clergymen and merchants who had prospered under the union, were jeered at by the working-class residents of the Old Town as they drilled and trained in the streets. Out in East Lothian, he observed that the common people 'had no aversion to the House of Stuart and, if their religion could be secured, would be happy to have them on the throne again'. He estimated that across Edinburgh as a whole, two-thirds of the male population was anti-Jacobite, while two-thirds of women were sympathetic to the rebellion.

Although women were never involved directly on the battlefield, they played a far bigger role in the rising than most historians have acknowledged. According to Maggie Craig, author of *Damn Rebel Bitches: Women of the '45*, women were less marginalised in the Jacobite movement than in the Hanoverian camp. Indeed, one of the heroes of the 1745 was a 46-year-old woman called Jenny Cameron, from Morvern, who raised a 300-strong regiment, and was subject to vile sexist abuse from the equivalent of the British tabloid press at the time. Another was Lady Anne Mackintosh, the 22-year old wife of the clan chief, who rallied 350 men from the Clan Chattan confederation to join the rising while her husband Angus was on overseas duty as commander of the British Government's Black Watch regiment. Isabel Haldane, wife of the chief of the Appin Stewarts, told her wavering husband: 'If you are not willing to take command of the Appin men, stay at home and take care of the house and I will go out and command them myself.' Then there was Charlotte Robertson, or Lady Lude as she was better known, a young widow from Perthshire who became notorious as a ruthless recruiter to the ranks to the Jacobite Army, forcing her tenants to join up or see their homes burned down. In recognition of her contribution, she was given the honour of firing the first shot during the unsuccessful Jacobite siege of Blair Castle, in Highland Perthshire.

The prominent role of women in participating and supporting the rising provoked a predictable cacophony of rage from male supporters of the government. Maggie Craig quotes from a pamphlet entitled *The Female Rebels*, widely circulated at the time, whose every phrase reverberates with fear and loathing:

> 'It is remarkable of the fairer sex that, whatever opinions they embrace, they assert themselves with greater constancy and violence than the greater generality of mankind. They seldom observe any medium in their passions, or set any reasonable bounds to those actions which result from them… They have generally speaking weak heads and warm hearts, and therefore we see this part of the species are the first proselytes to the most absurd doctrines, and in all changes of state or religion, the ladies are sure to lead the van.'

On a rather more balanced note, the veteran Jacobite Lord Pitsligo from Aberdeenshire, who had been driven into exile for his part in the 1715 rising, but nevertheless resumed arms in 1745 at the age of 67, wrote of women: 'They are more active, more foreseeing and better managers than we.'

None of this is to suggest that Jacobitism in 1745 was a bastion of progressive attitudes, but it does challenge the enduring belief that this was a clear-cut conflict between enlightened liberalism and dim-witted backwardness. Few in the Lowlands were prepared to lay down their lives for either the House of Stuart or the House of Hanover. Charlie's fine promise to restore the Scottish Parliament was popular in a country which had never supported the union in the first place. Even his religion no longer had the power to provoke mass hysteria. There was no longer any serious threat of counter-reformation; Catholicism now commanded the allegiance of barely 3 per cent of the population, mainly on the remote coastal fringes of the Highlands and Islands. The Jacobite army itself was predominantly Protestant, by a ratio of more than two to one, albeit of the Episcopalian rather than Presbyterian tradition.

At the same time, the once revolutionary Kirk, which in its early days had thundered against corruption and pioneered social reform, had ossified into a pillar of the establishment. Its support of the unpopular British state was unflinching. After the Act of Union, the Patronage Act of 1712 had reasserted the right of landowners to appoint ministers. Its abolition had been one of the progressive reforms of 1690, opening up a degree of democratic control and accountability over the clergy. The revival of patronage within the context of the British Union had altered the character of the Kirk. As historian TC Smout explains: 'The landowners were as a class increasingly looking to England for their cultural models, and therefore wanting to see someone in the manse as polite and friendly to the laird as the average Anglican parson was to the squire.' So controversial had been this power struggle between landowners and congregations that a minister, says Smout, 'was bound to see himself as the laird's creature... and to share the landowner's general outlook and social aims'.

By the 1740s, the Church of Scotland had even begun to fragment, with the emergence of four new dissenting Presbyterian churches, reflecting political as well as theological differences.

In the countryside and the towns, the Kirk had become an instrument of social control. In a changing society, fundamentalist Calvinism weighed down on communities like a gravestone. The misogyny of the church, its petty-minded intolerance, its suffocating interference in the everyday lives of its own people would later be lampooned by Robert Burns in poems such as *Holy Willie's Prayer*.

While historians tend to equate Jacobitism with tyranny, it is likely that many people, even in the Lowlands, saw the movement in a different light. In luminous contrast to the men in black, it projected an image of youthful glamour, colour and panache. When the Jacobite Army came to town, they did not carry out pillage or rape, nor round up political prisoners. Instead, they held victory dances.

500 miles – and 500 more

Less than a month after departing from Glenfinnan, Charlie's army marched triumphantly through the streets of Edinburgh. It had been an extraordinarily easy victory. From the mountains of Moidart to the shores of Loch Ness, across the Corrieyairack pass and down along the banks of the

Tay to Perth, then through Stirling and on to Edinburgh, this rag-bag force marched 150 miles without so much as a skirmish.

In the capital, Charles proclaimed his exiled father James VIII King of Scots, and declared Scotland an independent state. The Jacobites then threw a grand ball in the Palace of Holyroodhouse. It was, wrote Lord Rosebery who would become a Liberal Prime Minister in 1894, 'the most picturesque of all rebellions'. This mix of fearlessness and easy grace was intoxicating, cutting a sharp contrast to the grim conservatism of British rule. 'On one side there was enthusiasm,' said Rosebery. 'On the other, at most, staid conviction.' When a government army under General Sir John Cope mustered at Prestonpans, on the outskirts of the city, the Jacobites struck hard and fast at dawn. It was a rout. After the battle, Jacobite surgeons and physicians tended the wounded on both sides. In an act of humanitarianism, the Prince himself lent a helping hand. It would set the pattern for the behaviour of the rebels throughout the rest of the campaign.

The Highland clans who had marched with Montrose and Dundee the previous century had a notorious reputation for brutal, indiscriminate bloodletting. Across the Lowlands, they had inspired terror and contempt in equal measure. But the men of the '45 were disciplined, and behaved in an exemplary fashion towards those they defeated in battle. One fanatically pro-Hanoverian London newspaper would later admit that 'the rebels behaved tolerably well in their march southwards'.

Following Prestonpans, Charles was euphoric. He now had unassailable control of Scotland's capital city. Alas, Scotland was barely enough to satisfy the grandiose ambitions of the young prince. He wanted England too, with its wealth, empire, and international stature. He had all but promised the restoration of the Scottish parliament – but under a Stuart monarch. Now it seemed he also sought to seize the throne of the three kingdoms, where his ancestors had sat the previous century. Thus, intoxicated with a sense of his own destiny, Charles believed that the ocean was only knee-deep and the mountains shoulder-high. He convinced his troops that, when they crossed the border, they would be hailed as liberators; Jacobite risings would erupt across England, and a French invasion force would land on the south coast to meet them.

There was robust debate on 30 October 1745. General Lord George Murray, from the Atholl family in Perthshire, argued against an invasion of England. The Badenoch poet, Colonel John Roy Stuart, was vehement in his opposition. At the conclusion of a stormy army council, the prince won the day by a single vote. Not all those who supported the prince shared his wild optimism, but there was a hard-headed argument that the 50-year old union could not be dissolved by Scotland alone. Neither the crown nor parliament would recognise a breakaway Scotland any more than the young prince would have recognised a unilateral declaration of independence by Wales or Ireland. Strip away the bravado, and there remains a kernel of realism about what was necessary to carry this rebellion through to a successful conclusion.

In the north of England, the Jacobites encountered little hostility. If anything, they seemed to stir a buzz of excitement, and plenty of curiosity. When it became clear that these wild men from the north, bedecked in tartan plaids and blue bonnets, brandishing broadswords and speaking in an alien tongue, were not in town to lay waste, there was even some sympathy. By mid-November, they had surrounded Carlisle, the gateway to England. After a two day stand-off, the militia guarding the local castle surrendered, and the mayor delivered the keys of the city to Charles. Only one person died – a local soldier, accidentally shot by his own side. The Jacobites left behind a 100-strong garrison and proceeded to Manchester, a city with a sizeable Irish population even in the mid-eighteenth century. There they were greeted as heroes. As Maggie Craig points out, in her well-researched *Bare-Arsed Banditti: the Men of the '45*, 'Manchester had its own issues. It was growing rapidly, as was its textiles industry, yet it felt itself sidelined and distanced from those who held reins of power in London.' As in Scotland, Jacobitism was seen as something broader and more subversive than a vehicle for the dynastic ambitions of the Stuart family.

Billeted in the city on 30 November, St Andrew's Day, the Jacobites were joined in street celebrations by local people, some of the women having stitched together saltires to commemorate the occasion. While they were about it, the rebels raised the Jacobite Manchester Regiment, denounced by the national press as 'Irish rabble'. Maggie Craig suggests tentatively that 'in their belief that Charles Edward Stuart could deliver personal and political liberty, it could be argued that the officers of the Manchester Regiment were the forerunners of the political radicals which the cotton mills and factories of Manchester were later to produce in such abundance.'

In Preston, they paraded through the city to 'the loudest acclamation of the people you can imagine', according to one observer. Elsewhere in England, there was support for the Jacobites across the social spectrum, but especially amongst the lower classes. In the south-west, clothing workers, tin miners and fishermen turned against the House of Hanover, while in Yorkshire, colliers and ironworkers expressed sympathy with the Jacobites. Dave Douglas, a left-wing writer and former coal miner, suggests that there was also strong support for the Jacobite invasion of England amongst the pitmen, keelmen and sailors of Tyneside. In 1748, after the rising had been crushed, armed soldiers and sailors even took to the streets in solidarity with those slaughtered after Culloden, 'declaring Newcastle and Northumberland for Charles and Scotland'.

So detested was the Whig government in Westminster that the possibility of a near-bloodless coup appeared to loom closer every day. In early December, the Jacobites reached Derby, just 120 miles from London, significantly less than the distance between Inverness and Edinburgh. The capital of the British empire was in a state of panic as the upper-classes stashed their valuables before preparing to flee. Even King George, according to some reports, had two yachts crammed with the family silver, waiting at Tower Quay, on the Thames, ready to whisk him and his family over to Germany.

Then, all of a sudden, the Jacobite Army packed it all in, turned north, and began the long march back to Scotland. It was as though Andy Murray, after reaching his first Wimbledon final, had gone two sets ahead then thrown away his racquet and walked off the court. For someone who was feared as an autocratic tyrant ready to rule Britain like Genghis Khan, Charles Edward Stuart seems to have been pretty ineffective at imposing his will upon his own troops. He had wanted desperately to carry on to London – so desperately that he begged, wept and screamed at his officers when they argued in favour of retreat.

The mutiny was led by General Lord George Murray. He reminded Charles of his wildly optimistic promise that England would rise in support of the rebellion. As in the Lowlands of Scotland, the Jacobites had met little resistance on their long march south. They had even been greeted with sympathy in towns and villages along the way, for as Bruce Lenman comments, there was 'massive apathy of the British peoples towards their arrogant, unrepresentative and appallingly incompetent government'. But sympathy born of apathy is not easily turn into armed revolt, especially in a country where traitors regularly dangled from the gallows. In Scotland, thousands had enlisted in the Jacobite army; in England, the recruits could be numbered only in their hundreds.

Southern discontent with the Whig one-party state, and the House of Hanover, lacked one explosive ingredient: nationalism. In Scotland, the high-octane fuel that had powered the rebellion was the prospect of the repeal of the Act of Union, should the House of Stuart be restored. In England, the rebels had met with a reasonable response, but they had lit no bonfires of rebellion. Now the clan chiefs wanted to return to their northern stronghold. Decisive, perhaps, was the false information, supplied by a Hanoverian infiltrator, that 9,000 heavily-armed troops had massed at Northampton, blockading the road to London. Maybe the mission was doomed from the start. Or maybe, had the Jacobites pressed on to London, the government forces would have toppled like dead trees.

The working class and the poor of London hated the government and may even have risked joining the rebellion if it looked like it was winning. As Napoleon Bonaparte would later insist, the outcome of any battle depended one-tenth on technical superiority and nine-tenths on morale. The centuries are strewn with examples of might succumbing to zeal. In *The History of the Rebellion in the Year 1745*, John Home, who had fought against the Jacobites, wrote: 'There were moments when nothing seemed impossible; and to say truth, it was not easy to forecast, or to imagine, anything more unlikely than what had already happened.'

Horace Walpole MP, the son of the deceased Prime Minister, was mightily relieved by news of the retreat. 'No-one is afraid of a rebellion that runs away', he gloated. Just a few weeks earlier he had told a friend: 'Why really, Mr Montagu, this is not pleasant! I shall wonderfully dislike being a loyal sufferer in a threadbare coat, and shivering in an antechamber at Hanover, or reduced to teach Latin and English to the young princes at Copenhagen.'

The long march back up north was hardly the bedraggled retreat of a disintegrating army. Back on Scottish soil, Charles was able to mobilise his biggest force yet, 8,000-strong, to defeat the Hanoverians at the Battle of Falkirk Muir. But the Jacobites now had no strategy, nor even the faintest idea of what to do next.

While they had been in England, government forces had retaken Edinburgh Castle. The Highlanders argued for a return to the familiar territory of Inverness, but with no clearer purpose in mind than to recruit more troops. Lord George believed that their spectacular feat in reaching as far south as Derby would inspire tens of thousands in the Highlands to join up, now that the weakness of the opposition had been exposed. They underlined that point by capturing a chain of northern fortresses – Fort George, Fort Augustus, Fort William, and Ruthven Barracks. But morale had deteriorated, and Charles himself, the driving force of the movement, was despondent. His troops were now hungry and exhausted, and were beginning to drift back towards their homelands. They weren't deserting so much as taking a rest, as they had done before in previous campaigns. But there was one more battle left to fight.

12

DISGRACE OF THE VICTORS

Massacre on the moor

In 1745, at the height of the Jacobite offensive, a new verse was added to the British national anthem, and remained in the official Church of England hymnal until the late 1980s:

'Lord, grant that Marshal Wade,
May by thy mighty aid,
Victory bring.
May he sedition hush and like a torrent rush,
Rebellious Scots to crush,
God save the King.'

In the event, it was not Marshal George Wade who would play that role, but Prince William Augustus, the 25-year old brother of King George II. Better known as the Duke of Cumberland, he pursued the Jacobites right up to the Moray Firth, and by the spring of 1746, his redcoats had reached the town of Nairn – within striking distance of the Jacobites' makeshift HQ at Culloden House, on Drumossie Moor.

At dusk, on the evening of 15 April, the Jacobites set off on a 12-mile march, with the aim of a surprise night-time attack on the redcoat encampment. It was a miscalculation. The march through difficult moorland in the pitch black, trying to avoid government outposts, was chaotic. Just one hour before dawn, the Jacobites finally reached the outskirts of Nairn. But with the first faint glow of daylight visible over the North Sea, they knew they had lost the element of surprise. Furthermore, they were worn out and empty-bellied.

The offensive was called off, and the troops trudged back towards Culloden. By 11 o'clock that morning, the Hanoverian Army appeared at the edge of Drumossie moor, fighting fit, heavily armed, and with almost twice as many troops as the exhausted Jacobites, whose numbers were depleted by the deployment of four clan militias far to the north in Sutherland, and by the late arrival of the Clan MacPherson from Badenoch. It is incidentally both a myth and a cliché to say that more Scots fought on the government than on the Jacobite side. Of the 22 regiments commanded by the Duke of Cumberland, just four were Lowland Scots and Campbells, under 1,500 troops in total, out of 9,000. Of the 5,000 Jacobites, the vast majority were Scots, mainly Highlanders, supplemented by a small detachment of the Manchester Regiment and some Irish Franco-Scots forces.

On the bleakly exposed moor, the two sides lined up. On one side, the redcoats – fresh, fit, and armed with the latest in military technology. On the other, the weary Jacobites, sustained only by their fighting spirit, and armed with pretty much the contents of the kitchen cutlery drawer. Within an hour of the first charge, 1,200 corpses lay strewn across the battlefield. Most of them were Jacobites. And the trauma didn't end there. The fallen men, with their gruesome open wounds, were denied medical treatment and left to die in agony on the open moor. Those who surrendered were incarcerated in churches, cellars and other makeshift prisons in Inverness, before being hanged or deported.

For months afterwards, redcoats marauded across the north, on a vengeful spree against this race of vermin who had dared invade England. Entire villages were razed to the ground, women were raped, men were hanged or shot, livestock was stolen or slaughtered, crops were burned, tools confiscated. The supposedly backward, barbarian Jacobites had shown magnanimity and compassion in victory; the so-called modernising, civilised redcoats displayed nothing but brutish malevolence.

The man at the helm was to become known as Butcher Cumberland, often depicted in a bloody apron with a meat cleaver in his hand, and described by John MacLeod – author, *Daily Mail* columnist and fundamentalist Free Church Presbyterian – as 'the type that, two centuries later, in the name of law and order and racial hygiene, would cram Jews and Slavs into the gas chambers and neatly tot up the work in a ledger at day's end, and feel weary satisfaction at a job efficiently performed'. In London, Cumberland received a hero's welcome, and was rewarded with an extra £25,000 a year, worth not far short of £2 million in today's money, on top of his civil list allowance. To celebrate the British victory at Culloden, a special thanksgiving was held in St Paul's Cathedral, where a special oratorio, written by Handel in honour of Cumberland, was played for the first time. The composition, *Judas Maccabeus*, places the story of the great biblical warrior in the context of the Jacobite Rising, with a libretto that runs:

'See, the conquering hero returns!
Sound the trumpets! Beat the drums!
Sports prepare, the laurel bring!
Songs of triumph to him sing!'

Scotland did not rejoice, even the elements who had supported the House of Hanover. In the Highlands, Church of Scotland ministers gave refuge to fugitive Jacobites, while the Lowlands quivered with revulsion at the sheer savagery of the retribution. Duncan Forbes, Scotland's foremost legal brain, who had raised forces to resist the rising, was outspoken in his condemnation of the maltreatment of prisoners and other cruelties in the wake of Culloden. In response, Cumberland denounced him as 'that old woman who talked to me about humanity'.

Duncan Ban McIntyre, the accomplished Gaelic poet, had also fought on the side of the redcoats, in the Argyllshire Militia. His Hanoverian sympathies had been shaped during his early years, working as gamekeeper at Glen Orchy on the Duke of Argyll's estate. Now, he announced his regret that he had signed up to the Hanoverian army. In retrospect, his heart was with the Jacobites, he declared. In one poem, *Ode to the Trousers*, he laments the cultural oppression imposed on the Highlands as result of the defeat of the Jacobites.

'Fortune to us was bitter,
In an ill hour won Duke William,
Great the harm he's been to Scotland,
For the chieftains' lands are forfeit,
And the yeomen are disarmed.
Now we'll wear but hat and black coats,
In the place of checkered tartans.'

Revenge

In the wake of Culloden, anti-Scottish racism reached a crescendo. To be a Gael in London, or even a Presbyterian Scot, was possibly more dangerous even than being Irish in Birmingham after the pub bombings of the 1970s, or a Muslim in New York after 9/11. The British state now contemplated genocide. The Prime Minister demanded that the Highlands be 'utterly reduced'. Another government minister, Lord Chesterfield, the Viceroy of Ireland, called for all food supplies into Scotland to be stopped, and for a wholesale massacre of the Highland clans. The Duke of Cumberland contemplated deporting every single Gael to the colonies. Ultimately, they settled for the social and cultural obliteration of the Gàidhealtachd as the more politically acceptable option.

Highland dress was banned – an action akin to modern-day NATO forces in Afghanistan announcing the banning of the hijab. Bagpipes were prohibited as 'engines of war'. An Act of Parliament was rushed through to enforce the closure of every Episcopal church and meeting house whose clergy had refused to swear an oath of allegiance to the House of Hanover. Rebel clans had their lands forfeited. Almost a thousand prisoners were ordered to be transported to the Caribbean, though perhaps hundreds died in the fever-ridden prisons of the Highlands before they could be shipped overseas. Some of the Gaelic names in the West Indies today derive not from slave owners, but from exiled prisoners of war.

Notwithstanding the assertion of some left-wing historians, the merciless retribution visited upon the Highlands after Culloden was not part of a revolutionary war of capitalism against feudalism. Both social systems had co-existed peacefully in all parts of the British state since the 'Glorious Revolution' of 1688, which had in reality been a historic compromise between the landed aristocracy and the rising capitalist class.

In *The Isles – A History*, English historian Norman Davies makes the point that 'by the early twentieth century, many of the British peers had sat securely on their estates for two, three, four, five, six, or even seven hundred years'. Some still do. The biggest and richest feudal family in the Highlands, the Campbells of Argyll, provided a bedrock of support in Scotland for the House of Hanover, while some clans who had formerly supported King William against James II – for example, the Mackintoshes – fought with Bonnie Prince Charlie.

If anything, the annihilation of the clan system after Culloden secured the victory of feudalism over the older, more tribal social structure. New social relations were ushered in, based on money and private ownership of land rather than kinship. Those clans whose lands had been forfeited were transferred to new private landlords, while those who had supported the government – or those who had repented, such as Simon Fraser of Lovat, in the north-east Highlands – were co-opted, culturally and socially, into the anglicised British state. By the 1760s, their children were being schooled at Eton, Winchester and Oxford, where they were taught to speak in upper class English accents and to despise their own native tongue. They became aristocrats rather than patriarchal leaders of a community.

This social upheaval was primarily a bid to pacify the lawless Highlands, but it led to the north of Scotland becoming an exploited subsidiary of rising British capitalism. The replacement of the ramshackle clan structures with the strong arm of commercial feudalism became a necessary precondition for the later Highland Clearances, when the entire landscape was turned into a patchwork quilt of giant sheep farms providing wool for the rapidly growing textiles industry of northern England and Lowland Scotland. And a haunted landscape of ruined homesteads and ghost villages.

Jacobitism may have had a feudal figurehead in Bonnie Prince Charlie, but it was a complex phenomenon – perhaps most perceptively recognised by English historian Frank McLynn, whose wide-ranging and meticulous research led him to observe that 'surely no stranger political turnaround has been witnessed than that whereby the House of Stuart became in effect the standard-bearer for the very ideas it had fought against in the civil war of the 1640s'. McLynn quotes John Burton, an illustrious eighteenth-century scholar of Corpus Christi College, Oxford, and a staunch enemy of both Jacobitism and republicanism: 'What were republican principles in the last century are Jacobite principles in this.' Just as mass support for Hamas today in Gaza derives as much from the movement's militant anti-Zionism and its network of social programmes as its Islamist theology, Jacobitism contained both progressive and reactionary elements. Those on the political left who portray Culloden as regrettable collateral damage on the road to progress have – regrettably – lined themselves up on the same historical side as those who would welcome the crushing of the Palestinians by the Israeli state, the massacre of Native Americans at Wounded Knee, the Soviet invasions of Hungary, Czechoslovakia and Afghanistan in the twentieth century, and the recent wars waged by the US and UK against Iraq and Afghanistan – all in the name of progress.

Even some of the great industrial confrontations of the 1980s are now presented by pro-free market economists, politicians and historians as a struggle between the past and the future. The miners in 1984 were defending a dying industry and the printers, an obsolete trade. In economic and sociological terms, that argument could be valid. Yet those who resisted were on the side of humanity against cold-blooded free market economics. Had these trade unions succeeded, the industries and trades they fought for would still have withered on the vine, but at a more humane pace, leaving time to build alternatives, to adjust. Their defeat plunged these workers into sudden, disastrous change. Furthermore, it weakened deeper values such as social justice, community cohesion and solidarity, simultaneously strengthening the hand of those who measure the world in balance sheets and share prices.

The road not taken

Some insist that, had the Jacobites prevailed, the fortunes of the modern British state would have been disastrously reversed. The House of Commons would have been abolished, the industrial revolution would have ground to a halt, Britain would have been turned into a satellite of France, and the divine right of kings would have been revived as the foundation stone of governance. No-one can ever know for sure where that road that was not taken might have led. But any balanced speculation would refuse to take at face value these assertions, which were originated by eighteenth century Whig historians for propaganda purposes.

First, such an analysis ignores the context of the times. By the mid-eighteenth century, the concept of the divine right of kings to do as they please without any external control or accountability had already become an anachronism. It had reached its high tide under the tyrannical Louis XIV, who ruled France until his death in 1715; but three decades later the world had moved on. France was still formally an absolutist monarchy – and would continue to be so right up until the French Revolution of 1789 – but by the 1740s, King Louis XV was under huge pressure to share legislative power with the *parlements* – those decentralised political-legal institutions which pre-dated absolute monarchy.

The Stuart dynasty itself, like many other institutions through history, was capable of adapting itself to the changing context in which it operated. Right up to and beyond the Reformation, it had been a pillar of the Catholic Church in Scotland and staunchly pro-independence. Under James VI, it had become Protestant, pro-British and anti-Gaelic. Then it swung back again until, by the time of James VII of Scotland (and II of England), it was associated with Catholicism, with its strongest support base out on the Celtic fringes of Ireland and Highland Scotland. Bonnie Prince Charlie, and his father, were more than capable of accommodating themselves to the social changes that were underway in the 1740s.

Moreover, dynasties, like political parties, are influenced by the personalities and attitudes of those at the top. The Labour Party under Tony Blair was a quite different animal from that which had elected Michael Foot just twenty years earlier, while the Conservative Party of Margaret Thatcher was in marked contrast to that of Harold MacMillan. It is doubtful whether Bonnie Prince Charlie was seriously committed to any ideology. Nor was he particularly religious. A Catholic by birth and identity, he was privately cynical about all organised religion, and privately disdainful of superstition and all talk of the supernatural. In some of these personal beliefs, he seems to have been closer than some of his Whig enemies were to the later philosophers of the Enlightenment.

For the young prince, therefore, religion was a matter of expediency, not conviction. Not that he would be the last demagogue to use religion as a means of tapping into popular support. Even the modern secular state of America has its professional Christians vying for the White House. Four years after Culloden, in exile in France, Charles converted to Protestantism, hoping that it would improve his chances of recovering the crowns of England and Scotland. When that failed, he returned to the Catholic Church.

Nor did he strongly advocate the divine right of monarchy. The Glenfinnan Manifesto promised that the Jacobites would 'with all speed call a free parliament'. Charles later talked about cancelling Britain's national debt – the means of financing the state's colossal military apparatus – but made it clear that the proposals would first be referred to parliament. He also promised autonomy to the colonies, and guaranteed religious freedom to all minorities.

This was not an absolutist programme to establish a French-style tyranny in Britain, but a manifesto for reform. Later, in the wake of Culloden, the Jacobites were to unveil a radical programme of wealth redistribution and a proto-welfare state.

But more important than all of that was the dynamic of the rising itself.

The Jacobite Army was a people's army, drawn from the poorest clans in the Highlands and the ranks of working people in the north-east Lowlands. Had it marched on London, it could only have succeeded with the support of the broad mass of the population, particularly the working classes. Even if it had to rely on a *coup de grace* delivered by France, it seems unlikely that the advance of science, industry and technology would have been halted, parliament closed down, the Enlightenment cancelled and a one-man tyranny established.

More likely, Britain's imperial expansion – bought at such a high price, both in financial and human terms – would have been halted or at least slowed down. Paradoxically, without the plunder of the British Empire, the three ancient kingdoms of England, Scotland and Ireland may have become ripe for a republican transformation later in the eighteenth century, during the years of the American and French Revolutions. Furthermore, had the Hanoverian state been overthrown, England's centralised stranglehold over Scotland, Ireland and possibly even Wales would surely have been loosened. Had the Scottish Parliament been restored, the Gàidhealtachd may have been resurrected as a major force in Scottish culture and politics, given the central role of the Highland clans in that restoration. Instead, its heart was ripped out.

In Scotland, in the Lowlands as well as the Highlands, and in Canada, America, and wherever else Scots were flung like so much surplus humanity, popular sentiment has tended to sympathise with the losers of the '45 rather than the victors. Historians generally attribute this sense of solidarity with the Jacobites to the writings of Walter Scott. As the best-selling Borders novelist, the JK Rowling of the early nineteenth century, Scott was certainly influential. And he did help to romanticise the Jacobites, in a way that allowed even staunch Hanoverians to look back benignly on the movement as a colourful but hopeless and safely lost cause. He made the story all the more palatable by ignoring the vicious conduct of the British state, even to the point of omitting Culloden completely from his renowned historical novel of the times, *Waverley*. Yet others, coming from a polar opposite standpoint, including revolutionary Jacobins in France and radical Presbyterians involved in the United Irishmen, would also invoke the spirit of 1745. So too would striking workers in the north of England, who wove the songs and symbols of Jacobitism into their struggles. For a time, the white cockade of the Jacobites became the late eighteenth century equivalent of a Che Guevara t-shirt.

The appeal of Jacobitism might have diminished rapidly had the rising succeeded and the exiled James III and VIII, or his son Charles Edward Stuart, assumed the throne. The movement benefited from the luxury of generations of opposition. And its popularity was heightened by the fact that the 1745 Rising was the ultimate Glorious Failure. The day after Culloden, the shattered army miraculously regrouped at Ruthven Barracks, near Kingussie, in preparation for a final defiant onslaught against the House of Hanover. They dispersed only under orders from Charles to 'seek their own safety' rather than launch a suicide mission. The prince himself went on the run for six months, living in caves, bothies and in the open countryside of the West Highlands and Hebrides. Even with a bounty of £30,000 on his head, no-one betrayed him.

Part of the enduring attraction of the 1745 Jacobites was the impressive dignity with which they had behaved in both victory and defeat, in moving contrast to the soulless conduct of the triumphant Hanoverians. Sorley MacLean, the great Gaelic poet of the twentieth century, who while at school 'relinquished Calvinism for Socialism', summed it all up in his poignant bicentenary commemoration poem, *Culloden 16.4.1946*. He anguishes over the wisdom of a rebellion 'that left the Gaeldom of Scotland a home without people, fields haunted by ghosts, a pasture for sheep'. He acknowledges that 'the movement of history has given no proof or denial' of whether or not their 'undenied heroism' was misplaced. But 'if they made a mistake, they are not blamed by history, for they avoided the disgrace of the victors in that strife'.

13

THE EMPIRE STATE

Out of the night?

The crushing of the Gàidhealtachd after Culloden may not have been pretty, but for most modern historians – whether of the left, right or centre – it dragged Scotland out of the darkness into the bright of a glittering new world. When all is said and done, they argue, Culloden was a triumph for liberty, progress and civilisation against the forces of backwardness and reaction. It allowed Scotland to flourish by becoming fully incorporated into the British state, which in turn unlocked the key to the riches of the British Empire and paved the way for the Scottish Enlightenment and the industrial revolution.

In recent years, perhaps the most eloquent expression of that view was offered up in Arthur Herman's *The Scottish Enlightenment – the Scots' Invention of the Modern World*. Upon its publication in 2001, the book was acclaimed across the Scottish and UK media, the front cover of the paperback edition even emblazoned with a fulsome recommendation from Irvine Welsh: 'Every Scot should read it. Scotland now has the lively, provocative and positive history it deserves.'

Part of the book's attraction in Scotland derives from the adroit flattery employed by its American author. For page after page, chapter after chapter, the author lavishes praise upon little Scotland and its impact on the big wide world across a broad array of fields including philosophy, politics, economics, literature, medicine, physics, chemistry, engineering and mathematics. But every rainbow has a cloud. The central thesis of *The Scottish Enlightenment* is that these achievements would have been impossible without first the union, then the vanquishing of what Herman calls the 'deepest darkest aspect of Scotland's past'.

Curiously, in all the glittering reviews which accompanied the book's publication, little information was divulged about the author himself. The publishers of the British edition somehow managed to omit any reference to his previously published work. Perhaps that is because Herman's troublesome back-list includes a biographical rehabilitation of Senator Joe McCarthy, the orchestrator of the Hollywood witch-hunts, and a drooling eulogy to the British Empire, *To Rule the Waves*. Nor, at a time when the neo-conservative wing of the American ruling class was preparing a global bloodbath equivalent to a hundred Cullodens, did anyone mention that Professor Herman was up to his neck in the murky waters of the American Enterprise Institute, a right-wing think-tank that supplied over a dozen people to senior positions in the George W Bush administration, and whose board of trustees appears to be a collection of the leaders of the most powerful multinational corporations on the planet.

History can never be entirely detached from the present. Even the most scholarly and scrupulous professors interpret the past through a prism that reflects their own cultural, social and political influences. Just as there will always exist different political factions, tendencies or parties representing divergent groupings with different values and interests, so too there will always be conflict over the past. What is surprising is that Herman's analysis of the dynamic of Scottish history is widely accepted by the left and the centre as well as the right. He may be an accomplished writer and researcher, but Arthur Herman's interpretation of Scottish history is saturated with his own prejudices, and with a world-view that worships inequality, glorifies imperialism and elevates profit above humanity and nature.

So perhaps it's time to ask some searching questions. First, without the British state and the empire, would Scotland have become a barren and destitute outpost? If it hadn't been for the union, would Robert Burns have stuck to the plough, the whisky and the women and not bothered his backside writing poetry? Would James Watt's father have taught his son to play the bagpipes instead of instructing him in mathematics, woodcraft, metalwork and instrument making? Would the modern world have bypassed Scotland?

The Scottish Enlightenment may not have flourished so spectacularly without the empire to raise it onto the global stage, but neither would it have been drowned at birth. Scotland had one phenomenal advantage over most other European countries: its educational system was probably the most advanced in the world. It produced inventors, engineers, scientists and philosophers like Oxbridge today churns out BBC presenters. Prior to the Reformation, Scotland had already established three universities – one more than England – and a grammar school in every town of any size. The *Book of Discipline*, the manifesto of the Reformation, had then set out a vision of a school in every parish.

That programme of universal free education had begun, tentatively, as early as 1561, and was reinforced by a series of Acts of the Scottish Privy Council and Parliament in 1616, 1633, 1646 and 1696. Local landowners were compelled to pay taxes to support this vast network of schools and teachers. One distinguished twentieth century English historian, Sir George Norman Clark, went so far as to describe Scotland's rural population of the seventeenth century as 'the most enlightened peasantry in the world.'

In England, the education system was still steeped in elitism and snobbery. At its core were nine leading schools, seven of them boarding institutions, all of them serving the aristocracy and the wealthiest merchants. For the rest of the population, elementary education was rudimentary and piecemeal, based on charitable donations. Significantly, it would be a radical, Scots-born anti-slavery campaigner, Henry Brougham MP, who first opened up the debate in Westminster, when he presented a bill in favour of a free education system in 1811. In his supporting speech, he extolled the virtues of his own education in the High School of Edinburgh, whose greatest merit, he said, was that 'men of the highest and lowest rank of society send their children to be educated together'.

With or without the union, had Robert Burns been born a few hundred miles further south, he would almost certainly have been destined for a life of anonymous drudgery before disappearing forever into the black hole of historical anonymity.

Had Scotland been excluded from this global marketplace, it would undoubtedly have developed at a different pace. But historical progress is not like a single-track metro system, where each train must follow the one in front, and remain in front of the one behind. It is more like a jumbled network of roads, in which there are detours and diversions, breakdowns and collisions, overtaking and U-turns.

In the early 20th century, Leon Trotsky – the revolutionary who became the Soviet Union's first serious dissident – developed a theory which remains pertinent to this day. The Law of Uneven and Combined Development challenges the idea that human society progresses in a simple, linear fashion, where those who start ten years ahead will always be ten years ahead. The theory accepts that nations evolve at their own pace, subject to their own geographical and historical restraints – but they also adopt and absorb cultural, scientific, technological and political influences from elsewhere.

As a result, less developed countries can sometimes leapfrog over their more advanced neighbours by adopting superior techniques from elsewhere, effectively by-passing the tortuous processes of trial and error to get there. Thus, jungle-based tribes have been able to jump straight from fire to electricity, without going through the gas-lighting stage, while other primitive societies were able to replace bows and arrows with machine guns, ignoring all the intermediate weaponry.

Trotsky's law illuminates why Japan and Germany were able to rise from the ashes of national destitution after the Second World War to become leaders of industry and technology by the 1960s. While Britain was lumbered with antiquated equipment and infrastructure, Japanese and German industrialists, starting from scratch, were able to invest directly in the most sophisticated, cutting-edge machinery available.

This law also holds good, to draw on a more contemporary example, when considering how the 100-year-old Woolworth's chain could collapse in 2009, while 15-year-old Amazon soared into the stratosphere.

These same principles can be applied to constitutions and political systems. In the nineteenth and early twentieth centuries, a whole cluster of previously backward countries leapt ahead of Britain in the sphere of democracy. Why? Because these emerging countries were not lumbered with an archaic semi-feudal electoral system, under which voting rights were based on ownership of property. As a result, states such as Norway, Finland, Greece, the USA, Poland, Argentina, Denmark, Estonia, and the self-governing colonies of Australia and New Zealand were decades ahead of Britain in introducing universal male and female suffrage.

Without the union, Scotland would have had to find its own path to progress, probably with a more diversified and flexible economy. It may have set out a little later, but it is hardly credible that Scotland would not have found its own shortcuts into the modern world – perhaps with more humility and humanity than it could ever express as part of a state with ambitions to rule the planet.

'The dread and envy of them all'

In 1942, George Orwell wrote an essay analysing the poetry and politics of Rudyard Kipling. He observed how the celebrated bard of Imperial Britain could never quite understand that 'an empire is primarily a money-making concern. He believed imperialism was a sort of forced evangelising. You turn a Gatling gun at a mob of unarmed natives and then you establish the rule of law which includes roads, railways and a courthouse.'

Many others of Kipling's generation and class background sincerely believed the same thing. Generations of schoolchildren for two centuries were indoctrinated with the idea that the British Empire was kind of global state-sponsored charity, wiping out starvation, stamping out corruption, driving out tyranny and rooting out ignorance. The 'White Man's Burden' was a thankless task, unappreciated by the natives but driven by God and morality.

Even some of the most liberal voices of the nineteenth century sang the same tune. The philosopher John Stuart Mill, for example, was a champion of liberty, an enemy of slavery and a supporter of the rights of women. He also believed that some races were naturally barbarous and could not be left to fend for themselves. The Scottish Highlander, the Welshman, the Basque and the Breton, he said were 'the half-savage relic of past times, revolving in his own little mental orbit, without participation or interest in the general movement of the world'. It was right, he said, that they should be incorporated into large civilised states such as France and Britain rather than left to 'sulk on their own rocks'. He extended these same principles to the wider world. As one historian, Eileen P Sullivan, puts it, in Mill's eyes 'England had a right to rule despotically because it brought the benefits of higher civilization'.

During his entire professional life, spanning 35 years, Mills worked for the East India Company. Based in London, it presided over the colonisation of India, founded Hong Kong and Singapore, controlled the production of tea in India and China, and took over the textiles industry in Bengal. For a time in the eighteenth century, the company had even employed Captain Kidd to combat piracy on the high seas. Using brute power, including the staging of coups and the installation of puppet rulers across the East, the company was able to control supply and demand by buying up goods and raw materials cheaply and selling them for a handsome profit. In the 1780s it had taken advantage of a drought in Bengal to buy up all available grain and drive up prices to levels beyond the reach of the population, triggering a famine in which up to 10 million people perished. The British Empire may still bring tears of pride and regret to the eyes of elderly *Daily Telegraph* readers, but it was a ruthless operation, driven by private capital, whose main goal was to loot the resources of distant continents.

It would be foolish to pretend that there were no benefits bestowed on the natives. The British built schools, hospitals, roads and railways and other infrastructure. But the empire was no humanitarian mission. Every improvement introduced was an economic calculation. Roads and railways, for example, were designed to open up the interior of conquered territories to wider exploitation, while schools were a means of instilling a culture of discipline and deference.

On the other side of the balance sheet are the atrocities, direct and indirect, intentional and unintentional. And not just in the violent early days, when corpses of the conquered would be piled deep into unmarked graves. In the triumphalist words of *Rule Britannia* – written by the Borders-born son of a Presbyterian minister – Britain was 'the dread and envy of them all'. Some of the most grotesque crimes of the British Empire in the nineteenth century included the internment of the entire Afrikaaner population during the Boer War; the flooding of China with opium, and the subsequent slaughter of tens of thousands when the Chinese authorities declared the drugs illegal; and the manipulation of agriculture for profit which produced mass famines and the death of millions in India and Ireland.

In the twentieth century, the trail of destruction left by imperial Britain included the partition of Palestine, which produced generations of bloodshed in the Middle East, and the partition of India which provoked the biggest population upheaval in human history and the death of a million people.

As well as these catastrophic blunders, there were calculated, orchestrated outrages. The 1919 massacre at Amritsar in India, for example when soldiers under British command fired 1650 rounds of ammunition into an unarmed crowd, killing countless hundreds. Or the 1950s incarceration of 330,000 Kenyans into concentration camps and the sadistic torture of Mau Mau rebels, which included boring holes in prisoner's eardrums, slicing off their ears, fingers and testicles, and gouging out their eyeballs.

But for the elite at the top, the empire was a goldmine. It was guarded by warships and muskets to keep out intruders. And it spread across continents, stretching out, it seemed, to infinity, crossing the international dateline and dozens of time zones, prompting the cliché that the 'the sun never sets on the British empire'. Its bounty helped nourish mighty industries and great cities which would become a magnet for the rural poor at a time when population growth had begun to outstrip agricultural productivity. The spoils of the empire allowed the British ruling classes the financial leeway to make concessions when times got tough, blunting the edge of class conflict and avoiding the turbulence of revolution and counter-revolution that would convulse other parts of Europe.

The tobacco trade in Glasgow had started as an illicit smuggling operation in the seventeenth century at a time when Scotland was banned from trading with England's empire. Edward Randolph, the crown's colonial administrator in the Americas, wrote a stream of papers reporting on cargo ships laden with tobacco setting sail from hidden coves on the Delaware River bound for Scotland.

After the union, when Scotland could legally trade with the colonies, the tobacco trade became a more sophisticated operation. By the 1750s, the small port of Glasgow, with 3 per cent of London's population, was importing more tobacco than the rest of Britain combined, then re-exporting the golden weed to Europe at substantially higher prices. The route from the Clyde across the Atlantic was shorter and safer than from the main English ports, and the Glasgow merchants were ruthless in their dealings with rivals. They were also, like the bankers of the twenty-first century, prepared to take extreme financial risks by extending credit to their suppliers. Their prize was wealth on a scale that Scotland had never known.

The tobacco lords, as they became known, built great townhouses in Glasgow stuffed with ornate furniture and exquisite works of art, whose location can be roughly identified today by many of the street names in the city centre: Buchanan, Ingram, Wilson, Oswald, Dunlop, Cochrane. The grandest mansion of all belonged to the richest and most powerful tobacco lord of all, John Glassford. Originally from Paisley, his father was a magistrate and a merchant, so he was born into money. A charming man by all accounts – 'of very gentle, pleasing manners' and 'much energy of character' – he multiplied his wealth many times over by marrying first the daughter of another merchant, then the daughter of a baronet, and as a finale, the daughter of an earl, George Mackenzie of Cromartie. This allowed him to buy a fleet of 25 fast cargo ships which he plied back and forward across the Atlantic carrying immense quantities of the deadly herbal treasure.

But when the colonists whose forebears had crossed the Atlantic from Britain decided in 1775 to break free, the tobacco trade went up in smoke. Eight years later the revolution was complete and the independence of America finally recognised by Britain. The same year, John Glassford died in his grand mansion, leaving debts of almost £100,000 – the equivalent of around £6 million in today's money.

Other tobacco lords, however, had begun to move into the Caribbean. From way back before the Act of Union, England, backed by the gunboats of the British navy, had seized control of some of the most fertile sugar-producing territories in the West Indies which they staffed initially with white slaves, many of them political prisoners from Scotland and Ireland. But as the industry expanded, the white workforce was no longer big enough to cope with demand.

The labour shortage was solved when England followed in the footsteps of Portugal and Spain and entered the African slave trade. Half a century before the Treaty of Union, the port of Bristol was already well-established as the slave-trading centre of the world. On its quays, black captives were sold like cattle, and then transported in chains across the Atlantic.

Many Scots, including the descendants of servants and bonded labourers, would eventually rise to positions as managers of slave plantations, some of them while still in their late teens. Even the radical poet Robert Burns contemplated emigrating to become an assistant overseer on a West Indies plantation.

Scotland's empire?

A few years ago, the TV historian David Starkey sneered at Scotland as an 'insignificant little country that could never have built its own empire'. He may have a point, but the provocative right-wing academic fails to understand that without Scotland, Wales and Ireland, England on its own could never have carved out its fabulously wealthy empire which at its height embraced over one-fifth of the world's population. To conquer and to hold this vast expanse of the globe – spread over 200 times the land area of England – multitudes of military and civilian personnel were needed. Scotland and Ireland furnished more than their fair share.

The research of historian Tom Devine has been especially valuable in illuminating the participation of Scots in the colonies. *Scotland's Empire, 1600–1815*, for example, is a superb study of Scotland's role in the expansion of the British Empire during the eighteenth and nineteenth centuries. But its focus, which is on the Scots diaspora rather on the overall structure of the British Empire, can be misinterpreted as evidence that this was some kind of joint enterprise.

Scotland's role in the colonies was always subsidiary rather the primary. As one of the most literate countries on earth, it furnished the empire with a disproportionate number of doctors, teachers, missionaries, bookkeepers, administrators, and managers. The country did amass wealth from the British Empire, but mainly through trade rather than direct ownership of stolen land and plundered resources.

The Colonial State Papers – an archive of letters, minutes and other official documents concerning Britain's colonies in North America and the Caribbean during the eighteenth and nineteenth centuries – has more than 300 references to Scotland, often hostile, before 1707. After the Treaty of Union, when Scotland was supposed to have been admitted as a joint partner, this falls away to just 100. In contrast, there are more than 1,200 post-union references to the city of London. Albeit in crude statistics, these figures fairly reflect the real balance of power within the British Empire.

The square mile of the City of London was, in Georgian and Victorian times, the Rome of the modern world. From every direction, riches flowed into the narrow grid of streets on the north bank of the Thames. From the sixteenth century, it had been the headquarters of all the main joint-stock companies who were spearheading global plunder, including the Virginia Company, the Hudson Bay Company, the East India Company, the Honourable Irish Society, the Bermuda Company, the South Sea Company, and the Royal African Company of England (which directed the empire's role in the slave trade).

Although the British Empire was primarily driven by money, it had also acted from the start as a safety valve, releasing social pressure at home. The rather verbose title of the document proposing the first English colonisation of America blatantly declares that the 'King should make a plantation in Virginia by which the kingdom may annually be rid of 3,000 poor, and that each should have 20 acres of land, a house, and victuals out of the store for one year'. It further suggests that 'the prisons may be emptied, and much blood saved as well as relief given to many by sending them thither'.

Even those who voyaged voluntarily across the oceans did so, like hundreds of thousands before them and tens of millions since, in search of a better life. Travelling to the Caribbean in the eighteenth century was no luxury cruise. It was a dangerous venture that involved sailing through treacherous seas where pirate ships roamed, bound for unexplored islands where tropical diseases were rife and massacres of interlopers were commonplace. For some, the risk brought great rewards; for others it brought violence, disease and death.

For the poorest people in Scotland, even that escape route from the brutality of the factories and slums, and from the hunger of the villages and farms, was closed off. But there was one way out. An expanding empire needs soldiers and sailors, not just to conquer territory and subdue the natives, but to confront and defeat rivals.

Between 1756 and 1763, Britain waged a seven year war against France, Spain and the Netherlands, which raged across the Mediterranean, the Caribbean, the Pacific, the North Atlantic, the South Atlantic, Central Europe, North America, South America, West Africa, India and the Philippines. One million corpses later, Britain emerged victorious and now controlled the whole of America east of the Mississippi, plus a host of former French and Spanish colonies, including Canada, nine Caribbean islands, Manila in the Philippines, a chunk of India, and slave-trading centres in Senegal and other parts of West Africa.

And when that was over, Britain's own colonists turned against the crown in the first modern, democratic, anti-colonial revolution in history. Fought out on land and sea for 15 years between 1763 and 1778, the American Revolutionary War began with sporadic acts of civil disobedience against unfair taxes before gradually escalating into a full-scale war of independence. This would turn into a national humiliation, the British Empire's Vietnam. At its height, the equestrian statue of King George II was toppled in New York City in scenes similar to those that would become familiar in late twentieth century Eastern Europe.

With relish, the straight-talking American Declaration of Independence ripped into the king across the ocean: 'He has abdicated Government here... He has plundered our seas, ravaged our Coasts, burnt our towns, and destroyed the lives of our people.' What rankled more than anything was the fact that these insurgents spoke the same language as their colonial masters and worshipped in Protestant churches. Many were Ulster-Scots whose parents and grandparents had been part of the 200,000-strong influx of settlers that had arrived from the north of Ireland from 1717 onwards.

Ironically, many of the Gaelic Highlanders who had been driven from their homelands to the New World later in the century ended up fighting with the redcoats against the rebels. That reflected not so much gratitude or loyalty to the British state, but the fact that they were new, first generation immigrants in a foreign country, in contrast to the Presbyterian Ulster-Scots who had been there for two or three generations and now identified with the land of their birth.

For those that remained locked into the imperial state, there would be no respite from bloodshed and destruction. During the nineteenth century, Britain fought more than 40 international wars, either to defend or expand its empire. In that single century, Britain waged war for 77 years, and spent between 75 and 80 per cent of all its state expenditure maintaining its mighty war machine. Contrast that with Sweden, which fought its last ever war in 1814; or its enemy in that war, Norway, which would remain at peace until the outbreak of the second world war, a full 126 years later.

At the time, soldiers were regarded as the lowest of the low, the underclass, worse off than the lowest paid unskilled workers, and only marginally above paupers and vagrants on the social scale. So where better to find an endless supply of men with formidable fighting skills, courage and nothing to lose than in the Celtic fringes of Scotland, Ireland and Wales? These were the internal colonies of the British Empire, subjugated much more brutally than, for example, Britain's North American territories. Their poverty-stricken glens and valleys were brimming with teenagers and young adults for whom life in the army was at least one step above destitution. Earlier, the attitude of the ruling elite towards people they viewed as barbaric tribesmen had been summed up in the words of General Wolfe when he sent Highlanders into frontline at the battle of Quebec: it will be 'no great mischief if they fall'.

In the Napoleonic Wars of the early nineteenth century, close to 50,000 Gaels would fight in the ranks of the British Army, around half the eligible male population of the Highlands. By 1820, the total strength of the British armed forces stood at 400,000 strong – and one-third of its troops were from Scotland. Ireland would also supply vast numbers of fighting men to kill and die in foreign lands in the service of the British Empire. In 1830, over 40 per cent of soldiers in the British Army had been born in Ireland. In total, there were more Irish soldiers fighting for the empire at this point than English soldiers. Even James Connolly, the Edinburgh-born socialist who led the

Easter Rising in Dublin in 1916, had his first sight of Erin's Isle in a British army uniform, which he wore for seven years from the ages of 14 to 21 (he enlisted under false name and age).

Part of the *modus operandi* of the British Empire was to exploit the courage of those who had stood against them. In later centuries, Gurkhas, Sikhs, Afro-Carribbeans and others whose lands had been seized by Britain would also be turned into cannon-fodder.

Back home, Scotland wasn't exactly a blissful land of whistling working men in flat caps and happy housewives sending their children off to school with cheery smiles. 'No pen will ever paint even a dim picture of the horrors of the early years of the capitalist system', wrote Tom Johnston in *A History of the Working Classes in Scotland*. People lived in 'overcrowded, bleak and cheerless hovels'. They toiled 'from dawn to sunset, bullied and oppressed, the last ounce taken from their bodies by scarcely less oppressed overseers'. Their children were 'killed off like flies and they themselves emaciated, consumptive and without hope'. Their one day of relaxation was the Sabbath 'when a clergyman, voicing the desires of his chief paymaster in the raised pew, would urge submission to the present Hell as a qualification for the Paradise to come'.

But not even the threat of eternal damnation in Satan's raging furnaces could stop the tidal waves of heresy now besieging Britain and Ireland from America and France.

14

REASON IN REVOLT

A long habit of not thinking a thing wrong gives it a superficial appearance of being right.
– Thomas Paine

The Rights of Man

In 1791, a book published by an English-born journalist based in Paris became the bible of British radicalism for generations to come.

Thomas Paine had set sail across the Atlantic 15 years earlier, leaving a failed business and a broken marriage behind him. There he took up arms against his native country and became one of the most influential figures in the American Revolution. He subsequently moved to revolutionary France, where he published *The Rights of Man*. In clear, gripping language, written not for the academic elite but for the common people, it ripped into the injustices of British society and called for profound and sweeping changes which would shame most Westminster politicians even today.

It was generations ahead of its time, advocating progressive taxation, welfare benefits, wealth redistribution and the abolition of hereditary titles. It demanded universal child benefits for all under 14, and old-age pensions 'not of the nature of a charity, but of a right'. It denounced war as 'the curse of the age' and condemned the institution of monarchy as 'the master-fraud which shelters all others'.

It was incendiary. In London, Paine was tried in his absence and sentenced to hanging for seditious libel. Meanwhile, *The Rights of Man* sold by the hundreds of thousands across Britain, despite being banned. It was especially popular in Scotland, and even made it into Gaelic translation. Thomas Telford, the great civil engineer who built the Caledonian Canal, bought a batch of copies and sent them to his native Eskdale, in the Borders, to encourage the local people to take action in support of political reform.

Until recently, academic historians have largely agreed that, after the 1745 Jacobite rebellion, Britain became a secure, unified state, its population pacified by the fruits of imperial expansion. Within that state, Scotland was supposedly, as Tom Devine writes in his 1990 study *Conflict and Stability in Scottish Society 1700-1850*, 'a society of massive social stability, with three quarters of the population loyal to the British establishment'.

More recent historical research contradicts this view. Professor Christopher Whatley, notwithstanding his pro-union views, criticises what he calls 'historical complacency', arguing that there is 'voluminous evidence of deep social unease during this period'. If anything, the word 'unease', with its connotations of passive anxiety, underplays the scale and depth of the social strife that shattered Scotland, especially in the final decade of the eighteenth century. This was mutiny from stern to bow, except that Captain Bligh, in the shape of Henry Dundas – MP for Midlothian, British Home Secretary, and 'the Uncrowned King of Scotland' – held all the weapons.

For near on three decades, starting in 1760, the Scottish economy had prospered, thanks to a booming textile industry. Employers now faced labour shortages and collective demands for higher wages. But, as with the capitalist upswing of the mid-1990s to the late 2000s, economic growth generated runaway inequality. While the common people were thrown a few more scraps from the table, the landowners, merchants, bankers, and industrialists gorged themselves on gargantuan riches.

Then, in 1789, along came the French Revolution. As the monarchy toppled and the slogan *Liberté, Egalité, Fraternité* swept the old order away like a prophet clearing a money-lender's table, the British establishment trembled at the prospect of a French invasion. Banks stopped lending. Cash-flow diminished to a trickle. From 1790 to the end of the century, three recessions followed in quick succession, with barely a breathing space between. A sequence of hard winters produced food shortages, while in the countryside, landowners enclosed and annexed land that had always been held in common, for pasture, peat, wood and other vital resources. Up north, the Highland Clearances were just getting underway.

The movement for radical reform, inspired by events in Paris, multiplied like wild flowers in springtime. It fused with food riots and other expressions of social unrest on the streets, and served to polarise Scotland; on one side, the conservative defenders of the sanctity of inherited wealth and power, and on the other, the reformers seeking radical political and social change.

According to David Brown, the head of the Private Record Branch of the National Archives of Scotland, when revolutionary France conquered Belgium in November 1792, there were 'wild scenes of joy in many Scots towns, culminating in an eruption at Dundee where the burgh was lost to the mob for many days'. Across Scotland 'trees of liberty' – usually ash saplings – were planted in town and village squares to symbolise support for the ideals of the French Revolution, while effigies of Henry Dundas, the 'Great Tyrant', were set ablaze because of his opposition to political reform. This was not mindless anarchy. The so-called mob would chant slogans such as 'liberty, equality – and no king!'

The first Friends of the People group, as the official reform movement was called, was formed in Edinburgh in 1792 and soon spawned a multitude across Lowland Scotland. In Perth alone, according to one newspaper report, there were a thousand members of reform societies, mainly weavers and shopkeepers. At its peak, 123 societies operated in 66 Scottish towns and villages, and according to historian John Stevenson, weavers accounted for up to one-third of the membership of many groups.

Although led by middle-class professionals, the backbone of the movement was formed further down the social scale. As well as weavers, the most militant section of the working class, there were artisans in abundance, including tailors, cobblers, bakers, tanners, brewers, butchers and hairdressers. The movement was less successful, however, in recruiting labourers, colliers, foundrymen, and stone-masons, all probably too exhausted and focused on day-to-day survival to get involved in substantial numbers.

Nonetheless the movement in Scotland appears to have been both more proletarian and more radical than its English counterpart. Initially, the Friends of the People had substantial backing from the well-heeled, such as lawyers and politicians from the Whig party who were by now in opposition within the House of Commons. But as historian TC Smout observed, 'Each convention and its aftermath frightened away more and more of the upper middle classes from both the reform movement as a whole and from the ranks of the Friends of the People.' The men of property lost their early enthusiasm, 'disturbed by new forces which threatened to overthrow not just the Balance of Power but to take the power themselves'.

The organisation had moved beyond timid reforms, such as modest widening of the franchise, to demands that struck at the heart of the entire political system. These included universal male suffrage, annual parliaments and even abolition of the monarchy. It took up social and economic demands, highlighting the poverty, disease and starvation stalking a land where whole swathes of the population were forced to subsist on bread and potatoes.

In common with the radical movement elsewhere, including France, it had little to say about the rights of women. In London, the first stirrings of feminism were expressed in the writings of Mary Wollstonecraft, the daughter of an East London handkerchief weaver. In 1790, she anonymously published the pamphlet *A Vindication of the Rights of Men*, which attacked the aristocracy, monarchy and slavery. Her follow-up book, *A Vindication of the Rights of Woman*, called for women to be allowed access to public education. It was tame by today's standards, but in 1792, it was inflammatory. From pulpits and printing presses across the land, she was reviled. The Whig politician, Horace Walpole, whose father had been the first-ever British Prime Minster, famously denounced her as a 'hyena in petticoats'.

More sensational still was her posthumously published novel, *The Wrongs of Women, or Maria*, which shocked even many in the radical movement with its sympathetic portrayal of an adulterous middle-class woman and a working-class prostitute, and its depiction of the institution of marriage as a form of slavery. Her character was defamed and her name blackened for the best part of two centuries, until 1970s feminism found and cherished her. The rights of women was an idea whose time was yet to come. But in the 1790s, the struggle for political rights was restricted to half the population. That was more than enough to provoke hysteria in the ruling circles of the day.

In Scotland, material recently uncovered by archivist David Brown offers revealing insights into the mindset of those at the top of society. In a report to the Duke of Buccleuch, Sir William Maxwell of Langholm warns that 'unknown emissaries of sedition have persuaded the lower orders to believe that monarchy should be abolished and that the common people will infallibly obtain justice, freedom, equality and a division of landed property'. Maxwell goes on to express his horror at the 'spirit of equality and licentiousness which seems everywhere to prevail in these kingdoms amongst the lowest classes of the people'.

Meanwhile Henry Dundas himself, the supreme commander of conservative reaction in Scotland, spearheaded the campaign to counter the growing influence of the radicals. 'The contest here', he wrote, 'is with the lower orders of the people whose minds are poisoned up to the point of Liberty, Equality and an agrarian law.' Central to his strategy were the clergy, the press and a network of spies.

Church of Scotland pulpits were turned into political soapboxes from which ministers damned the wickedness of reform. The smaller churches that had broken away from the Church of Scotland, however, tended to be on the side of the radicals. The press presented a more difficult challenge. At the start of the 1780s, before the French Revolution electrified political debate in Scotland, there were only eight newspapers published in Scotland, mostly local gossip-sheets. By the 1790s, there were 27, all of them fiercely partisan. Some were passionately pro-reform, others staunch supporters of the status quo.

These days politicians employ spin doctors to influence the media, but Dundas had a more direct approach. Evidence has been uncovered of substantial sums of money paid by the government to two prominent pro-reform newspapers, the *Edinburgh Herald* and *Caledonian Mercury*. The state also bankrolled a pro-government pamphleteer to publish a newspaper, *The Patriot's Weekly Chronicle.*

On top of which, Dundas ran a spy ring to penetrate the radical movement, feeding back information on the people involved and their activities. Because it was paid on the basis of piecework, they were guaranteed to be deluged with information, some of it no doubt accurate, but much of it simply invented.

The unique flavour of Scottish radicalism

In recent years, mainstream academic history has tended to minimise the strength of national feeling in Scotland during the glory years of the empire, implying that, the odd wee bicker notwithstanding, Great Britain was riveted together like the mighty Clyde-built ocean liners that would one day be launched from Glasgow, the Second City of the Empire. The popular movements for political reform, from the republican Friends of the People of the 1790s to the Chartists of the 1840s, and the emerging labour movement of the later nineteenth and early twentieth centuries, are portrayed as British through and through, unbesmirched by vulgarities such as national sentiment.

It is true that the social struggles that erupted in Scotland during these decades were part of a wider movement across Britain and Ireland. In contrast to the Jacobites, they did not explicitly advocate the break-up of the union.

But to grasp the complexity of any movement, it is not enough to focus only on its stated aims.

A future historian researching the anti-Poll Tax struggle in Scotland, for example, would find little published evidence of support for independence, or even devolution, within the movement. Yet those who attended the public meetings, or marched on the demos, or campaigned on the streets, were well aware that the campaign was a lightning conductor for a multitude of other grievances against the Westminster Tory government, not least the sense that Scotland had been effectively disenfranchised by a south-east of England block vote that had delivered Thatcher three successive general election victories.

The demand for more political power for Scotland may not have been spelled out in bold headlines on the official leaflets, but the Poll Tax movement was galvanised by the mood of national alienation that had gradually seeped into the bones of Scotland throughout the 1980s. And paradoxically, the sheer strength and success of the movement in Scotland, bolstered by national discontent, inspired the wider struggle that spread across England and Wales a year later.

Political upheaval in Scotland in the late eighteenth and nineteenth century also focused on clear, short-term goals that could only be achieved by piling pressure upon, or bringing down, the government in London. Yet these movements too were fuelled by the sense of national injustice that had pervaded Scotland since 1707, and a burning hatred of the Hanoverian Government.

But no democratic channel existed through which to achieve independence or even Home Rule. The British state had an iron grip. Of Scotland's 45 MPs, 30 were elected by just 3,000 landowners, with the other 15 chosen by the corrupt elite who ran Scotland's towns and burghs. This tiny electorate, just 0.3 per cent of Scotland's population, was solidly unionist, bound by golden chains of privilege to the British establishment. And in any case, Scotland's 45 MPs were swamped by over 500 English MPs.

Nor was armed insurrection feasible. The Jacobite Rebellion had been drowned in its own blood; since then, the British state had built up a mighty military machine backed by an iron phalanx of repression. Any attempt to head for the exit would be futile, if not suicidal.

The radical movement in Scotland was closely intertwined with radical movements in England, and Ireland. But unlike, for example, the Westminster political parties today, or even most modern trade unions, it was not run from London, but fully controlled from within Scotland. Although ideas were shared by correspondence, and attempts made to find common ground, it had no Britain-wide structure.

The character of the three movements in Scotland, England and Ireland were quite distinct. In England, the Society of the Friends of the People was led by Whig MPs and peers, and operated as an exclusive club drawn from the upper middle classes and aristocracy. Other organisations proliferated across England that were more militant and more representative, notably the London Corresponding Society, which forged links with Scottish and Irish radicals. In Ireland, the movement had been formed by a small group of Protestant liberals. Once it became clear that lobbying for constitutional reform was a dead end, the movement evolved towards revolutionary republicanism.

In Scotland, the movement had its own unique characteristics, which drew from different, even conflicting traditions. Nowhere are the ambiguities and paradoxes of Scottish radicalism expressed with more feeling than in the poetry of Robert Burns. On Hogmanay 1787, he had attended a secret celebration of the final birthday of the exiled Prince Charles Edward Stuart, and wrote a poem for the occasion – *Birthday Ode to 31st December 1787* – praising the memory of Jacobite heroes such as Viscount Dundee and Lord Balmerino. Earlier that year, he had engraved, with a diamond, a pro-Jacobite verse on the window of a Stirling inn, which he later published under the initials RB:

'The injur'd Stewart-line are gone,
A Race outlandish fill their throne
An idiot race, to honour lost
Who know them best despise them most.'

He continued to write streams of verse expressing historical sympathy with the House of Stuart and the Jacobites, with such partisan titles as *Lament of Mary Queen of Scots on the Approach of Spring; It Was A' for Our Rightfu' King; The Highland Widow's Lament; Charlie He's My Darling; and Awa' Whigs Awa'*. Yet these sentimental odes were counterbalanced with the kind of hard-headed scepticism, laced with pacifism, of *Ye Jacobites By Name* – 'So let your schemes alone; adore the rising sun; and leave a man undone to his fate.'

Burns was not writing about dim and distant history – he was born just 13 years after Culloden, and his father had migrated to Ayrshire from the Jacobite stronghold of north-east Scotland. The poet also paid his respects to a tradition whose stronghold had been his own backyard, the south-west of Scotland:

'The Solemn League and Covenant
Now brings a smile, now brings a tear.
But sacred Freedom, too, was theirs;
If thou 'rt a slave, indulge thy sneer.'

The Covenanters and Jacobites represented the duality of Scotland at the time. They had been irreconcilable enemies, yet Burns managed to assimilate both traditions within his own philosophy by embracing the radical and rebellious elements of each current, and discarding what was reactionary.

Burns' most famous works, however, were directly inspired by the revolutionary storms that blasted through Scotland in the 1790s. *Scots Wha Hae* directly links the medieval Wars of Independence with the struggle against tyranny then raging in 1793:

'Lay the proud usurpers low
Tyrants fall in every foe!
Liberty's in every blow
Let us do or die.'

The final line is a barely disguised reference – in a time of savage repression – to the Friends of the People toast, declared at the close of every gathering: 'Live Free or Die!' A couple of years later, Burns published his famous anthem of equality and internationalism, *A Man's A Man for A' That*, which mocks the aristocracy and looks forward to a new world free of hierarchy.

The radical movement too was a product of these eclectic influences and traditions. Despite its size, Scotland had always been an extraordinarily diverse and complex nation. It had a composite national identity that could never be reduced to blood, language or religion. Its easy access from the north, south, east and west meant that its ethnic DNA was as scrambled as a kaleidoscope. Since medieval times, it had spoken three languages – Scots, Gaelic and English, seasoned with a rich range of local dialects. It was the birthplace and stronghold of Presbyterianism, yet the eighteenth century movements to defend Scotland's nationhood and restore its independence were associated with Catholicism and Episcopalianism.

The northern half of the country had a strong cultural affinity with Catholic Ireland, while the southern half had become complicit in the oppression of both the Scottish and Irish Gaels. Scotland had benefited from being part of the British Empire yet its people and resources had been exploited and oppressed by England, who held tight the reins of that vast international network of colonies. No wonder Scottish radicalism was confused.

The Friends of the People did, however, unravel some of it, drawing on the egalitarian traditions of Presbyterianism, whilst rejecting its sectarian dimension and supporting Catholic emancipation and religious tolerance. Although rooted in the towns and burghs of the Lowlands, the Friends of the People respected the Gaelic component of Scotland's national make-up, supported Ireland's bid for freedom from the British Empire and, though regretting Scotland's loss of sovereignty, channelled its energies into uniting with English radicals to force political reform at Westminster. Nonetheless, divisions opened up over the national question. At a General Convention of the Friends of the People in Edinburgh in November 1792, a faction of the leadership tried to prevent Thomas Muir, a talented advocate and leader, from reading out a greeting to the conference from the United Irishmen:

> 'We greatly rejoice that the spirit of freedom moves over the face of Scotland… a country so respectable for her attainments in science, in arts and in arms… We rejoice that you do not consider yourselves as merged and melted down into another country… you are still Scotland. The land where Buchanan* wrote and Fletcher spoke and Wallace fought.'

Muir's opponents had seen the statement in advance and argued that it amounted to 'Treason against the union with England'. The overwhelming mass of delegates, however, voted for Muir to read it out. Within a few

* The sixteenth century humanist poet and Protestant theologian who defended the right of people to rise up against tyrannical monarchs.

months, it would be used as evidence against him in one of the most famous trials in Scottish legal history.

One of those who objected to the greeting being read out was Lord Daer, a close friend of Robert Burns who was embarrassed by his inherited feudal title and preferred to be known as 'Citizen Douglas'. A few months later he wrote a letter pleading with English radicals to continue the fight for reform at a time when they were wavering, simultaneously urging them to recognise the strength of national feeling north of the border:

> 'Scotland has long groaned under the chains of England and knows that its connection there has been the cause of its greatest misfortunes… We have existed a conquered province these two centuries. We trace our bondage from the Union of Crowns and find it little alleviated by the Union of Kingdoms [i.e. Parliaments]… You may say we have joined emancipation from feudal tyranny. I would believe most deliberately that had no Union ever taken place, we should, in that respect, have been more emancipated than we are. Left to ourselves, we should probably have had a progression towards liberty not less than yours... the Friends of Liberty in Scotland have almost universally been enemies to the Union with England.'

Tyranny of the wigs and gowns

In time, this movement for political reform was crushed by brute force. Thomas Muir, who came from Bishopbriggs on the northern outskirts of Glasgow, was arrested and dragged before the High Court in Edinburgh in August 1793. He was accused of 'delivering seditious speeches and harangues', and 'wickedly and feloniously advising and exhorting persons to peruse seditious and wicked publications and writings calculated to produce a spirit of disloyalty and disaffection to the King and Government'. The charge sheet was lengthy and detailed, and included the greeting he had read from the United Irishmen.

The presiding judge, Lord Braxfield, was notorious for his cruel humour and savage sentencing, delivered in brutal, broad Scots. 'If ye hing a thief in the mornin', he'll no' get up to much mischief in the efternin', he advised his colleagues, and famously told one unfortunate offender, 'Ye'll be be nane the worse o' a guid hingin'. Now he turned to the Edinburgh jury – 15 'men of proper principles', hand-picked by the Crown. 'This is the question for your conseederation. Is the panel guilty of sedition or is he not? Afore this question can be decidit, ah hae twa things tae say that require nae proof. The first is that the British constitution is the best that ever wis since the creation of the world and it is no' possible to make it any better.'

He then dazzled the courtroom with his sophisticated grasp of the intricacies of international affairs: 'Ah never liked the French a' ma days and noo ah hate them. In ma conseedered judgement, the French are the monsters o' human nature.'

Faced with such sophisticated arguments, it was nae wunner Muir was condemned. He gave a rip-roaring speech from the dock, defiant and brave – though perhaps on the reckless side in a country suffocating in the chill fog of repression. He did not seek to cover up his actions, nor to blame others, telling the court:

> 'I am careless and indifferent to my fate. I can look danger and I can look death in the face for I am shielded by the consciousness of my own rectitude. I may be condemned to languish in the recesses of a dungeon. I may be doomed to ascend the scaffold. Nothing can deprive me of the recollection of the past, nothing can destroy my inward peace of mind arising from the remembrance of having discharged my duty.'

Sentenced to 14 years' transportation, in February 1794, aged just 28, Muir set sail from Merseyside in a ship called the *Surprize* along with a group of 93 other convicts, including 17 Scots, bound for Sydney. He was in Australia barely a year before escaping to America. He then returned to Europe, via Mexico and Cuba, to spend the last couple of years of his life in revolutionary France, dropping dead suddenly at the age of 34.

Back in Edinburgh, radicals hatched a plan for an armed uprising. Their strategy was first to light a bonfire near the customs and excise building in St Andrews Square, and to deliver a letter to the castle signed, ostensibly, by the Lord Provost asking the troops to go and extinguish the blaze. They would then try, by force of argument, to win over the soldiers.

Their next move was to peacefully detain the key officials in the city, including judges, magistrates and councillors. This done, they planned to occupy strategic buildings in the city – the castle, the excise, the banks and the post office, giving them control over the army, the economy and communications. Meantime, messengers would have been dispatched to Dublin and London, in the hope that a simultaneous uprising could be coordinated in the three main cities of the British Empire.

In retrospect, it all seems like hapless bravado born out of desperation. Nevertheless, the reaction of the state was ice cold fury. After a show trial, two of the leaders were sentenced to the same fate as William Wallace.

Half a millennium had elapsed since Stirling Bridge. A religious reformation had swept through northern Europe. The Glorious Revolution had triumphed against the divine right of kings. Universal education had banished ignorance among the mass of the population. The industrial revolution had begun. The Enlightenment was in full flow.

Yet here in the very heart of city where a galaxy of philosophers, poets, and scientists were pouring out manifestos for a new, tolerant and humane world, a black-capped judge pronounced that the guilty men be 'drawn on a hurdle to the place of execution, hanged but not until you are dead, and that being alive you be cut down and your bowel taken out and burned before your face. That your heads be severed from your bodies and your bodies be divided into four parts, and that your heads and quarters be disposed of as the king thinks fit.'

One of the two accused, David Downie, a Catholic goldsmith, had his sentence commuted to permanent transportation to Australia after the jury appealed for mercy. The other, Robert Watt, had, ironically, first become involved in the reform movement as a spy, providing information to the state before going native. Perhaps it was that betrayal that sealed his fate. At 1.30pm on 16 October 1794, the grisly execution took place.

It was a time of savage repression. Among the middle-upper classes, early enthusiasm for the French revolution had evaporated as news came of the French king's execution. Day in, day out, the now heavily state-controlled media ran blood-curdling tales of the Jacobin Reign of Terror across the Channel. A fiendish new device designed for instant executions called the guillotine aroused widespread public revulsion, precious few seeming to recognise this as a more humane method of carrying out a death sentence than the crude butchery favoured in Britain. Most terrifying of all was the constant fear of a French invasion. In such a heightened atmosphere, where menace seemed to lurk around every corner and ooze from every crack and crevice, the judges treated dissidents as though they were cockroaches, to be stamped out without pity.

Such was the fever of the times that even Burns seems, on the face of it, to have been affected. In 1795, he signed up for the Dumfries Volunteers, one of a number of part-time militias springing up around the country to defend Britain against France. His decision remains murky and controversial – just four months before enlisting, he had smuggled four cannonades to France at great personal risk in the draconian atmosphere of the times. A year later, a private journal of James MacDonald, an acquaintance of Burns, describes meeting the poet and a friend in Dumfries. These were dangerous times to be known as a radical. Yet Burns and his friend were both, according to MacDonald, 'staunch republicans'.

It may be that, as an excise man employed by the government on a comfortable of salary of £50 a week – double the average income at the time – Burns would have been expected, if not compelled, to join his local militia. Others, however, including the twentieth century poet Hugh MacDiarmid, are convinced that he joined up, as did many radicals, to gain access to weapons, ammunition and training, in preparation for a future showdown.

By this time, the Friends of the People had been crushed, along with the radical reform forces in England. As a general rule, people tend to learn more effectively from defeats than victories, forcing them to analyse what went wrong, and to seek out new paths. One lesson drawn by Scottish radicals in the mid-1790s was that trying to persuade the entrenched British state to reform itself was like trying to make a river run uphill. Pamphlets, petitions and public rallies had achieved nothing but mass arrests, show trials, jailings and deportations.

The aims remained the same, but the strategy to achieve these aims had to change.

15

OUT OF THE DEPTHS

No conscription!

In the centre of Tranent, the oldest mining town in Scotland, stands a striking statue of a woman striding resolutely forward, a drum under her left arm, her clenched right fist raised to the sky, her face etched with defiance. By her side, a child is running to keep up.

This is Joan Crookston – better known as Jackie – as she appeared on 29 August 1797. That morning, she led 2,000 people through the town, in protest against the Militia Act. It was the last day of her life.

The full title of the Westminster legislation was an *Act to Raise a Militia Force, in the part of the kingdom of Great Britain called Scotland*. Its purpose was to raise a 6,000-strong military force in Scotland by conscripting all young men between the ages of 19 and 23, excluding schoolmasters, professors, clergy, parish constables and those with the wealth to buy their way out.

The British state and its henchmen in Scotland were deeply unpopular, and resistance erupted in towns and villages across the land. In Tranent, the huge assembly of colliers and servants, predominantly female, converged on the town square, all set to tear down the list of those chosen by ballot to be conscripted. When he saw the size of the hostile crowd, the commander of the recruitment squad, Major Andrew Wight, called for reinforcements. From barracks in nearby Musselburgh, the Pembroke Yeomanry from Wales and the Cinque Port Cavalry from the south coast of England marched into town and, in the words of labour historian Tom Johnston, began 'shooting, spearing, slashing and riding down a populace armed only with stones'. By the time they'd finished, the streets were strewn with a dozen corpses and countless wounded. One of those killed was Jackie Crookston.

As with Bloody Sunday in Derry, in 1972, no-one was ever convicted. The Lord Advocate, Robert Dundas, the brother of the Secretary of State for Scotland, refused to take any action, declaring that the action of the soldiers had been justified in the face of 'such a dangerous mob as deserved more properly the name of an insurrection'.

A few days after the Tranent massacre, a regional uprising blew a hole in Highland Perthshire. This was frontier territory, the start of the Highlands, a bilingual region where people would slip effortlessly from Gaelic to Scots and back again without missing a beat. It had been a stronghold of the Jacobites half a century before. The subsequent High Court indictment of the two men identified as the ringleaders, Angus Cameron and James Menzies, describes how a large crowd first surrounded the home of the minister in Weem, Aberfeldy, and invited him, none too politely, to join their march on nearby Castle Menzies, the residence of the Lord Lieutenant of the County of Perth.

Here, the 'riotous and disorderly mob, their number amounting to upwards of a thousand, mostly armed with sticks and bludgeons', pressed the Lord Lieutenant to have no part in this reviled Militia Act. And as an added incentive to comply, they made it clear that his castle would be be burned to ashes should he refuse.

The protest was bolstered when a contingent arrived from Grandtully, about six miles away, swelling the crowd to 'upwards of two thousand'. Unsurprisingly, the Lord Lieutenant, Sir John Menzies, now agreed to sign a statement. Dictated by Angus Cameron, it pledged that there would be no conscription in Perthshire and that the Lord Lieutenant would petition the government demanding the repeal of the Militia Act. Just for good measure, the statement guaranteed that there would be no arrests or imprisonments of anyone involved in the protest.

According to the aforementioned indictment, Angus Cameron then climbed on one of the pillars of the castle gate and 'did most seditiously and wickedly administer an oath to the people thus riotously assembled, to stand by one another in their illegal endeavours to resist the authority of the established law of the country'.

The gathering, now three times larger than the entire Perthshire regiment of the British Army, began to spread across the region. As the crowds marched north-eastwards towards Blair Castle, the stronghold of the Duke of Atholl, it strong-armed local lairds, gentry and ministers along the way to sign the pledge. At its height, the rebels claimed to have mobilised more than 16,000 people; for a time, the established authorities disintegrated, leaving the people in control.

Alas, there was no clear strategy about what to do next. According to court testimony, Angus Cameron proposed raiding the armouries at Taymouth and Castle Menzies, then taking to the surrounding hills in small guerilla detachments, ready to swoop on the forces of the crown as they arrived to restore order.

Though their blood was up, the rebels failed to organise themselves sufficiently, and a potential uprising was reduced to a series of torchlit protests, which were quelled ten days later when a detachment of English troops – the Windsor Foresters from Berkshire – stormed Angus Cameron's house in Weem.

The report of the arrest by the commanding officer, Captain Colberg, described the unsuccessful effort by the people to liberate their leader as they transported him by coach through the winding back roads of Perthshire. 'We observed hundreds of people with forks, fowling pieces, pikes and scythes fixed on poles, pouring from the mountains and water side and the road was covered with men women and children'.

Along with one of his associates, James Menzies, Angus Cameron appeared in the High Court on 15 January 1798 charged with sedition, mobbing and rioting. After pleading Not Guilty, the two men were, surprisingly, granted bail – and vanished into thin air. Cameron appears to have fled to London to join the active community of radical Scots outlaws who had taken advantage of the less oppressive climate of the English capital. Scotland had a more draconian judicial system by far – perhaps because the Edinburgh establishment was still haunted by the ghosts of ragged Highland clansmen seizing Edinburgh Castle and Holyrood Palace within living memory.

The United Scotsmen

Angus Cameron, it would later emerge, was one of the leaders of a new underground resistance movement called the Society of the United Scotsmen. According to government reports, riots against the Militia Act broke out in 70 towns and villages from New Galloway in the far south-west to Strathtay in the southern Highlands. The United Scotsmen organisation appears to have played a major part in coordinating this mass movement.

Dismissed by some mainstream historians as a fringe organisation, the United Scotsmen had a membership of over 3,000 by the mid-1790s – which was more than the entire electorate of Scotland at the time, and proportional to today's population, comparable with major parties such as the SNP and Scottish Labour. Not bad really, for an illegal organisation, membership of which could land you with a one-way ticket to Botany Bay.

Yet the secret society remains something of a mystery. Operating in the deep, dark shadows, under conditions of severe repression, no minutes or membership lists existed, and few written records survive. Members were under strict instruction to destroy all letters after reading them. As a result, much of what is known about the United Scotsmen has been pieced together from court records and government intelligence reports.

In January 1798, one of its most prominent leaders, George Mealmaker, was tried at the High Court for 'Sedition and administering unlawful Oaths'. The transcripts of his trial provide an illuminating insight into the structure and strength of the organisation. Its members were charged a 6d entry fee – two and half pence in today's currency – plus a further 3d annual subscription, which funded a network of travelling agitators and organisers, who spread across the country recruiting new forces. Each new member swore an oath, pledging to fight for 'equal political franchise', and used a system of secret handshakes and coded phrases to identify one another.

The movement had, according to court records, 'small clubs or societies in various parts of the country, with officers belonging to them chosen by ballot as president, secretary and treasurer'. When an individual club reached 16 members, it would divide in two to minimise the possibility of mass arrests. The organisation was overseen by geographically-based committees – parish, county, provincial and national – with a seven-strong 'Secret Committee' in overall control. In Coupar Angus, according to police reports, there were 12 clubs, which means that a large proportion of the town's male population must have been members.

It would have come as no great surprise when the Edinburgh jury of seven merchants, five bankers, a solicitor, a bookbinder and a printer, delivered a unanimous guilty verdict after just half an hour's deliberation. Like Thomas Muir, Mealmaker was sentenced to transportation to Botany Bay for 14 years.

Some historians point to the absence of any formal written declaration in favour of independence by the movement as evidence that no such appetite existed. But the clandestine nature of the United Scotsmen meant that its political strategy was thrashed out in secrecy. If one of their goals was to break the union, it could only be achieved by armed insurrection, tantamount to High Treason – and punishable by the grisly ritual of hanging, drawing and quartering on the testimony of two witnesses.

The state certainly suspected that the United Scotsmen was more than just a movement for political reform. Mealmaker's charge sheet read:

'The object and purpose of [the United Scotsmen] was, under the pretext of reform, and the obtaining of annual parliaments and universal suffrage, to create in the minds of the people a spirit of disaffection and disloyalty to the king, and the established government, and ultimately to excite them and stir them up to acts of violence and opposition to the laws and constitution of this country.'

Political statements from abroad, unconstrained as they were by fear of persecution, suggest that the radical struggle in Scotland had a strong national dimension. In 1793, Armand de Kersaint had told the French National Convention that Scotland and Ireland were conquered nations:

'The English people, like all conquerors, have long oppressed Scotland and Ireland; but it should be noted that these two nations, always restive, and secretly in revolt against the injustices of the dominating race, have acquired at different epochs concessions which have engendered the hope of ultimately regaining their independence… Since the union, Scotland has been represented in Parliament, but out of such proportion to its wealth, its extent and its population that it does not conceal the fact that it is nothing but a dependent colony of the English Government.'

A few years later, the French revolutionary regime sent Jean Mengaud to England, Scotland and Ireland to assess the prospects for revolution. The Frenchman reported that the Scots, especially in Glasgow, were favourable, and that 'this feeling had existed since the union of Scotland and England.'

By now Thomas Muir was explicit in his support for an independent republic of Scotland. Just before arriving in France he had written a letter stating:

'The people of Scotland have long groaned under the most hideous oppression. Their ancient rights have been ravished away. Their ancient laws have been insulted. Of their ancient constitution, at this hour they possess not even the shadow. This brave and high-spirited people have made exertions to break their chains.'

And when he arrived in France in 1797, Pierre David, a poet and diplomat, wrote in the main newspaper of revolutionary France:

'The Scots have never forgotten their ancient independence, the massacre of their ancestors, the tragic death of their last Queen, the expulsion of the Stuarts from the throne of Great Britain: these memories, the consciousness of their want, the shocking contrast of English luxury, perhaps finally the example of our revolution, were the causes of the revolutionary movements which appeared in Scotland in 1792, in which Thomas Muir played one of the premier roles.'

From Paris, Muir himself then wrote a document on the state of Scotland, tracing the nation's woes back to the Union of Crowns and suggesting – in a flight of wild optimism, perhaps – that if there was a French invasion of Britain, it could expect the support of 50,000 Scottish Highlanders and 100,000 Scottish patriots in total.

At the start of the following year, 1798, plans were floated from Paris for the establishment of a Scottish Directory to oversee a republic. The title of the proposed body derived from French Directory, which held executive power at the time in revolutionary France. Its planned Scottish equivalent would be chaired by Muir, and would include a Neil Cameron, who is believed to be Angus Cameron, who had led the uprising in Highland Perthshire against the Militia Act. James Kennedy, another exiled Scot who had been a weaver, a poet and republican activist in Paisley, was also listed as a potential member of the Scottish Directory.

By the early summer of that year, the ruling elite in London would be shaken to its core by a violent insurrection on a scale not seen for half a century. But the shockwaves came not from the Scottish Highlands, but from across the Irish Sea.

The thistle and the shamrock

Every summer for more than a century, Irish republicans and nationalists have flocked to a small churchyard in County Kildare, to pay homage to the most high profile leader of the 1798 Irish rebellion.

Theobold Wolfe Tone was a Dublin lawyer, a supporter of the French Revolution, and a founder of Ireland's first-ever movement for an independent republic, the United Irishmen. And like most of the other leaders in Dublin, he was a Protestant, from the Anglican Church of Ireland tradition.

In another cemetery, just off the Antrim Road in North Belfast, stands the gravestone of another great hero of the 1798 Irish rebellion. Today, there's a pub in the city named after him, and a republican flute band that bears his name.

Although Henry Joy McCracken was the son of a Belfast industrialist, he was the most left wing of all the prominent figures of the United Irishman. He was also a Protestant, whose paternal ancestors had been driven from Wigtownshire during the persecution of the Galloway Covenanters by Bonnie Dundee.

Wolfe Tone and Henry Joy McCracken were typical of two of the key strands of this first wave of Irish republicanism. In the south, most of its leaders were progressive liberals, from Cromwellian plantation stock; in the north, its roots were steeped in the egalitarian, anti-hierarchical culture of the Covenanters.

One of its strongest pillars of support was the Reformed Presbyterian Church, which had been founded by Covenanter settlers from Scotland. Because they were banned from taking oaths, members of the church did not formally join the United Irishmen, but provided political support and large numbers of activists for the rising in Antrim.

The bond between Scotland and Ireland has been strong since time immemorial. Just 11 miles separate the Mull of Kintyre, in Argyll, and the north coast of Ireland, while the east coast of Antrim is but 20 miles from Wigtownshire. By the nineteenth century, a daily ferry shuttled back and forth from Portpartick to Donaghadee, filled with migrant workers, traders, farmers and students.

In her 1994 book, *Ireland and Scotland in the Age of Revolution*, Elaine MacFarland, a historian at Glasgow Caledonian University, reveals a multitude of previously hidden connections between Irish and Scottish republicanism in the final decade of the eighteenth century, some of which can be traced back to the influence of a Glasgow University lecturer who died in 1746, the year of Culloden. Francis Hutchison, born in Ulster of Scottish parents, is hailed by many historians today as the 'Father of the Scottish Enlightenment'. His philosophy was rooted in the Covenanting tradition, his brand of humanitarian theology fusing Presbyterianism with religious tolerance and radical ideas, such as freedom of opinion, the right of resistance to tyranny, and the right of citizens to bear arms in defence of civil liberties. A brilliant orator, inspirational and influential, his ideas endured for decades after his death.

Because Ireland's only university, Trinity College in Dublin, admitted only Anglicans until the end of the eighteenth century, Glasgow University became a magnet for the more academically inclined sons of Ulster Presbyterian farmers and artisans. According to a study of university records by MacFarland, almost 17 per cent of all students who matriculated at Glasgow during the eighteenth century were from the four north-eastern counties of Ulster.

On returning home, many become involved in the Society of United Irishmen. Formed in 1791, two years after the French Revolution, its membership, initially, was overwhelmingly Protestant, especially in Belfast. Like the United Scotsmen, it even became entangled with freemasonry, utilising the clandestine nature of the lodges, at the time awash with radical ideas, as a cloak for illegal revolutionary activity.

In recent years, some Northern Ireland loyalists have attempted to lay claim to the United Irishmen. One Progressive Unionist Party activist, the late Billy McCaughey, a former Royal Ulster Constabulary officer and Ulster Volunteer Force gunman, even tried to organise an annual loyalist pilgrimage in honour of the United Irishmen. But the movement's central goal was irreconcilable with unionism of any brand. At the heart of its founding programme was the statement:

> 'We have no national government; we are ruled by Englishmen and thus servants of Englishmen whose object is the interest of another country, whose instrument is corruption; whose strength is the weakness of Ireland.'

It also supported religious equality and Catholic emancipation, even expressing sympathy with feminism, centuries before the word was coined. The society's newspaper, the Belfast-based *Northern Star*, published Mary Wollstonecraft's *Vindication of the Rights of Woman*, and in some areas women played a key in the movement – most notably, Mary Ann McCracken, the sister of Henry Joy, who in 1796 founded a Society of United Irishwomen.

By the time of the rising in 1798, the movement had succeeded in unifying urban Protestants, inspired by the French and American revolutions, with the Catholic rural poor, who had suffered merciless oppression at the hands of the English ruling classes for centuries. The two strongholds of the rising were Wexford in the south-east, where 30,000 rebels were commanded by a parish priest, Father John Murphy, and Antrim and Down in the north-east, where Henry Joy McCracken led 22,000 men into battle.

But the insurrection in Dublin was stillborn. In what should have been the epicentre of the rebellion, the authorities were able take preemptive action after successfully infiltrating the movement with spies and informers. To add to the chaos, the promised assistance from France and the Dutch Republic failed to materialise until it was too late. And across the land, some of the wealthier landlords and merchants who had pledged support for the rebellion drew back, prompting Henry Joy McCracken to rue the fact – in a letter to his sister – that 'the rich always betray the poor'.

After six weeks of bloody clashes, the rising was crushed, brutally. In scenes reminiscent of the aftermath of Culloden, rebel captives were massacred by the British and, in some cases, burned alive. Thousands of people in the poorer quarters of Dublin were rounded up and tortured to extract confessions of their involvement with the United Irishmen.

In the north, the British crown mobilised the Orange Order, which had been formed just three years before to counter the rising tide of republicanism within the Protestant community. Hundreds of Protestant rebels were imprisoned, tortured or murdered, while thousands of Catholics were driven out of Antrim and Down and forced to flee west. In their hundreds, and perhaps thousands, rebel prisoners were press-ganged into the Royal Navy, or sent to the West Indies as part of Britain's colonial occupation force in the Caribbean.

Thirty four leaders of the rising were executed. Henry Joy McCracken was hanged in the centre of Belfast, in a public square donated to the city by his great-grandfather, while Wolfe Tone died of a neck wound, probably self-inflicted, as he awaited execution in Dublin's Mountjoy Jail.

According to Elaine MacFarland's research, at least 23 licensed Presbyterian ministers, plus another seven probationers, were arrested and charged with participation in the rising. Some were transported and at least one was hanged. Of those ministers arrested, no fewer than 19 had been educated at Glasgow University. Many more are likely to have taken part in the insurrection.

The rebellion led directly to the 1801 Act of Union, in which Ireland was fully incorporated into the British state on the same basis as Scotland. Ireland would now directly elect 100 MPs to Westminster, and to forestall further unrest, there was promise of Catholic emancipation – although King George III and his successor George IV blocked its implementation for a further 28 years.

In Scotland, radical republicanism was weaker. Although the nation had lost its political and economic autonomy, it had not been vanquished and tyrannised as Ireland had. It had retained its own national church, in contrast to Ireland where 90 per cent of the population were treated as the enemy within, and deprived of even the most basic rights because of their religion. Only in the Highlands had the population suffered anything like the cultural persecution inflicted on Ireland, and by the 1790s the Gàidhealtachd was too consumed in its own struggle for survival against native landowners to be part of any wider movement. There was nonetheless an affinity between the radical currents in both nations, expressed, for example, in a subversive poem of the times, *The Social Thistle and Shamrock*, which condemns the reign of England over Scotland and Ireland.

In September 1798, two Dunfermline weavers, James Paterson and David Black, appeared before the High Court charged with sedition and membership of the United Scotsmen. Among a litany of other offences, their charge sheet states that they 'did most wickedly and feloniously' attempt to recruit one Henry Keys or Kees, a soldier in the West Lowlands fencible regiment, attempting 'by inflammatory harangues [to] prevail on him to join their wicked association and turn their guns against his king and country'. On top of which, they 'had the audacity to vindicate the unnatural rebellion which has broken out in Ireland, and to present the Irish insurgents as people groaning under oppression and struggling in defence of their just rights'. While Black appears to have escaped and gone on the run, Paterson was found guilty and ordered to be 'transported beyond the seas for five years'.

According to Elaine MacFarland, Glasgow radicals also attempted to spread mutiny among local regiments who were about to be mobilised to Ireland to crush the rebellion, while in Ayrshire, there were reports of troops coming under fire *en route* to Portpatrick. Had the 1798 rebellion succeeded and an Irish republic established, it would surely have electrified Scotland, especially given the key role of northern Presbyterians.

Instead, the crushing of Ireland, coming just 50 years after Culloden, underlined the supremacy of the British state and the futility of all attempts to break it. Under these grim conditions, the radical movement in Scotland could have sunk without trace. Instead, the Society of United Scotsman remained active, its forces replenished by the great river of radicalised and militant refugees from Ireland that poured into Portpatrick and spread across the Lowlands, seeking work in Scotland's burgeoning weaving industry.

Broken by an emperor

In 1800, a fresh outbreak of disturbances erupted across the south-west of Scotland, with riots reported in Ayrshire, Renfrewshire, Glasgow, and Pollokshaws, all important centres of the weaving trade. Although these were triggered by genuine grievances over savage price increases, the authorities were convinced, probably with some justification, that radical activists were once again fomenting unrest.

Elaine MacFarland offers evidence of correspondence between the Lord Advocate of Scotland, Charles Hope, and the British Home Secretary, Lord Pelham, which suggests that there was deep unease at the highest levels of government – enough to merit launching a serious drive to infiltrate the movement as they had done with striking success in Dublin. In a letter dated 1801, Hope expressed regret that, for all the efforts of his spies, they had never yet been able to penetrate the Glasgow-based executive of the United Scotsmen. In a letter the following year, also to the Home Secretary, he warned that the United Scotsmen were regrouping in Fife and planning a rising. The rebel strategy involved obtaining arms and munitions from local fencible regiments, then capturing Edinburgh Castle with the support of soldiers in the garrison who were secret members of the United Scotsmen. Fencibles, it should be explained, were not swordsmen, but British Army regiments raised for the purpose of defence (ie defencibles) against foreign invasion.

By this time, Hope was able to supply some membership figures for the United Scotsmen in Perthshire. In Perth itself, there were 483 registered members. In Crieff, 133. In Auchterarder, where there was also reported to be a secret pike factory, 93. In Dunning there were 59, and in Foulis, 29, while in Auchermuchty and Strathmigo, there were reckoned to be 1,000. Unless this was a transcription error, the authorities had serious grounds for concern. Even if it was, the strength of the movement in Perthshire was clearly considerable, especially given the scale of repression by the authorities. Indeed, by the spring of 1803, the Lord Advocate reported that the Societies in Scotland 'were all alive again', and its central leadership as impenetrable as ever.

That same year, a further failed rising was launched in Dublin, leading to the execution of Robert Emmet. In Scotland, meanwhile, there was intense anxiety in state circles over the activities of Irish migrants, especially in the industrial villages of South Ayrshire. These were both and Catholic and

Protestant, but the Scottish authorities, making no distinction between the denominations, busied itself stirring up anti-Irish racism.

In Glasgow, where 10,000 people were of Irish birth – more than one in eight of the total population – the Lord Provost vented his fear and fury like a *Daily Mail* columnist with his trousers alight: 'Almost all are of the suspicious character and very many known to be old rebels not in the least reformed.' He warned the Lord Advocate that 'if a French force were to appear on the west coast of Scotland, those Irish would rise to a man.'

What the British state could not destroy by repression was weakened almost mortally, however, by a French general. Napoleon Bonaparte, was a fanatical, risk-taking genius with little interest in the ideals of liberty and equality. His victories on the battlefield had catapulted him to national stardom, allowing him to concentrate more and more political power into his own hands. In 1804, he delivered the final *coup de grace* to the revolutionary regime by crowning himself Emperor of France and restoring the principle of hereditary monarchy.

By this time, the exhilaration of the early days of the French revolution had long since worn off. But while it remained a republic, France still offered a sparkle of hope that a more equal world was 'coming yet for a' that'. Diseased though the French Revolution may have become, its final demise looked like the lights had now gone across Europe. For the best part of a decade, radicalism fell to its knees as the government in London successfully rallied the masses, the poor and the rich, the desperate and the despicable, against the fearsome dictator in Paris.

16

THE LAND AND THE PEOPLE

Roots of ruination

At the official opening of the Scottish Parliament building in 2004, the singer Eddi Reader captured the essence of something in Scotland's sense of identity with a beautiful rendition of a contemporary song written by John Douglas, *Wild Mountainside*. The harsh Highland landscape is almost imprinted on our psyche, and regarded, dreamed about, referred to, around the world. Tourists cash in their life savings to come to this place that attracts adventurers, photographers, writers, film-makers, and has inspired poems, songs, stories, novels, through centuries, in Gaelic, English and Scots.

This is not, however, a pristine wilderness, a Caledonian Yosemite of ancient, unspoilt beauty. It is, as explained by Aldo Leopold, the pioneering American environmentalist, an ecologically wrecked locality, that is also a beautiful one. The soaring magnificence of this northern outpost tends to camouflage the fact that this is a damaged landscape. The glens and straths that once supported a third of Scotland's population are lonely and silent, while the native trees, birds, animals and plants that once thrived on the lower and mid slopes of these hillsides are lifeless and bare. Apart from those enclaves where conservationists have battled bravely to restore natural balance, this is a wasteland of ecological plunder, a barren desert grazed to death by sheep and deer.

Over the centuries, the thread that binds the land and the people has snapped. Most of the landmass of the Highlands, now covered by sporting estates – the ultimate status symbol of the British upper classes – was once the legendary Caledonian forest, a sea of rowan and birch, aspen, Scots Pine, hazel and juniper: a rich ecosystem that sustained people and communities as well as supporting circle upon circle of fascinating wildlife. And the people, drawing on generations of ecological wisdom, sustained the forest. Trees and their associated habitats were vital to daily life in the Highlands, and in other areas such as Galloway. They provided winter shelter and spring grazing for cattle, and were an important source of nutrition – plants, berries, even bark for winter-hungry deer and wild boar, whose descendants are emaciated scavengers by comparison, with only bare hillsides to sustain them.

Trees supplied the raw materials for house building, agricultural equipment, furniture, bowls, barrels, baskets and dyes. Bark was used to tan leather; ash to make shinty sticks; birch twigs to weave ropes and reins; alder to build roofs. Oak, the most valuable wood of all, was used to build robust boats, sturdy bridges, and upmarket furniture and panelling in castles, mansions and manses.

The Highlanders preserved the fertility of the soil by using sustainable agricultural practices. They tended black cattle, in small numbers, and used the manure to fertilise the soil. During the summer months, they took them high into the uplands to graze by the shielings, allowing the woodlands and glens to regenerate. During the growing season, trees, grasses, shrubs and wild flowers were left to flourish and replenish the soils with valuable nutrients.

It was a harsh life of constant toil and bare subsistence, but it was sustainable and able to support a population of hundreds of thousands. In 1755, over half of Scotland's population – 650,000 out of 1.2 million – lived north of the Highland line. But then came the sheep and 50 years of human and ecological catastrophe.

In the late nineteenth century, Friedrich Engels – Karl Marx's friend and collaborator – made a general observation about nature which was light-years ahead of its time.

> 'Let us not flatter ourselves overmuch on account of our human victories over nature. For each such victory takes revenge on us... The people who in Mesopotamia, Greece, Asia Minor and elsewhere, destroyed the forests to obtain cultivable land, never dreamed that by removing along with the forests the collecting centre and reservoirs of moisture, they were laying the basis for the present forlorn state of these countries... Thus at every step we are reminded that we by no means rule over nature like a conqueror over a foreign people, like someone standing outside nature – but that we, with our flesh, blood and brain, belong to nature and exist in its midst, and that we have the advantage over all other creatures of being able to learn its laws and apply them correctly.'

But commercial capitalism, from its inception to the present day, has always had a triumphalist disregard for nature and a callously arrogant attitude towards people, except when these can be exploited for profit.

A huge demand had arisen across the British Empire for wool and mutton, and sheep needed vast acreages for grazing. By the late eighteenth century, they had overrun the south of Scotland, while the people were eased off the land, many to work in the weaving industry. Thus the sheep were moved north in droves, vast flocks of Cheviot from the Southern Uplands. To make way for this woollen wave, the people were swept from their native wooded glens out to the barren coastal fringes on the North Sea, the Pentland Firth and the Atlantic, or across the ocean to the USA and Canada, or into the British Army to kill and die on foreign fields.

For a time, the post-Culloden landlords and their industrialist allies in the south amassed mind-blowing profits. They were able to do so by taking advantage of the native Highlanders' expert stewardship of the land, and the relatively healthy and fertile ecosystem they had left behind. This bonanza lasted for around 50 years, until the sheep devoured everything of value and rendered the land sterile. In a small country, this was a human and ecological catastrophe on an epic scale, and it would distort Scotland socially, economically and culturally for centuries to come.

Year of the Sheep

The magnificent Balnagown Castle in Easter Ross has been owned since the 1970s by the flamboyant Egyptian-born business magnate, Mohammed al-Fayed. Desirable it may be, this ancestral home of the chiefs of Clan Ross, but it harbours a dark secret.

In 1760, after the sudden death of his elder brother, it was inherited by Admiral John Lockhart, who added his mother's name to reflect his new status. The following year, he was elected MP for Linlithgow Burghs and Lanarkshire. And the year after, 1762, he raised the rents of his tenants and brought in sheep farmers from the Lowlands. At the time, the change went through almost unnoticed beyond the boundaries of the Balnagown estate, but eventually, in decades to come, it would bring about cataclysmic change.

By the 1780s the most extensive of the early Highland Clearances kicked off in Lochaber, in the lands of Duncan MacDonnell of Glengarry. This had been a Jacobite stronghold, and one of the few Catholic enclaves in Scotland. MacDonnell's father had been killed at Falkirk fighting for Prince Charlie, and his uncle, the previous clan chief, had fallen at Culloden. But the old clan system had perished on the same battlefield, dismantled by the British state and replaced with commercial feudalism. Just as many of the old communist commissars were co-opted into the international capitalist elite after the collapse of the Soviet Union, so a new generation of clan chiefs were absorbed into the British aristocracy.

Ancient clan lands, belonging to no-one and everyone, were converted into the personal private property of this new caste of feudal chieftains. As they clambered up the social ladder, they turned their backs on the culture from which they had sprung, ashamed of their old language and embarrassed by the rough and ready ways of the glens. Adopting the abrasive accent of the English public schools, they sent their sons to Eton, Harrow and Oxbridge, and married their daughters off to wealthy southern families. Their forefathers had valued land by the number of people it could support; they valued land by the amount of profit that could be extracted from it.

In 1785, under the supervision of Glengarry's wife Marjorie, herself from another feudalised Highland family, the Chisholms, 500 tenants were cleared from Glen Quoich, the land that lies between Glen Shiel and Knoydart. Further clearances followed, mainly south of the Great Glen.

The word 'cleared' may be a little innocuous to describe what actually took place when tenants were evicted from their homes. Their roofs – the most valuable part of the structure, given the paucity of trees by this time – were ignited, dogs were sent in, and sometimes the houses were set alight with people still inside them. These were savage, almost vengeful clearances, and those evicted had almost nowhere to go – just barren shorelines, or the New World of Canada and America which, from an eighteenth century perspective, was tantamount to the ends of the earth.

Then came 1792, the Bliadhna nan Caorach, or Year of the Sheep. While the reverberations of the French Revolution sent tremors across Europe, and Thomas Muir rallied the Scottish Friends of the People in Edinburgh some 175 miles to the north, the first great upsurge of resistance was erupting.

Strathrusdale is today a quiet corner of Scotland, where local residents invoke the spirit of 1792 in opposition to a giant wind farm on the surrounding hillsides that is being driven by an American multinational corporation and an absentee landowner who refuses planning permission for local people to build houses. Back in the summer of 1792, a landowner in the neighbouring Kildermorie estate cleared a cluster of tenants to make way for a sheep farm run by two brothers, Allan and Alexander Cameron. Relations soon turned sour when the sheep farmers began to seize cattle which had strayed onto their land, and refused to release them until their owners made cash payment. Sick and tired of this, the people of Strathrusdale decided to physically liberate any impounded cattle, but when a group arrived to confront the sheep farmers, Allan Cameron appeared with a gun in one hand and a dagger in the other, threatening to 'shoot like birds' anyone who dared enter his farm. Any survivors, he warned, would be transported to Botany Bay. The gang of Strathrusdale men listened to his bluster, then moved to disarm him, before giving him a beating.

Two days later, at a local wedding, over pitchers of home-brewed ale, the men of Strathrusdale gleefully recounted the humiliation of Allan Cameron. As often happens when these kinds of conversations run rampant, and ale oils their wheels, the talk expanded and before long, they were drawing up a grand plan to rid the Highlands of the mutton-headed interlopers. Thus, on Sunday 29 July, these self-same bodies read a proclamation in Gaelic outside 13 churches across an area that stretched 30 miles from Alness in Easter Ross to Lairg in Sutherland, calling upon every able-bodied man to join an insurrection to clear every sheep out of the two counties. The declaration ended with the words, 'The curse of the children not yet born, and their generation, will be placed upon such as would not cheerfully go and banish the sheep out of the country.'

By the Tuesday, 400 men had been mobilised and began to drive 6,000 sheep out of the area southwards towards Beauly, 20 miles away. For days, the procession continued. A summit of 23 of the most powerful men in Ross, chaired by Sir Hugh Munro of Foulis, gathered in panic. The man in charge of law and order, the Sheriff Depute, Donald Macleod, reported 'disturbances and tumultuous associations in every part of the county'. It showed 'a turbulent spirit of anarchy affecting the greatest numbers of the lower class'. That night Sir Hugh Munro wrote a letter to the Lord Advocate describing the situation: 'We are so completely under the heel of the populace that, should they come to burn our houses and destroy our property, we are incapable of resistance.'

The Lord Advocate, Robert Dundas, agreed that the rebels should be 'crushed to the last extremity', that it was necessary to take 'the most vigorous and effective measures' in order to send a message to the lower orders that such acts 'will not be suffered with impunity'. Had the Starthrusdale revolt been allowed to spread, especially in a nationwide climate of rebellion, who could tell where it would lead?

For the people of the straths and glens on the borderlands between Ross and Sutherland, this was a local battle for survival, a last stand in defence of a way of life that was facing extinction. But for the authorities it was an uprising that struck at the heart of landed power. 'It created anxiety even in London', says Emeritus Professor of History, Eric Richards, in his book *The Highland Clearances*. 'It was certainly the most alarming news from the Highlands since Culloden.'

And it was all the more serious because of the revolutionary spirit of the times. The people were ascendant and the old order was starting to look precarious. Protests had been held across Scotland in support of the French Revolution, and trees of liberty planted in town squares – including one in Cromarty, just across the nearby firth and almost within sight of Strathrusdale. Thomas Paine's *Rights of Man* had been translated into Gaelic.

Inevitably, the rising was quelled, by three companies from the Black Watch, and the ringleaders arrested. Years later, after the natives of Ross and Sutherland had all but been replaced by sheep, one of the soldiers would write of his regret at being part of the clampdown. 'The manner in which the people gave vent to their grief and rage when driven from their ancient homes showed that they did not merit this treatment and that an improper estimate had been made of their character', this David Stewart lamented.

Five men were identified as ringleaders and brought to court in Inverness. In Ross, the landowners wanted the most extreme punishment available for what they denounced as 'Sedition, Insurrection and Rebellion', but in these dangerous times, the court was wary of inflaming the people. Hugh Breac MacKenzie and John Aird were sentenced to seven years' transportation. Malcolm Ross was fined £50 – the equivalent of £3,000 in today's money – and would remain in prison until it was paid. Donald Munro and Alexander MacKay were banished from Scotland for life, and William Cunningham received a three month jail sentence.

But there was a further twist when the two men due to be transported to Botany Bay managed to flee from the Tolbooth in Inverness. The exact circumstances of their escape were hushed up by the authorities, but according to accounts, members of the public had torn open the gates, and the men were then sheltered and looked after by local people.

The great sheep rebellion had been a heroic gesture. It had, for a time, struck fear into the heart of the northern feudal establishment, and inspired the peasantry of the north. As Red Clydeside resonates today in the peoples' culture of the West of Scotland, the Year of the Sheep remains rooted in Highland folklore. Both episodes are, alas, part of that wider Scottish tradition of glorious failures. After the rebellion, the sheep kept coming, and the Highlands was transformed, utterly. There was resistance, but it was now defensive and mainly led by women.

It was an unequal contest. Scattered villagers were ranged against the combined might of feudal landowners, industrial capitalists and the imperial British state. And by the turn of the century, the blue skies of reform had turned leaden grey, and repression rained down, seemingly forever.

Sutherland no more

In the Lismore Bar near Partick Cross in Glasgow, each of the urinals in the gents toilets is engraved with the name and description of one of the infamous figures of the Highland Clearances. Customers using the facilities are invited to pay their appropriate respects to George Granville; his evictor-in-chief, Patrick Sellar; and the man who spearheaded the clearances on the island of Lismore after which the pub is named, Colonel Fell.

Granville – or to give him his full name, George Granville Leveson-Gower, the Marquis of Stafford and, in 1833, the first Duke of Sutherland – is also commemorated in a more reverential way. For almost 180 years, a giant red sandstone statue of a figure in a Roman emperor's toga has faced out to the North Sea from the summit of Ben Bhraggie, 1,300 feet above the town of Golspie.

The Marquis of Stafford was the richest man in the world in the nineteenth century. He had inherited vast family lands in Staffordshire, Shropshire and Yorkshire, and the Orleans Collection – the most lucrative art collection ever assembled. He also owned the Bridgewater Canal in the north-west of England, a number of coal-mines, and a major stake in the new Liverpool to Manchester railway. And on top of that, he had married Elizabeth Gordon, the 19th Countess of Sutherland, who owned of a million acres of land in the northern county and controlled the lives of thousands of tenants.

Had anyone known of Stafford's past activities in the English Midlands, they might well have had a foretaste of what was to come when he moved north. Thomas Bakewell, a journalist from Staffordshire, would later describe how his callous treatment of his tenants had made him a figure of hatred: 'He ejected a poor man, his wife and six children from their humble cottage upon Tittensor hills, in a cold season of the year... I found them encamped in the open air like gypsies.'

If it was a bad time to be poor – and when would be a good time? – it was a great time to be a powerful landowner in the Highlands. The spectre of revolution that had haunted Europe around the time of the Year of the Sheep was now a dim memory. The ideals of liberty and equality that had once inspired millions had been ground to fine powder beneath the iron heel of Napoleon Bonaparte. The French dictator was on the rampage, the war drums were beating furiously and British patriotism was in full flow. And the glens were empty of young men.

Since the pacification of the Highlands after Culloden and the dismantling of the clan system, the north of Scotland had become a fruitful recruiting ground for the imperial army. The British state had been impressed by the military prowess of the rebel Highland clans during the '45 Rebellion, and was now desperate for manpower to fight the Napoleonic Wars.

In the south, the new industries, hungry for labour, were prepared to pay higher wages than anything a rank and file soldier could ever hope to earn. According to the *Oxford History of the British Army*, in 1807, an unskilled dockworker could earn 28 shillings (£1.40), while a private in the armed forces was paid just 7 shillings (35p). Unable to compete, the recruiting sergeants looked north to the Highlands, and west to rural Ireland.

Up in Sutherland, the Countess had already expressed venomous anger at her tenants for refusing to enlist in great numbers to fight the French Wars. This was a matter of honour and prestige. At times of conflict, the aristocracy was always determined to fight to the last drop of their tenants' blood. The more bodies they could mobilise, the greater their own glory. The local people, wrote the Countess, 'need no longer be considered as a credit to Sutherland or an advantage over sheep or any useful animal'. As later events would testify, this was no angry slip of the tongue.

But by the time the northern clearances got into full swing, a dozen or so years later, huge numbers of young men from the far northern counties were fighting and dying for the British Empire in the humid swamplands of the Mississippi Basin. The Sutherland Clearances, the most brutal of all, had been devised as part of a grand plan to forcibly industrialise the north of Scotland.

It involved turning the interior of the county into a giant sheep farm, and moving the population out to new towns scattered around the coastline, where they would be employed in factories producing or processing salt, kelp, fish, bricks, lime, flax and wool.

The first obstacle blocking this Stalin-esque vision was the people. But these were repressive times and the odds were heavily stacked in favour of what Robert Southey, the Poet Laureate of the time, called the 'Fifty Land Leviathans' who owned the Highlands. In some areas, tenants – often with women at the forefront – put up courageous but futile resistance. In other areas, they went sullenly to their seemingly inevitable fate.

Years later, one law officer involved, a Mr J. Campbell of Lairg, wrote to the *Inverness Courier* describing an incident he witnessed at an isolated cluster of crofts in Strathfleet:

> 'They burned the rest of them, and this crofter's was the last. He pleaded hard to be left in the house till his wife was well. The factor did not heed him, but ordered the house to be burned over him. The crofter was in the house, determined not to quit until the fire compelled him. The factor told us the plan we were to take – namely, to cut the rafters and then set fire to the thatch. This we did, but I shall never forget the sight. The man, seeing it was now no use to persist, wrapped his wife in the blankets and brought her out. For two nights did that woman sleep in a sheep cot, and on the third, she gave birth to a son. That son, I believe, still lives, and is in America. That is only one instance. I could give many more should space permit.'

While some tenants were appeased by promises of industrial prosperity to come, others stayed and fought against all the odds. In the Strath of Kildonan, the hirelings of Stafford confronted six weeks of sustained resistance. One law officer warned his superiors that the tenants could mobilise a thousand men, including army veterans, to resist evictions. They also reported talk of a general rising in the area.

The authorities hated the people of Kildonan with a ferocious passion. William Young, a henchman of Patrick Sellar, described them as 'savages' and 'banditti' who were worse than the Red Indians of America and 'absolutely a century behind'. He lamented that 'the whole population feel desirous of success to the Rioters, knowing that they have common interest in the expulsion of the Strangers', and advised Stafford to send in armed forces to sort out the glen.

Their hatred was fuelled by Kildonan's reputation for illicit activities, including smuggling. This may explain why resistance there was so strong: no resettlement options were offered to those who had been convicted of poaching, trespass, smuggling, illegal fishing or other such offences. That would probably account for the majority of the population in the Kildonan, many of whom emigrated to the Red River Valley in Canada where they established a settlement named after the strath of their birth.

The most infamous clearances of all took place on the banks of the eighteen-mile long River Naver, in the far north. Stafford's most feared enforcer, Patrick Sellar, had bought the lease for Strathnaver at an auction in the Golspie Inn, and now set about removing the people like a man possessed. With a dozen agents under his command, he moved from one township to the next, terrorising people into submission. They beat women and children, as well as men, with fists and staves for the crime of disobedience. They seized the cattle and other possessions of those who had fallen into arrears after their rents were driven up to exorbitant levels.

And when the time came to clear a settlement, they set about the evacuation with clinical efficiency. Most people resigned themselves to their fate. But others tried to stay, usually because they were too old or too sick to uproot themselves. They were treated with heartless cruelty. One eye witness described the scene at a typical eviction:

> 'The consternation and confusion were extreme. Little or no time was given for the removal of persons or property, the people striving to remove the sick and the helpless before the fire should reach them. The cries of the women and children, the roaring of the affrighted cattle, hunted at the same time by the yelling dogs of the shepherds, amid the smoke and fire, altogether presented a scene that completely baffles description... The conflagration lasted six days, till the whole of the dwellings were reduced to ashes or smoking ruins.'

And when the people were gone, every barn, byre and stable would be razed to the ground to make sure no-one could ever return.

After one especially ugly piece of violent thuggery, at an isolated hamlet in

Strtahnaver, Sellar found himself in deep trouble. His men had first turfed out 80 year old Donald MacKay to sleep in the woods. Then they removed Barbara MacKay, who was pregnant. They tore down Donald Beath's home around him as lay on his sick bed; exposed to the wind and rain, he died a few days later. Finally, they torched 90 year old Margaret MacKay's home while she was still inside. They did, heroically, drag her out just prior to her certain incineration, but the old woman was understandably, and fatally, traumatised, dying some five days later.

Even by the standards of Patrick Sellar, this had been a sadistic piece of work. In one isolated little settlement, two people had been left dead and three others severely injured. This time, he had overstepped the mark – and there was one man in Sutherland determined to bring him to justice.

Robert McKid, the Sheriff Substitute of Sutherland, had tangled with Sellar in the past. Although a lawyer by profession, he had a sentimental attachment to the old ways, when deer, hare and grouse belonged to no-one, and he regularly indulged his passion for poaching. On three occasions Patrick Sellar had tried and failed to nail the maverick lawman for illegal hunting. Now McKid took his revenge. The process was lengthy and tortuous, but a year later, on 23 April 1816, Patrick Sellar appeared before the Circuit Court in Inverness Court charged with 'culpable homicide, as also oppression and real injury' plus 'wickedly and maliciously setting on fire and burning'. It seemed as though a glimmer of daylight had broken through the dark Sutherland skies. But it was just a flicker of brightness, short-lived.

As the trial proceeded, the judge dismissed one after another of the long list of charges that had taken two hours to read out in court. All that remained for the jury to decide was the culpable homicide of Margaret MacKay. It all hinged on the evidence of one witness, the dead woman's son-in-law, William Chisholm. But he was a tinker, and therefore the lowest of the low in the eyes of a genteel jury of eight landowners plus seven assorted merchants and magistrates. It took them all of 15 minutes to deliver a Not Guilty verdict.

For the landowning classes across the north, the acquittal of Sellar was like a royal jubilee. For the rest, it was more akin to the funeral of all their hopes.

Sellar took out his revenge, forcing Sheriff MacKid to write a grovelling apology and pay substantial damages. Although Sellar gingerly stepped aside from the frontline of the eviction crusade, his successors now had carte blanche to go on the rampage. Evictions escalated, reaching their peak in the Whitsun clearances of 1819 and 1820, when between four and five thousand people were driven out of their homes.

When the dust finally settled over the last burnt-out township, the old Sutherland was dead, and the grand plan for industry and employment was stillborn. Instead of new-fangled factories, the people were left dangling on the edge of starvation on meagre plots of land, strung along narrow strips of barely fertile coastline, many perched precariously at the edge of towering cliffs. Sutherland had been improved into a desert, said Hugh Miller of Cromarty, the astute geologist and writer.

But the fight for the northern glens was not over. In early 1820, Hugh Munro, the landowner of the Novar estate, just across the county border in Easter Ross, moved to evict 600 of his tenants in Strathoykel. According to the local minister, 100 of them were old and bedridden. But Munro had a taste for expensive art, ultimately assembling a world-famous collection of paintings. So when a sheep farmer offered him more than three times the total rent paid by existing tenants, it was a no-brainer for the sensitive art collector.

On a cold February day, agents arrived at the township of Culrain to issue Writs of Removal. According to an outraged letter from Sheriff Macleod, published in the *Inverness Courier*, the officers were 'pursued off the bounds of the property, threatened that if they returned their lives would be taken and themselves thrown into the Kyle of Firth… and one of the Witnesses, who had run away from the terror, was pursued and struck with stones to the danger of his life.'

A month later, Sheriff Macleod arrived in the township of Culrain in person, along with 40 constables and the entire Easter Ross Regiment of Militia, resplendent in their red coats and black breeches and armed with muskets. But the people were not going down without a fight. The landowner had not arranged resettlement on the coast or anywhere else. The stark choice facing the tenants was starvation or emigration.

Angry, distressed women blocked the road, crying that they would rather die here, where their mothers and fathers and grandparents were buried, than on foreign soil thousands of miles across the ocean. They armed themselves with sticks and stones, while their menfolk lay in wait behind the dry stone wall lining the road.

It turned into a pitched battle. The soldiers fired blanks to intimidate the crowd, and when that failed, a drummer opened fire with live ammunition, killing one of the women. Enraged, the women turned fearlessly on their oppressors. They overturned and smashed to pieces Sheriff Macleod's carriage while he and his men fled. The women, with men and children now joining the fray, chased the constables and militia men four miles down the strath to the village of Ardgay, where they barricaded themselves inside the local inn. The people laid siege to the building, pelting it with stones, before returning to Culrain in triumph. It had been a brave and defiant fight back. But it was to be their last stand. What the militia men failed to subjugate would be overpowered by a minister of religion.

'The men of cloth they failed again', sings the Irish folk musician, Christie Moore, of the bishops who blessed the fascist blueshirts as they sailed from Galway to fight for General Franco in the Spanish Civil War. In the Highlands, the men of cloth were of a different denomination, but they failed just as dismally, again and again, in parishes across the north.

In one grimly humorous scene in John McGrath's *The Cheviot, the Stag and the Black, Black Oil*, a ranting, over-the-top minister tries to put the fear of everlasting hellfire into female members of his congregation 'who have wandered from the path of righteousness and into the tents of iniquity':

> 'Oh guilty sinners, turn from your evil ways. How many times and on how many Sabbaths have I warned you from this very pulpit of your wickedness and of the wrath of the Almighty? Some of you today are so far from the fold, have so far neglected the dignity of your womanhood, that you have risen up to curse your masters and violate the laws of the land... Unless you repent there will be much wailing and weeping and gnashing of teeth...'

The minister in Strathoykel, the Reverend Alexander MacBean, wrote to the *Inverness Courier* condemning Sheriff Macleod for acting against the people as though they were an invading army. But Reverend MacBean's words were like those of a modern trade union leader who criticises the employer before selling out the employees. No sooner was his letter published than he rode along the strath from township to township, using his formidable oratorical powers to convince his flock to obey God's will and accept the Writs of Removal. Within 48 hours, it was all over bar the long sorrowful voyage to the land beyond the sea.

The press, printed in an alien tongue, had far less impact on the people than the preachers. Its role was more indirect. The mission of the most influential newspaper in the Highlands, the *Inverness Courier*, had been to inoculate respectable public opinion against the disease of sympathy. When it was all over, the editorial columns gushed with patronising satisfaction at the outcome. These poor wretched creatures, suggested the *Courier*, had no doubt been acting in good faith, but malevolent forces had duped them into believing they were the victims of some kind of injustice.

> 'Unhappily, their weak side was found out and their credulity worked upon until they were impressed by the belief that they were barbarously treated and that they should… retain possession of their ancient settlements, which it was not possible for them to do without violating the laws of the country and bringing misery and destruction upon their own heads. Hence has arisen all the shameful riots and illegal acts committed in these parts during these two years past.'

The people had been defeated by the combined power of the pulpit, the law and the armed bodies of men who could be mobilised if all else failed. Now all was deathly still in the Highlands. But in the decades to come, the flame of resistance would burn again.

17

DARK SATANIC MILLS

The weaving of the working class

As the lifeblood was being drained from the Highlands, a huge industrial city was rising rapidly in the south-west. Within a century, 700,000 people would be crammed into three square miles of squalor, making Glasgow 20,000 times more densely populated than the vast land mass that stretched northwards from the Great Glen to the Pentland Firth.

By the end of the first wave of the Highland Clearances, the population of the city had already hit 150,000, a heaving, seething mass of humanity concentrated into a narrow grid of streets on the banks of the Clyde. They had gravitated to the city from across the Lowlands and the Southern Uplands, where new agricultural machinery was turning out whole swathes of the rural population onto the destitute streets of the city. Some had been evicted from their Highland homes to make way for sheep. Others came from Ireland, the advance guard of the multitudes who would pour into the city in the middle years of the century.

By this time, the mill owners had replaced merchants as the masters of the economy, wielding the kind of power that today's energy giants or communications companies might recognise. Almost overnight, small-time local entrepreneurs turned into the equivalent of today's billionaires.

Robert Owen, whose name would later become synonymous with social reform and the cooperative movement, was anything but a typical nineteenth-century entrepreneur, yet his rapid rise from obscurity to a position of immense power and wealth was emblematic of the times. After starting his working life as a draper's assistant in Wales, he borrowed £100 in 1779 to start a textiles business in Manchester. Just ten years later, he bought over the New Lanark Mills for £84,000, cash up front – the equivalent of £677 million in today's money.

By the early decades of the nineteenth century, the weaving industry had begun to coalesce around two main centres. Lancashire and the West of Scotland were perfectly located to take advantage of the rising new industry, with their high levels of rainfall and raging rivers to power the mills. Later, when steam-powered machines began to take over, they had great coalfields in their backyards. And they were within easy striking distance of Ireland, North Wales and the Highlands, with their endless supplies of destitute humanity.

Around this industry, a numerically powerful new social class arose – the industrial proletariat, as it was called by the German-speaking Karl Marx. The canyons in which they toiled morning, noon and night soon replaced village alehouses and Edinburgh coffee shops as the focal points for social disaffection.

Strikes, martyrs and intrigue

Glasgow's first ever industrial strike broke out in 1787, two years before the French Revolution. For four months, from June to October, the Clyde Valley Weavers Association had organised a shutdown of the weaving factories in the Calton area of Glasgow against proposed wage cuts.

It reached its violent climax on 3 September, when several hundred strikers gathered in Wellhouse, near the Tennent Caledonian brewery, just east of the city centre. When a delegation of magistrates, headed by the Lord Provost, arrived at the assembly and tried to arrest the leaders, the weavers turned on them, with sticks, stones and other missiles. When the dignitaries later returned accompanied by the 39th Regiment of Foot, the crowd, including women and children, stood its ground. Then the troops opened fire.

When it was all over, three weavers lay dead and scores more were wounded. In the days that followed, another three weavers died of their injuries. It was the first ever incidence in Britain of trade unionists being mown down by the forces of the state. Over 6,000 people attended the burial of the six 'Calton Martyrs' in the local cemetery.

None of those who carried out this indiscriminate murder were ever prosecuted. But six weavers were arrested and charged with rioting. Five failed to appear at the High Court, so were declared fugitives. The other, James Granger, did face trial, and in July 1788 was found guilty of 'having taken an active part in the combination among the operative weavers, and the riots which afterwards took place in Glasgow in September last'. This was before the first Combination Act was passed by Westminster in 1799, which means that James Granger may well have been the first man in Britain to be convicted for belonging to a trade union.

He was sentenced to be publicly whipped through the streets of the Edinburgh by the public executioner and then banished from Scotland for seven years. But 38-year-old Granger, who had six children, returned home illicitly. He was re-arrested and ordered by the High Court to be whipped once again through the streets of the capital for 'returning from banishment'. This wasn't to be his last brush with the law. Twenty-five years later, at the age of 63, the irrepressible activist was jailed for four months at the High Court, along with a group of others, for 'illegal combination or conspiracy'.

By 1811, the economy was overheating. Prices were rising almost daily, while wages were being hammered down by the advance of labour-saving machinery that could be operated by young children. In England, the infamous Luddite movement was on the march, breaking into factories in the dead of night to smash up the hated machines which were throwing able-bodied men into the poorhouses.

In Scotland, resistance was more organised and disciplined, partly because of the more advanced level of literacy and education among the working class. In every factory, there was at least a strong nucleus of articulate, well-read weavers, a product of the progressive Calvinist education system. When some years later, a number of Scottish weavers appeared as defence witnesses in a libel trial, taken out at the Court of Exchequer in London by a notorious Glasgow-based spy, Alexander Richmond, the Spectator magazine expressed surprise at how capable these common workmen were:

> 'The witnesses for the defendants, though mostly men in humble life, had a very respectable appearance. They received their expenses and the same wages as they would have earned in Glasgow. Their manner of delivering their evidence was exceedingly clear and impressive, in many passages resembling the Scottish dialogues in the Waverley Novels; and their sharp replies told upon the Court and the Jury.'

Although the Combination Act of 1799 had driven trade unions underground, from 1808 a weavers organisation, whose structures would become the prototype for the future trade union movement, had taken shape in the West of Scotland. To circumvent the law, it was financed through legally recognised friendly societies, the forerunner of today's mutual insurance companies. Among those funders listed in the High Court during the trial of James Granger were the Hibernia Friendly Society, the First Volunteer Regiment Friendly Society, the Lanark and Fife Friendly Society, the Ayr and Ayrshire Friendly Society and the Drygate Youths Friendly Society (whose name refers to an area just east of Glasgow city centre). A network of district organisations would send delegates to a weekly general meeting in Glasgow to thrash out strategy and to draw up plans, coordinated by two central committees, one in the city centre, the other in Paisley.

Towards the end of 1812, a protracted cold war between the weavers' union and the employers erupted into all-out conflict. In what may have been the biggest industrial strike ever seen in Europe, 40,000 weavers across 80 towns and villages brought virtually every loom in the West of Scotland to a standstill. At its peak, the strike took in the east and north coasts, including Aberdeen.

Desperate attempts were made to smash the movement. The authorities posted a proclamation prohibiting all meetings and declaring the strike a criminal act. They ordered all available troops in Scotland into the weaving areas of the west to intimidate the workers into surrender. But the weavers stood firm from November 1812 until February 1813, when 14 strike leaders were arrested. The group included James Granger and Alexander Richmond, a weaver from the village of Pollokshaws, three miles south of Glasgow. Highly intelligent and articulate, Richmond had emerged as one of the most prominent leaders of the struggle. But later he would become a notorious spy and agent provocateur, with connections to the highest levels of the British state. After his spymasters failed to deliver the lavish financial rewards he had been led to expect, however, Richmond would expose his own role in the disruption of the workers' movement in Scotland from within.

During the earlier negotiations preceding the strike, Richmond had been part of a small delegation of weavers who had met with a team of Glasgow magistrates, including the city's Lord Provost Kirkham Finlay, soon to be elected as a Tory MP with close links to Lord Sidmouth and Viscount Castlereagh, the high priests of reaction in London. It was at this meeting, according to his own published account, that his gradual slide over to the dark side began. 'He [Kirkham Finlay] said he had formed such a favourable opinion of me that if I could point out any way in which he could be of service, promoting my views in life, I might fully command his interest, as he would feel pleasure in exerting it', recalled Richmond, who claimed to be unmoved by such flattery.

During the great strike of 1812-13, Finlay approached Richmond again, and was once more refused. Then Richmond was arrested for his role in the strike, and Finlay moved in again, his language threatening, rather than persuasive: 'By persisting (in refusing to cooperate), I would ruin my family and my prospects in life – that I was much more blameable than those who had acted from ignorance as I was capable of taking a more enlarged view of the subject and therefore more culpable and my punishment would be more severe.' Richmond again claims to have resisted, instead jumping bail and heading for Manchester, then Dublin, before returning to Clydeside. According to his own account, this time he initiated contact with Finlay, and was received 'in a very flattering manner'.

Following this meeting, Richmond gave himself up and confessed his guilt to most of the charges set out in his original indictment. His sentence – a month's imprisonment – was surprisingly lenient. From then on, he appears to have been on the payroll of the government, working under the direction of Kirkham Finlay, who in turn reported to Lord Sidmouth, the Home Secretary in London. His malign activity would become one of the key weapons in the armoury of the employers and the political establishment in London.

Ablaze with rebellion

Just as surely as the human body can only survive by inhaling oxygen and exhaling carbon dioxide, capitalism cannot exist without alternating cycles of boom and bust. But back in the early nineteenth century, no-one really understood why capitalism had this infuriating habit of going to pieces just when everything in the garden was rosy. It was not until 1867, when Karl Mark published *Das Kapital*, that the workings of capitalism were explained in logical, scientific terms.

In a system based on the exploitation of labour for private profit, the global workforce can never be paid enough to buy back the sum total of the goods they produce, otherwise there would be no surplus left for the investors. As a result, every so often vast mountains of goods pile up which can never be sold. Profits turn to losses, businesses fail, share prices plummet, unemployment rises, factories turn silent and trade shrivels. Through artificial measures, such as allowing debt to keep on rising, it's possible to delay a recession in the same way that it's possible to delay a hangover by staying on the bottle. But as Gordon Brown discovered to his surprise when he was Chancellor of the Exchequer, 'no more boom and bust' is a capitalistic contradiction in terms.

By 1816, the feverish upswing in the weaving industry had turned into a catastrophic slump. Mass bankruptcies, factory closures and lay-offs had created an army of 10,000 unemployed workers in Glasgow and the surrounding suburbs. Those lucky enough to avoid redundancy were reduced to semi-starvation wages. Under these conditions, there could be no return to the industrial militancy of five years earlier. Instead, the working class of the west of Scotland sought to escape their misery by fighting for political reform.

On 29 October, over 40,000 people marched to a field on the northern outskirts of Glasgow. Proportional to the population, it would be the equivalent of 250,000 marching today – double the size of the colossal 2003 march in Glasgow against the Iraq war.

The plan had been to hold an indoor rally in the Trades Hall in George Square, but the city's magistrates banned the event. The organisers then applied for permission for an outdoor rally on Glasgow Green, but that too was refused. But then a pro-reform businessman came to the rescue. He owned an estate called Thrushgrove, extending across an area that today incorporates the housing schemes of Royston and Sighthill.

The Thrushgrove Meeting, as it became known, was the largest political rally Britain had ever seen. Some carried banners demanding political reform; some held brooms, symbolising the sweeping away of the old order; some wore the Cap of Liberty, the brimless felt halt popular during the American and French revolutions. Speakers railed against a political system under which the government of the day was elected by a minuscule group of wealthy men. In the whole of Scotland there were just 4,000 people eligible to vote – one-tenth of the numbers attending this rally.

The protest also had an economic dimension. As a result of the Napoleonic Wars, Britain's national debt had shot into the stratosphere. Yet under pressure from the bankers and traders of the City of London Corporation, the House of Commons had voted to abolish income tax. As a result, the burden of taxation was shifted onto the poor in the form of excise duties on basic commodities such as salt, candles, leather, beer, soap, and starch.

Radical and Whig opposition politicians had begun to thunder against war and waste. The French Wars were over, but a bloated elite was growing in London, nourished by lavish salaries, sinecures, expenses and pensions. By unanimous acclaim, resolutions were carried at the Thrushgrove Meeting in favour of universal suffrage and an end to the decadent culture of profligacy surrounding the London elite, both elements summed up in the slogan 'Retrenchment and Reform'.

A surviving set of minutes of a radical public meeting in Pollokshaws a few weeks later sums up the political essence of the progressive movement at that point. The first of a series of fourteen resolutions – all passed unanimously – talks of the 'corrupt House of Commons' and calls for 'equal, fair and free representation of the people'. The second resolution lashes out at 'public money notoriously squandered among a host of sinecure pensioners who are rolling in splendour', while poor working people 'are loaded with the most grievous and intolerable taxation'. A third resolution could have been drafted anytime in the twenty-first century. 'Our blood and treasure have been wasted in an unjust and unnecessary war... subversive of the right of nations and disgraceful to our country'. Resolution four warns of ministers 'making dangerous strides towards a military government by tenaciously upholding a powerful and expensive army.'

The growing grassroots movement began to get itself organised along similar lines as the now defunct United Scotsmen. Across the west of Scotland, a network of Workers' Union Societies and Radical Committees began to take shape, coordinated by a Scottish National Committee.

Other parts of Britain, especially the mill towns of northern England, were also ablaze with rebellion. At the heart of the British state, plans were being hatched to derail these struggles. And Scotland, especially Clydeside, with its vast concentration of mills, was a prime target for the men in dark cloaks operating in the shadows.

Trickery and treachery

By now 'Richmond the Spy' was in full throttle. At the Thrushgrove Meeting, he struck up a conversation with Robert Craig and invited him to a local tavern for a drink. He told him in conspiratorial tones that there were 100,000 radicals ready to launch an armed insurrection. He encouraged the Parkhead weaver to 'take a position of responsibility' in the movement, but Craig's instincts told him to steer well clear. Richmond approached others, with varying degrees of success, insinuating that a well-armed organisation in Glasgow was preparing to overthrow the government.

He was reporting to Finlay at least two or three times a week. The Tory MP supplied him with a stash of cash to recruit a small of group of four *agents provo-*

cateurs, who in turn assembled around them a wider group of a dozen or more, who had no idea they were being lured into a trap. They signed oaths pledging to 'support, to the utmost of my power, either by moral or physical strength or force' the struggle for 'free and equal representation and annual parliaments'.

Finlay, in turn, reported back to his masters in London, and on 19 February 1817, a secret committee of the House of Commons drew up a report claiming there was a plan for general insurrection across Northern England and Scotland. In Glasgow and surrounding towns, it claimed, secret societies with access to arms were operating under the cloak of the reform movement.

Three days later, just before midnight on Saturday 22 February 1817, the authorities swooped. Accompanied by a gang of constables, the Glasgow Procurator Fiscal, George Salmond, raided a meeting in a house in the Old Wynd, a few hundred yards east of St Enoch's Square. Fourteen men were arrested on the spot, the rest rounded up at various addresses throughout the city. Those detained were mainly weavers and cotton-spinners, but included a teacher, a divinity student, a manufacturer, a teacher, a clerk and a spirit dealer.

The following week, Westminster debated suspending the Habeas Corpus Act, amid public hysteria akin to the aftermath of the London bombings of 2005. The emergency legislation would allow suspects to be arrested and interned indefinitely without trial, no matter how flimsy the evidence.

On the Monday, Kirkham Finlay intervened in the debate with his dire warning regarding the existence of secret societies in Glasgow and other Scottish towns. A few days later, on 28 February, the Lord Advocate of Scotland, Alexander Maconochie – a staunch Tory landowner – stood up, clutching a copy of an oath, supposedly written by the radicals but later revealed to have been devised by Finlay and Richmond. As he read out the section pledging physical force, there was uproar. But there was more to come.

There was now a major conspiracy against the state underway in the west of Scotland, according to the Lord Advocate, involving thousands of people including 'many of the higher orders of society'. This was all based on a few dozen working men discussing political reform, while the 'higher orders of society' were the teacher, the small manufacturer and the spirit dealer. But greater tales have been woven from thinner threads than this, and the shocking revelation silenced all dissent. The Bill was passed by Parliament on 28 February 1817. Exactly one week later, Scotland's first sedition trial in 15 years began. Alexander

MacLaren was accused of delivering 'seditious and inflammatory speeches' after addressing a public meeting in the town's Dean Park, while Thomas Hardie, the owner of a small print business, was accused of publishing the subversive oration. Fortunately for the duo, the presiding judge, Lord Gillies, had pro-reform leanings and had once been a friend of Thomas Muir. He sentenced them each to six months in prison.

At a further trial in May 1817, Reverend Neil Douglas, a 69-year-old pacifist and fluent Gaelic speaker, who was described by his defence counsel as 'old, deaf, dogged, honest and respectable', stood accused of dishonouring the monarchy. He had preached a sermon in Glasgow comparing George III to Nebuchadnezzar, the vainglorious King of Babylon, who in the Book of Daniel builds a gold statue of himself and demands that all his people bow down before it, or be thrown into a blazing furnace. Then, just for good measure, he further likened him to Bacchus, the Greek god of drunken revelry. The chief witnesses were three government spies who had been sent to gather evidence, but their findings were so contradictory that the defence advocate, the reformer Francis Jeffrey, took them to pieces in his summing up and the case against Douglas was thrown out.

As the wave of trials continued, the public mood began to swing against the underhand tactics of the government, prompting questions in Parliament by reform-minded MPs. Earl Grey, a future Whig Prime Minister – although better known today as the namesake of a fragrant tea – told the House of Lords on June 16 that 'Glasgow was one of the places where treasonable practices were said, in the Report of the Secret Committee of both Houses, to prevail to the greatest degree; but there could no longer be any doubt that the alleged treasonable oaths were administered by hired spies and informers'.

A few days later, Lord Archibald Hamilton, the Whig MP for Lanarkshire, complained of the 'oppressive and arbitrary' nature of the proceedings undertaken against some of the prisoners and attacked the insidious tactics of the authorities and the 'system by which the sources of their information prove to be the cause of the very evils of which they complain'.

The state ploughed ahead regardless. Already, twenty radicals were in jail, convicted on the worthless evidence of paid informers. The Lord Advocate had a further list of so-called suspects who had been ensnared by Richmond, and might be arrested at any time.

Why did the authorities persist? Because the aim of the radicals was so repugnant to those who benefited from the status quo that it had to be quashed by any means necessary. Speaking at the infamous (and failed) trial of Andrew McKinlay, an Irishman charged with administering the fictitious oath to several hundred people, the alcoholic Lord Hermand declared: 'Nothing more unconstitutional, nothing more absurd, nothing more mischievous, nothing more necessarily leading to despotism and to the destruction of the liberties of the country could be suggested than this proposal of universal suffrage and annual parliaments.' He added, 'Figure the effect of this universal suffrage and these annual parliaments – that is annual *elections*, not annual *sessions* of Parliament. The life of the king and every other good man would be in the situation of republican France. Every revolution begins with the lowest of the people... it is absurd therefore to believe that legal means can be used for such a deplorable end.'

Richmond's shadowy spy ring was to collapse amid a wrangle over money. Although he was paid thousands of pounds in cash, and offered an area of land around the Cape of Good Hope, plus a letter of introduction to the Colonial Governor there, Richmond claimed he had been promised a bank draft for 'any money I required'.

The whole affair of Richmond the Spy was raised in the House of Commons by Lord Archibald Hamilton, the Whig MP for Lanark, who was promptly shouted down by the assembled ranks of Tory MPs. Much of the detail, however, would subsequently emerge, as Richmond took out two failed libel cases in London against Scottish radical newspapers which had exposed his role as a spy and *agent provocateur*.

With Richmond out of the picture by 1817, the Scottish radical movement grew stronger, and the mood of militancy across Britain deepened. With its back to the wall, the government and the crown lashed out venomously.

From pleas to pikes

In *The Scottish Insurrection of 1820*, a classic work of people's history first published in 1970, Peter Berresford Ellis and Seumas Mac a' Ghobhainn shone light on a mine of information that had been sealed for generations. Two powerful points emerge from their research.

First, the cutting edge of Scottish radicalism was the rising working class. While the merchants and manufacturers focused on reform of the burghs and the rooting out of local corruption, the weavers and cotton-spinners struck at the heart of the power structures of society by demanding universal suffrage, annual parliaments and secret ballots. It was, in essence, a class movement that sought to wrench political power from the landowners and industrialists and place it in the hands of the people.

Second, the movement was informed by a sense of national injustice, which in turn drew inspiration from Scotland's history of resistance to tyranny, strengthening the intensity of the struggle north of the border. The battle anthem of Scottish radicalism, *Scots Wha Hae*, became so closely associated with working class struggle that it would later be adopted by Lancashire cotton-spinners and Tyneside colliers influenced by migrant Scots workers. Its heroes were Robert the Bruce and especially William Wallace, whose image adorned banners and placards like the Che Guevara of the industrial revolution. And its most hated enemy was the mighty British state, controlled from London by the crown and Westminster, and shielding the Scottish elite from the rebellious masses.

That is not to suggest that this was a movement focused on the single issue of independence. Most of the resolutions, manifestos and other written records that survive concern themselves with the wider democratic demands that were simultaneously being pursued south of the border. That has led some historians to ignore and even repudiate any national dimension within the movement. Ellis and Mac a' Ghobhainn provide a necessary corrective, bringing out an underlying antagonism towards the remote and alien British state, that in turn sharpened the edge of working class disaffection in Scotland

At this time, Scottish radicalism had no clear strategy. The slogans of the movement were inconsistent, even contradictory. In the prevailing climate of the times, Scottish independence was unimaginable. Within living memory, the British state had mercilessly crushed even the formidable United Irishmen, who were backed by revolutionary France. Now, since the Bonapartist counter-revolution, there was no sympathetic state ready to aid a republican breakaway in Ireland or Scotland. Nor was there any viable constitutional route towards the repeal of the union. The only people entitled to vote in Scotland were the landowning and commercial elite, a bloc that was tied by a thousand threads to London.

For the mainstream reform movement in Scotland, the only realistic way of bringing about change was through Britain-wide pressure on Westminster.

During its decades in opposition, especially after the seismic shock of the French Revolution, the Whig party had shifted to the left. Whiggism had always been a vaguely defined political current rather than a coherent party underpinned by a clear ideology. It now advocated limited electoral reform, restrictions on crown power, the abolition of slavery, and an end to discrimination against Catholics and other religious minorities.

A strong extra-parliamentary reform movement had also emerged in England around people like William Cobbett, an influential former Tory who had gradually shifted towards radicalism over the years. Yet a more militant section of the movement in Scotland looked to escape the straitjacket of the British state, fired up by fury at brutal poverty, lack of democratic rights, an entrenched and despised Tory Government in Westminster, and an acute sense of national oppression.

At a radical public meeting in 1816, in Tarbolton, Ayrshire – consisting of 'men of no higher rank in society than that of farmers, mechanics and labourers' – one speaker told the audience: 'If the calamities of Scotland are not sufficient to wake the people to the need of Reform, let them glance for a moment to those scenes of blood and horror committed in India [where] English dominion is founded on tyranny, on violence and terror'. He also invoked the plight of the Irish who 'are in a worse condition than the slaves of any country, and still they are styled free!'

And in a key passage of the Kilmarnock speech that had led to a double trial for sedition, Alexander Maclaren had asked the crowd:

> 'Shall we, whose forefathers set limits to the all-grasping power of Rome; shall we, whose forefathers on the never-to-be-forgotten field of Bannockburn, told the mighty Edward, "Hitherto shalt thou come and no farther"; shall we, whose forefathers defied the efforts of foreign tyranny to enslave our beloved country, meanly permit, in our day, without a murmur, a base oligarchy to feed their filthy vermin on our vitals and rule us as they will?'

By 1819, lack of progress towards political reform at Westminster was provoking profound changes within the workers' movement. In his *History of Paisley*, written in 1837 – easily within living memory of the events he recounts – John Parkhill wrote that 'by the beginning of 1819, the agitation became intense;

unions were established, and a vast number of members were enrolled, and these unions spread throughout Renfrewshire, Ayrshire, Lanarkshire and Dunbartonshire. The ostensible principle of these associations was reform of the Commons House of Parliament, not by petitioning however, but by force of arms.'

The leaders were all young men, according to Parkhill, and 'in the ardour of youth, considered that all talking was useless and action was necessary'. He describes the structure of the unions: each branch was made of 10 to 20 members who would meet in the factory when the working day was over. 'At these meetings, pistols and pikes were paraded and sometimes guns. Pikes, a very dangerous weapon, were made in various parts of the country, as well as in the town.'

On 17 July 1819, under blue skies and blazing sunshine, at least 30,000 people, according to Parkhill, gathered at Meikleriggs Muir on the outskirts of Paisley for a rally chaired by a Mr James Allison. The Paisley Radical Committee brought forward a series of resolutions 'petitioning the Prince Regent (soon to be crowned George IV), for a redress of grievances'. But militancy was rising, and there was now a widespread understanding that trying to reform the political system by peaceful pleas and petitions was like trying to demolish stone walls with feather pillows. The rally voted down the resolutions – 'the Houses of Parliament not being thought worthy of petitioning', according to Parkhill – and 'an address to the nation was substituted in their place which contended for universal suffrage, annual parliaments, and election by ballot'.

If anyone still had any illusions that the Prince Regent and his Government could be persuaded to sign their own death warrants by introducing democracy, these would be blown away exactly one month later, at another rally, in another field, 200 miles away.

18

THE RADICAL WAR

Manchester massacre

One of the greatest poems ever written in the English language was composed in commemoration of one of the greatest atrocities ever committed on English soil. Its stirring final stanza resonates with oppressed peoples everywhere, even today, urging them to rise up against those who would enslave them.

> 'Rise like lions after slumber
> In unvanquishable numbers
> Shake your chains to earth like dew
> Which in sleep had fallen on you
> Ye are many — they are few.'

Such was the scale of political repression in Britain in 1819 that *Mask of Anarchy* remained unpublished for another thirteen years, only seeing the light of day a full decade after the death of its brilliant young author, Percy Shelley.

He wrote his masterpiece in a state of shock and fury. On 16 August 1819, 60,000 people turned out in St Peter's Field near Manchester for a peaceful, pro-reform carnival.

By the end of the day, the field resembled a battleground after a troop of cavalry charged into the crowd, hacking them down with sabres. In all, 15 were dead, and over 500 wounded.

Shelley's poem is something akin to an updated version of the biblical Four Horsemen of the Apocalypse, recounting the tale of a sinister pageant in which three Tory Ministers and the King ride past dressed as Murder, Fraud, Hypocrisy and Anarchy:

> 'I met Murder on the way
> He had a mask like Castlereagh -
> Very smooth he looked, yet grim
> Seven blood-hounds followed him.

All were fat; and well they might
Be in admirable plight
For one by one, and two by two
He tossed them human hearts to chew

Last came Anarchy: he rode
On a white horse, splashed with blood;
He was pale even to the lips,
Like Death in the Apocalypse.

And he wore a kingly crown;
And in his grasp a sceptre shone;
On his brow this mark I saw—
"I AM GOD, AND KING, AND LAW!"'

The front page of the *Manchester Observer* ran the headline 'Peterloo Massacre' – a darkly sarcastic reference to Britain's celebrated wartime triumph at Waterloo. The name stuck.

But the state turned its fury against the protesters. The Prince Regent and the Home Secretary sent messages of congratulation to Manchester magistrates who had ordered in the cavalry. The organisers of the rally, including the rousing radical orator, Henry Hunt, were charged with 'assembling with unlawful banners at an unlawful meeting for the purpose of exciting discontent'. The government then railroaded through six acts of parliament banning public meetings, silencing radical newspapers and bringing in harsher penalties for sedition.

In towns and cities across Scotland, collections were made to aid the relatives of the victims, while rallies and marches were organised to voice their protest at the atrocity. On Saturday 11 September, a sombre procession, with contingents from all over the west of Scotland, converged again on Meikle Muir near Paisley.

Local magistrates had prohibited flags and banners, but a 300-strong contingent form Glasgow defied the ban, and came bearing flags edged with black borders. After the rally dispersed, a posse of special constables attacked the contingent as it reached Paisley Cross. John Parkhill was there to tell the tale: 'The first flag was seized there, a scuffle ensued, a crowd collected in a moment, and a dreadful riot began; the council chambers windows were smashed and similar outrages were committed in other parts of the town. The Riot Act was read at 10 o'clock and the cavalry were sent for, and arrived at 1 o'clock. There was a great deal of rioting during the Sabbath, and at 7 o'clock, it became serious and general. The rioters were augmented by strong reinforcements from the villages to the West, who became active partisans.'

Despite repeated recitations of the Riot Act, the voice of protest only became stronger. By the week's end, the chaos had subsided, but the unions were growing in strength.

On 1 November, another great radical meeting was held in Renfrewshire, this time in Johnstone. In his *History of Paisley*, John Parkhill notes: 'The meeting was large, and Mr Brodie, merchant, Kilbarchan, was called to the chair, and a handsome young woman placed a splendid cap of liberty upon his head amidst the cheers of the meeting. The speeches were brief and few, as the day was cold; there were evidently a great number of pistols in the meeting, and all the men were armed with sticks; there were a great number of women on the hustings, and five caps of liberty.'

By now, it seems, women were at least more visible in the movement. And the mood was growing more militant – a point later reinforced by Parkhill, who describes the manufacturing of bullets and other missiles and the military drilling and training that took place in the dead of night, under the supervision of army veterans.

Following the rally, the demonstrators marched the mile or so to Elderslie, and stopped beneath the ancient yew tree, which, according to local legend, had been planted by William Wallace five centuries earlier. After the band played *Scots Wha Hae*, a volley of pistol shots were fired fire into the air.

Some of the banners and slogans listed by an observer further underlined the national dimension to the radical struggle in Scotland. One banner, for example, displayed a portrait of Wallace along with the inscription, *'Sir William Wallace, like our ancestors, we'll defend our liberty and laws.'* Another carried an image of a thistle and a harp intertwined, along with the message *'May our union be firm.'*

At another meeting in Kirkcaldy two days later, attended by around 6,000, a Mr Mitchell moved a 14-point resolution expressing abhorrence of the bloodshed in Manchester and proposing that 'a subscription be opened for the purpose of bringing to justice the inhuman perpetrators of the deeds done at Manchester'. He later asked the crowd, rhetorically, what Scotland had gained from the union with England: 'the massacre of our people; the debasement of our national character; the accumulation of a debt beyond all spendthrift precedent; famine in our streets and fever in our houses; the establishment in Europe of a military despotism which leaves the very name of freedom a mockery; the payment of war taxes in the time of peace… this has been our dearly bought indemnity.'

By early 1820, Britain was heading for all-out class war. For a decade, King George III had suffered from dementia, leaving his son, the Prince Regent, in charge. The heir to the throne had flirted with the Whigs in his younger days, before the French Revolution. But as he grew older he hardened into a bigoted reactionary, ranting against Catholic equality, denouncing wicked reformers, and waging a vendetta against his estranged wife. But most of the time, he merely indulged himself in grotesque acts of drunken debauchery. Then, on 29 January, his father died and George IV became king.

Two weeks later, 14 police officers, with a company of the Coldstream Guards as back-up, raided a house just off Edgware Road in London. In the loft of the house, a group of 25 men had gathered to finalise plans to assassinate the entire British cabinet at a dinner party in nearby Grosvenor Square. In the chaos that ensued, shots were exchanged and one police officer was killed when the leader of the group, Arthur Thistlewood, plunged him with a sword. Ten working men were arrested – four shoemakers, a few carpenters, a butcher and a tailor – and a cache of arms and ammunition was recovered, including pistols, muskets, carbines, broadswords, blunderbusses and stiletto knives. The others escaped, including Thistlewood, but were later arrested.

After a sensational trial, five of the men were publicly hanged and another five transported. But the architect of the plot had been absent during the raid, and now vanished into thin air. George Edwards had been Thistlewood's right-hand man. He had paid for the arms and ammunition. He had persuaded the rest of the group to plan the mass assassination. And, as it transpired at the trial, he was an *agent provocateur*, on the payroll of the government, who had whisked him off to Guernsey, before resettling him in South Africa under a new name. The whole affair had been engineered by the state to provoke fear and hysteria among the population at large, and to isolate and demoralise the radical wing of the reform movement in London.

Meanwhile, 400 miles away, the British state's men in Edinburgh and Glasgow were planning their own campaign of entrapment designed to decapitate the strongest, best organised and most militant working class movement anywhere in Europe.

'Lured out of their lairs'

By March 1820, the simmering political unrest in the west of Scotland was about to blow its lid. In three villages in Galloway, workers set fire to the mills. In Paisley, angry weavers torched another mill and attacked soldiers with stones. Ayrshire was ablaze with mass meetings and radical rallies.

Colonel Alexander Boswell, the commander of the Ayrshire Yeomanry, and Tory MP for a Devon seat, provided a stream of reports to the Home Secretary, Lord Sidmouth, about the state of affairs in his area. His father James, the famous sidekick and biographer of Dr Samuel Johnson, had been a cantankerous reactionary, whose poem *No Abolition of Slavery; or the Universal Empire of Love* was a celebration of the joys of bondage: 'The cheerful gang! – The negroes see; Perform the task of industry. Ev'n at their labour hear them sing, While time flies quick on downy wing.'

Boswell Junior seems to have inherited not just his father's flair for invective, but also his contempt for reform. He wrote of villages such as Newmiln and Galston in Ayrshire being 'contaminated' and 'poisoned' by the 'festering evil' of radicalism. And he warned that 'in all the villages where there are weavers of cotton goods, a large proportion are radicals'.

But the most dangerous centre of revolution anywhere in the empire was the densely packed city on the Clyde, with its flammable cocktail of Irish migrants with rebel hearts, Highlanders burned out of their homes and driven from their lands, and Lowland Scots steeped in the militant egalitarianism of the Covenanters.

On 18 March, the Glasgow Police Commander, Captain James Mitchell, wrote to the Home Secretary in London warning him of plans for an armed uprising:

> 'The Scottish radicals have been making preparations for some little time now for a general rising in Scotland and to this end they have kept in close communication with the disaffected in England. Their plan is to set up a Scottish Assembly or Parliament in Edinburgh, likewise similar assemblies are to be set up by the dis-

affected in England and Ireland. As far as can be gathered by our informants they are imbibed with the republican ideals that were preached by that odious band of disaffected called United Scotsmen, who, after their abortive attempt to overthrow Government in '97, it was generally accepted, had disappeared at the beginning of the century, but whose aim was also the destruction of the unity of our kingdoms.'

The message was based on detailed intelligence provided by spies who had infiltrated the central leadership of the radical movement in the west of Scotland, a 28-strong 'Committee for Organising a Provisional Government'. The body was due to meet in a few days' time, said Mitchell.

His information was accurate. Three days later, on the evening of Tuesday 21 March, the committee, made up of delegates from local radical groups, met in a tavern in the Gallowgate. One of those present, John King, was a shady character. He called himself a weaver, but according to observers, he 'had no conspicuous occupation', and sometimes used the name John Andrews. Just before 9 o'clock, he excused himself from the meeting with some vague excuse about other business elsewhere.

A few minutes later, a large body of police officers and soldiers, led by Glasgow magistrate Baillie James Hunter, smashed their way in and arrested everyone present. They seized some documents, though many were thrown in the fire and burned before they could be confiscated. The raid was kept secret from the press and the public.

A week later, on 29 March, the Glasgow Police Commander sent a further letter to Lord Sidmouth, urging the Home Secretary 'that action must be taken immediately to quench the treasonable ardours of the disaffected before they grow too strong'. He went on to report the successful rounding-up of the radical leadership, which he explained was 'due solely to the efforts of an informant who has served his Government well'.

He also reported a confession they had managed to extract from the leader of the group, who admitted to 'an audacious plot to sever the kingdom of Scotland from that of England and restore the ancient Scottish Parliament'. He continued:

'We know many of the vipers involved in this treasonable plot but I would say, indeed I would stake all on such a hazard that the disaffected are too weak and disorganised at this date to carry out their wicked intent. Thus my lord, if some plan were conceived by which the disaffected could be lured out of their lairs – being made to think that the day of "liberty" had come – we would catch them abroad and undefended. The military in North Britain is more than adequate to round up such vermin. Our intelligence leads us to believe that few know of the apprehension of the leaders in this odious treasonable plot and so no suspicion would attach itself to the plan at all. I have given instructions to our informants on these lines – all good men, and true to our principles, who at tremendous hazard to their life and limb, have infiltrated the disaffected's committees and organisation, and in a few days you shall judge the results. It would, by the severity of their punishment which must be harsh – quench all thought of patriotic pride and Radical feeling among the disaffected.'

A few days later the disaffected were lured out of their lairs. In the dead of night, sometime between Saturday 1 and Sunday 2 April, an *Address to the Inhabitants of Great Britain and Northern Ireland* appeared on hoardings, gable ends and even church walls across Glasgow, Paisley, Kilmarnock, Girvan, Strathaven, Hamilton, Airdrie, Kilsyth and Dumbarton. It purported to come from the 'Committee of Reformation for Forming a Provisional Government', and called for nothing less than violent revolution, urging not just the people to rise up, but for the army to join them.

The language of the proclamation was clumsy and tedious, in contrast to the highly literate pamphlets and speeches that were the hallmarks of the radical movement in Scotland during these years. It lacked any clear demands, making do with vague, hasty demands for 'just and equal laws'. Tellingly, it threatened the 'severest punishment' to anyone who violated private property; hardly the pressing issue for desperate radicals with no private property to speak of.

Again rather oddly, rather than appeal to the spirit of Wallace and Bruce, which was almost obligatory for radical gatherings and publications in Scotland, it invoked the *Magna Carta* – the charter of rights agreed by King John and his nobles half a millennium before Britain even existed. The fact that it was addressed to the people of Great Britain and Ireland seems to imply that the proclamation had been posted across both islands, and that a simultaneous rising had been declared across Scotland, England and Ireland.

None of it proves conclusively that the address was a forgery. But research conducted at the time by journalist and pro-reform activist Peter MacKenzie, and augmented by the work of Ellis and Mac a' Ghobhainn, seems to prove beyond all reasonable doubt that the proclamation was the work of a group of *agents provocateurs* run by Captain Mitchell and Captain James Brown, the Superintendent of Edinburgh City Police, who in turn reported to the Lord Advocate. The four spies have been identified as John King; Duncan Turner, a tinsmith; John Craig, a weaver from Anderston; and Thomas or Robert Lees, a solicitor from England, and unofficially credited as the author of the proclamation.

It was an audacious plan to incite a premature, chaotic and leaderless rising, solely to draw out and isolate the most radical elements of the working class. With Habeas Corpus long since suspended, the militants could be rounded up and interned. Some at least could be prosecuted for High Treason, and a few executions would surely extinguish the fire in the belly of even the most ardent radical?

That Sunday morning in Glasgow, the 1st Rifle Brigade set up cannons on every bridge across the Clyde to stop any mobilisation of insurgents into the city centre. At the same time, the volunteer Glasgow Yeomanry – commanded by Samuel Hunter, the 18-stone editor of the pro-Tory *Glasgow Herald* – surrounded and barricaded the city's treasury, the Royal Bank in Queen Street. Just after noon, the Commander-in-Chief of the Army in Scotland, Sir Thomas Bradford, set off on horseback from Edinburgh Castle along with his entire General Staff, protected by a 60-strong squadron of the 10th Hussars.

Seven miles away in Paisley, radicals gathered with the few bits and pieces of ammunition they could muster, to await instructions from the Provisional Government in Glasgow. All across west-central Scotland, fragmented bands of radicals gathered in their hundreds, in town and village squares, waiting for messengers that never came.

For those who had set the trap, everything was going to plan. But those pulling the strings from on high had underestimated the hunger for radical change and were about to discover the law of unintended consequences. Events began to escalate beyond their control, rapidly. The proclamation may have been a fake, but there was nothing artificial about the general strike that it incited. Journalists and historians would later pore over the text of the proclamation, searching for clues that might help them piece together its origins. But the mass of people had seen only the bold headlines and the rousing call to action – 'Liberty or Death!'

By Monday morning, the whole of west and central Scotland – a heavily populated area covering almost 3,000 square miles – had ground to a standstill. The press estimated that 60,000 workers joined the general strike, though the real figure was probably higher still. Upwards of 5,000 troops – all the regulars available in Scotland – were flooded into Glasgow, Paisley and other strongholds of the rebellion, while English regiments were mobilised north to defend Edinburgh. Major-General Bradford sent a message to London urgently requesting 10,000 flintlock firearms and half a million ball cartridges.

The atmosphere of dread was expressed tersely in an anonymous eye-witness report sent to the Duke of Hamilton from 'A British Subject', who is now thought to be the eminent geographer and journalist James MacQueen. Under the heading *Events of the Late Rebellion in the West of Scotland*, the letter describes how radical leaders immediately denounced the proclamation as an effort by 'Government spies to trap the people'. Nonetheless, on the first day of the strike, 'almost all the labouring population abandoned their work'. Horrified by this colossal mutiny, panic-stricken employers, fearing retribution, sent home those few who had run the gauntlet of the picket lines, and locked up their factories.

According to MacQueen, 'the manufacture of arms was continued by night and by day with astonishing celerity and perseverance'. Pikes, pistols, muskets, catapults, lead-weighted darts and ammunition were being churned out in huge quantities in makeshift workshops across the Lowlands. Raiding parties roamed the countryside, scouring farm buildings for firearms.

Meanwhile, radicals were preparing to defend themselves against a bloodbath. 'Drilling in large bodies at all hours was open, extensive and undisguised. Parties of many hundreds drilled during the day in the Green of Glasgow, at Dalmarnock Ford, at the Point House, at Tollcross, and many other places without interruption.' MacQueen goes on to describe how respectable families fled Paisley and other towns in terror, as 'workmen openly and boldly declared to their masters that they would work no more till the Government of the country was changed.'

The crisis provided a glimpse of the potential power of the fledgling Scottish working class. Janet Hamilton, who became a prominent working class poet during the Victorian era, was 25 years old at the time, and living in Monklands. In her *Reminiscences of the Radical Time in 1819-20*, she describes how local radicals advised that 'when the rising took place, every man should help himself as best he could to the possessions of the rich and that property of every kind was no longer to be monopolised by the few but divided among the many'. She also underlined the extraordinarily advanced cultural level of the west of Scotland weavers – 'the most intelligent, enlightened and by far the most independent body of working men in the Kingdom'. In her own local library, founded by weavers, 'half the books were works of divinity, then biography, travel, voyages, and several sets of the British Essayist, a fair proportion of history and geography'.

For the Tory Government in London, and their henchmen in Edinburgh and Glasgow, the existence of this huge concentration of highly literate and politically militant workers represented a mortal danger to the status quo. Thus, a public meeting of 'prominent citizens' was called to 'consider what steps it may be proper to take regarding the future employment of those who have obeyed the command of a treasonable confederacy to desist from their normal labour'. Addressing the meeting, the commander of the Glasgow Yeomanry warned that 'all the lower classes are contaminated and ready to enter any plan of rebellion'.

The gathering agreed on a declaration, signed by 155 employers, that they would 'withdraw our employment and support from every person who may have lent, or who in the future shall lend, his aid to the purpose of their wicked and treasonable conspiracy'. It resolved not to employ anyone who took part in the strike – a bellicose piece of rhetoric which would have been to impossible to implement without sacking almost every weaver in the west of Scotland.

But key government figures had other tricks up their sleeves. As Tom Johnston notes in his *History of the Working Classes in Scotland*, 'The Government was in no hurry; the troops could bide their time until a Radical army of ill-armed, ill-disciplined rebel weavers had been gathered, and then, in one great carnage, would be taught a lesson that would serve to humiliate two or three generations of the discontented common folk.'

The Battle of Bonnymuir

Meanwhile, the state agents who had penetrated the inner circle of the radical movement worked in the background, almost certainly under orders from the Home Secretary in Westminster, to bring it all to a head.

John King reported to the authorities that the radicals were planning two simultaneous armed offensives on Wednesday 5 April. One unit would lay siege to Glasgow city centre; the other would attempt to seize control of Carron Iron Works in Falkirk, the biggest heavy industrial factory in Europe, with a 2,000-strong workforce. The ironworks specialised in manufacturing firearms and ammunition, and was famed for developing the pioneering short naval cannon, which became known as the 'carronade'.

King, along with his tightly-knit band of spies, then set about provoking the raids. His right-hand man Duncan Turner met with the radical committee in the north of Glasgow and told them an insurrection was now underway in England and in other parts of Scotland. Claiming to speak for the Provisional Government, he reported that the workforce of Carron Iron Works had joined the strike, and seized several cannons and a hoard of other arms. He assured the group that if they marched on the factory 'there was no doubt whatsoever of their success'.

But Dougald Smith, the leader of the radical forces in the area, was adamant that the group was too small to carry out such a mission. When the promised reinforcements from Anderston, on the western edge of Glasgow, failed to appear, he outright refused to take command of the operation. After a heated debate, the men split into groups. One stayed with Smith, while a small faction of around 30 – commanded by Andrew Hardie from Castle Street, near the site of Glasgow Royal Infirmary – set off on the 35-mile hike to Falkirk.

En route, they passed through the village of Condorrat, now part of Cumbernauld new town. Before they arrived, John King had appeared at the door of two brothers in the town, John and Robert Baird, to persuade them to join the attack on Carron Iron Works. To gain entry, he had shown them a headed manuscript from the Provisional Government of Scotland, apparently signed by a number of well-known radicals. He told them that a successful rising had already taken place in England, and that the Provisional Government had robust intelligence that the magistrates of Glasgow and other parts of Scotland were ready to support an insurrection in Scotland. Even the military were ready to switch sides. By way of icing on the cake, he even produced a letter confirming these facts from the 'Secret Committee of the Provisional Government'.

Robert Baird, a married man, was suspicious. But his brother John, a veteran of the Napoleonic Wars and the key leader of the radical movement in the area, was fired up. He agreed to raise a group of local activists to join Andrew Hardie's men in a march on the Carron Iron Works.

It was, of course, a trap. As they headed east to Falkirk, two troops of light cavalry were riding south from Perth. One took position inside the Carron

Iron Works, while the other, the 10th Hussars, commanded by Lieutenant Ellis Hodgson, teamed up with the Stirling Yeomanry to halt the insurgents in their tracks. They confronted each other on a desolate stretch of open moorland outside Falkirk.

On the spectrum of military conflict, the Battle of Bonnymuir was closer in scale to a 1970s Glasgow gang fight than to Stalingrad. The few dozen who marched under Baird and Hardie believed they were participating in a wholesale rising to overthrow the British state. In reality, the movement was without any central leadership. There was no strategy, no tactics, and no clear goal. It was a premature rebellion, doomed from its inception. The ragged band of exhausted, half-starving weavers, armed mainly with pikes, were no match for the professional cavalry.

They fought bravely, refusing repeated demands by Hodgson to surrender, and at one point charging down a hill straight towards the Hussars while cheering. But it was a kamikaze action. Had it been left to the Stirling Yeomanry, who by all accounts were thirsting for blood, they would in all probability have been massacred on the spot. But Lieutenant Hodgson seems to have been a humane man. Or perhaps he was under orders to bring back the leaders alive, to be tried for High Treason and hung from the gallows as a warning to any future would-be rebels, rather than be slaughtered on the battlefield as martyrs. Either way, there were no fatalities.

After a brief skirmish, 18 radicals were arrested, the rest escaping. When the prisoners arrived at Stirling Castle, John Baird made a short plea to the Fort-Major: 'Sir, if there is to be any severity exercised towards us, let it be on me. I am their leader, and have caused them being here. I hope that I alone may suffer.' He then asked for food and treatment for the wounded men.

According to Ellis and Mac a' Ghobhainn, when the news reached Glasgow, 'there was great excitement and the church bells were rung as if another Waterloo had been won. Public meetings were afterwards held by merchants and manufacturers, and resolutions adopted congratulating the Government and their success.' The Home Secretary, Lord Sidmouth, sent a letter of thanks to the Yeoman of Stirlingshire, and published an 'Extraordinary Bulletin' to all parts of the British empire to celebrate the fact that 'Our glorious constitution in Church and State, the envy of surrounding nations and the admiration of the world, is still to be inviolably preserved for all posterity.'

'Scotland free or a desert'

Elsewhere there were sporadic shows of strength by armed groups of radicals. On the Wednesday night, as the Bonnymuir prisoners were being locked up in Stirling Castle, around 500 weavers armed with muskets, pikes and pistols gathered under a Saltire and a radical banner in the Bridgeton-Calton area. In Tollcross, men, women and children began to arm themselves after hearing that a radical army had defeated government troops at Bonnymuir. In the early hours of Thursday, after receiving a report that radicals planned to seize Dumbarton Castle, the Dunbartonshire Fencibles threw a cordon around the town of Duntocher, and arrested eight radical leaders.

In the absence of a cohesive leadership, rumours and misinformation spread like fireweed. According to one story, Marshall MacDonald – an ex-general in Napoleon's army and the son of one of Bonnie Prince Charlie's closest aides – had arrived on the Ayrshire coast with a shipload of arms and cash to support the rising. The day after the Bonnymuir arrests, a messenger arrived in the town of Strathaven, a weaving town steeped in radicalism, with a slightly different version of the rumour. James Shields brought information, supposedly from the Provisional Government, that George Kinloch, a radical laird living in exile in France, had returned to Scotland and set up camp on Cathkin Braes, to the south of Glasgow, with between 5,000 and 7,000 troops. Meanwhile, another army was said to be gathering on the Campsie Fells, to the north of the city.

Shields, by all accounts, had acted in good faith. Some historians, including Peter MacKenzie and the authors of *The Scottish Insurrection of 1820*, argue that he had been duped by John King. Others, including John Stevenson, a local radical activist who later penned his own personal account of events, dismissed suggestions that government agents played a role locally.

Whatever the circumstances, the news created a buzz amongst the radicals of the town. James Wilson was a 60-year-old grandfather, poet, clockmaker, tinsmith and doctor and, according to John Stevenson, 'a man of much reading and reflection, his natural abilities placed him above mediocrity'. Wilson greeted the news from Shields with elation: 'I am glad to hear that my countrymen are resolved to act like men. We are seeking nothing but the rights of our forefathers – liberty is not worth having if it's not worth fighting for.' That night his home was turned into a miniature pike-making factory.

But the women of the town were more sceptical, and by the following morning enthusiasm for the mission had dwindled. In *A True Narrative of the Radical Rising in Strathaven*, Stevenson wrote:

> 'The night was dark and comfortless; we however succeeded in procuring a number of guns; and there was a good deal of bustle and confusion during the night. Mothers, with maternal solitude, were inquiring after their sons; wives were exhorting and entreating their husbands to return home. In short, the screams of women might occasionally be heard... Although our number at one time amounted to nearly one hundred, by the time the sun rose on morning of the 6th, we could scarcely muster twenty-five; the wetness of the night, the sagacious advice of friends, and the report that all was quiet in Glasgow, will account for the desertion of three quarters of our number; the rest of us, however, were firmly resolved to join the division which Shields positively assured us were to rendezvous on Cathkin that morning.'

The next morning a group of 25 men, with pikes, three guns and a broken sword brandished by James Wilson, marched towards the nearby towns of Kilbride and Maxwellton, hoping to raise reinforcements. They carried a banner which on one side carried the words 'Strathaven Union Society' and, on the other, 'Scotland Free or a Desert'. But no new recruits were forthcoming. By this time, the stirring news of an army of thousands mustered on the Cathkin Braes was beginning to look like either a flight of fancy or disinformation.

As it became apparent that they had been misled, Wilson and others returned to Strathaven, but a dozen or so carried on, including John Stevenson and James Shields, hope prevailing over realism. After seeing for themselves the deserted hillside, they hid their weapons among the bracken and returned home, dejected. The last man to leave the scene was Shields, desperately apologetic, blaming himself for the debacle.

In contrast to Bonnymuir, there was no cavalry or yeomanry there to arrest the insurgents, a fact that lends some weight to John Stevenson's argument that they had been victims of nothing more sinister than wishful thinking. Yet as he wrote in his memoirs, they returned home with a sense of dread:

> 'We left the hill with fearful prognostics of the future. We knew well the vindictive disposition of the old monarchial governments, and that they rarely for-

> give those who have the hardihood to rise in arms against their despotic proceedings; and while we were hurrying down the hill I felt a strong presentiment that some of us would expiate this on the scaffold.'

His 'presentiment' was well-founded. Fourteen of the Strathaven rebels were arrested that night, while the remainder fled the country. In all, 88 people across the west of Scotland would be charged in the next few days with the capital offence of High Treason, and hundreds more with lesser offences. Three would face the scaffold. Yet the rebels had killed no-one during the Radical War. Their firearms and pikes had been carried for defensive purposes. The influential pro-reform *Edinburgh Review* described the episode as 'a war of the rich against the poor – of the Government and soldiery against the people'.

The punishments were atrocious and disproportionate, and yet the greatest atrocity of all went unpunished. The incident began when a troop of soldiers from the Port Glasgow Militia was asked to remove five 'prominent Radical leaders' from the now overcrowded Paisley prison and escort them to Greenock Jail. As the regiment marched into the busy port town at 5 o'clock on Saturday 8 April, they were jeered by local bystanders. As the troops reached Cathcart Street in the town centre, a few stones were thrown from the sidelines. The soldiers responded with a volley of shots into the air, wounding a few protesters. But instead of dispersing, the crowd turned on the troops, pelting them with debris. Discipline went to hell, and the soldiers fired indiscriminately. Eight people were killed, including an 8-year-old boy and a 65-year-old man. Another 10 were seriously wounded, including a 65-year-old woman who had to have her leg amputated.

At 7 o'clock, an enraged horde marched on the heavily guarded prison, smashed open the wooden gates and released the five radicals, leaving the non-political prisoners locked up in their cells. Rumours now spread across Scotland that the radicals had captured Greenock. In the early hours of the morning, two troops of cavalry galloped into town, and a few hours later a steamboat packed with footsoldiers arrived from Glasgow. But all was quiet.

Across the west of Scotland, the state forces now went to town. In Glasgow alone, 100 radicals were arrested in dawn raids by the army, while others managed to flee. Although there were still a few splutters of resistance to come, it was all over bar the brutal recriminations.

The summer of retribution

James Wilson was hanged on Wednesday 20 August outside the High Court of Glasgow, facing south across the River Clyde. A sullen, hostile assembly of over 20,000 had gathered in bright sunshine to witness the execution of the prisoner, who was dressed in a white suit trimmed with black. 'Did you ever see sic a crowd, Tammas?' he asked the nervous executioner, a 20-year-old medical student called Thomas Moore.

Wilson was now a hero of the working people. Before being condemned to death, he had told his judges:

> 'My gory head may in a few days fall upon the scaffold and be exposed as the head of traitor, but I appeal with confidence to posterity. When my countrymen will have exalted their voices in bold proclamation of the rights and dignity of humanity, and enforced their claim by the extermination of their oppressors, then, and not till then, will some future historian do my memory justice, then will my name and suffering be recorded in Scottish history…'

At his execution, leaflets were circulated, printed with the words, 'May the ghost of the butchered Wilson haunt the pillows of relentless jurors – Murder! Murder! Murder!' The cry was taken up by sections of the gathering as Wilson mounted the scaffold at 2.55pm. Amid scream and hisses, groups of cavalry charged the crowd, fearing attempts to liberate the condemned man.

The *Glasgow Chronicle* reported that 'Wilson was especially cheered when he came to the scaffold, and the sentiments of the mob showed that they regarded him in quite a different light from that of a traitor. Cries of 'he's died for his country' and 'he's murdered' were quite general.' After the hanging, Wilson's body lay for half an hour before it was beheaded by the executioner. 'This is the head of a traitor!' he roared, as was a customary part of the ritual fashion. But the crowd roared back, 'He is a martyr!'

Wilson's corpse was taken to the Cathedral and contemptuously thrown into a pauper's grave. But that night, his daughter and niece dug up the turf and carried his remains back for a proper burial in his beloved Strathaven.

Eighteen days later, at 1 o'clock on Friday 8 September, John Baird and Andrew Hardie, dressed in black, were taken in a horse-drawn hurdle from their cells in Stirling Castle to Broad Street. Along the way, women lined the streets in tears. At the scaffold, both briefly addressed the 2,000-strong crowd, defending their role in 'the cause of truth and justice'. As in Glasgow, there were hisses and cries of 'Murder!'

Eighteen others had also been condemned to death, but feeling the heat from below, the authorities commuted their sentences to transportation to New South Wales. Hundreds more were jailed for lesser charges. Although the government had been given a fright, the objectives of the British state had been achieved. The radical workers' movement on Clydeside had been left decapitated and demoralised. The executions ushered in a decade of grim reaction.

Yet as with the 1916 Easter Rising in Dublin, the 1960 Sharpeville Massacre in South Africa, or the 1930s Spanish Civil War, history would later honour the vanquished and shame the victors. Those who conspired to crush the radical weavers have long since been judged as backward bigots, defenders of an oppressive and decaying political system. In contrast, those who were sent to the scaffold are commemorated as the Nelson Mandelas of their day, placing their lives and their liberty on the line to overthrow tyranny.

Indeed, in 1832, an absolute pardon was granted to all those who had been transported for their part in the 1820 insurrection. By that time, only 10 could be traced; the others had either died or disappeared. Almost two centuries after their judicial murder, John Baird, Andrew Hardie and James Wilson are commemorated in marches and rallies, songs and poetry. As James Wilson prophesied, they were, ultimately, vindicated by posterity.

Their persecutors have become a footnote in history. The spies and *agents provocateurs* vanished into the mist. Lord Sidmouth died in 1844, a bitter opponent of Catholic Emancipation and an enemy even of the gutless 1832 Reform Act. In 1822, his associate, Lord Castlereagh, cut his own throat.

19

DAYS OF HOPE

Whiggery pokery

Speaking in a debate in the Scottish Parliament to commemorate the 1820 Insurrection, Tory MSP Brian Monteith dismissed the role of working class action, insisting that 'it was the social reform of the Conservative Party, rather than revolution, that enshrined the rights of trade union members'. He continued: 'It is by the often bitter experience of a turbulent history that Scots have learned that the surest road to social progress lies through reform and not through revolution. The reformers offered the remedy of the pursuit of progress by constitutional means. In 1832, twelve years after Bonnymuir, the first Reform Act was passed and the political life of modern Scotland was created.'

The former MSP's views are pretty much in tune with mainstream opinion, which apparently regards British history as one long, relatively peaceful march towards freedom and human rights. The Glorious Revolution, the Act of Union, the Monarchy, and the Mother of Parliaments all played a central part in making Britain Great. The ruling elites, brimming with intelligence, vision and generosity, reshaped society by instalments, gradually moulding the modern, *civilised* democracy we know today.

Alas, the aforementioned is but a piece of historical fiction to rival anything ever written by Walter Scott. The democratic rights we have today, from voting to free speech and the right to strike, were not handed out like birthday presents by the beneficent British state. In truth, every inch of progress was fought for long and hard. People were jailed, transported, shot down and hung from the gallows before the British ruling classes conceded, grudgingly, morsel by morsel, the human rights we have today.

The Chartists of the mid-nineteenth century were ferociously opposed by the crown, the House of Commons, the House of Lords, the landowners, the industrialists, the churches and the official press. Their central demand, for universal suffrage, was denounced as a fiendish fantasy which would lead to mob rule. And it took best part of a century before it was finally achieved in full. Before that, it took a century and half of struggle after the Glorious Revolution of King William III for the first feeble Reform Act to be accepted by Westminster. Up until then, the British state had been run since its formation as the private club of a clique of wealthy landowners, via a corrupt electoral system and a parliament that might as well have been located on Jupiter for all it understood the lives of the mass of people it ruled over.

By the end of the 1820s, Scotland had fewer than 4,500 voters out of a population of over 2.5 million. Yet the only section of society calling for democracy max, via universal suffrage and secret ballots, were the common people, the lower orders, the riff-raff. The working class, as it later became, was always the main driving force for democratic and human rights. Politicians, landowners, monarchs, merchants, clergy and mill owners were swept along by great rivers of protest from below, going with the flow only as an alternative to drowning.

By 1830, the Whig Party, which represented the rising middle classes, had positioned itself in the centre ground of politics, between what it viewed as two extremist forces. On the one side, the dyed-in-the-wool reactionaries of the Tory Party, who opposed any attempt to dilute the power of the landowning elite; on the other, the revolutionary extremists in the factories, with their outlandish demand for universal suffrage. Thomas Macaulay, the famous historian and sometime MP for Edinburgh, insisted that the right to vote for all adult males would 'lead to the destruction of civilisation and a return to barbarism'. And he was a Whig – supposedly the most progressive faction in the House of Commons. The mildly pro-reform *Scotsman* newspaper ridiculed universal voting rights in the kind of language that the *Daily Mail* might use today to attack Scottish independence. Supporters of general suffrage were, said the paper of the Edinburgh Whig establishment, 'quacks and adventurers, fools and charlatans'.

The catalyst for the rise of the pro-reform movement was a change in the balance of forces at Westminster. For almost half a century, the Tories had controlled both the House of Commons and the House of Lords, except for a brief interruption in the early nineteenth century, when they lost their overall majority for a year. But by the end of 1830, as they tore themselves apart over Catholic Emancipation, Earl Grey slipped into 10 Downing Street via the back door – the first Whig Prime Minister for several generations. He pledged to go to the country the following year to seek a mandate for electoral reform.

In Scotland, a proliferation of organisations demanded varying degrees of electoral and political reform. Three broad groups emerged. The Reform Association was middle class and cautious, and included in its ranks the prominent industrialist Charles Tennant, the owner of the St Rollox chemical works on the north side of Glasgow, and James Oswald, a merchant and mill owner. Confusingly, its more militant rival was called the Reform Committee, established by West of Scotland trade unions. Somewhere in between the two was the Political Union, whose members included the big landowner John Maxwell of Pollok, whose twentieth century descendants would bequeath the family's ancestral lands to Glasgow Corporation.

When the Whigs won a 136-seat majority over the Tories in June 1831, it looked as though Britain was about to be transformed. But the new government was terrified that democracy would mean the end of private wealth and privilege, and that it would sweep away many of the central pillars of the British state, such as the House of Lords and the monarchy. The Whigs were the party of the manufacturers and merchants, the business elite, and the urban professional classes. They loathed the big Tory landowners, but not half as much as they feared the great unwashed rabble.

When the Government brought forward two timid reform bills, one after another, calling for merely an extension of the franchise, the disappointment within the reform movement was profound. That disappointment soon turned to anger when even these meagre concessions were blocked by the Tory House of Lords. Across Britain, the mood began to turn militant. A demonstration in Glasgow, called at just 18 hours' notice, mobilised between 100,000 and 200,000 protesters, many carrying black flags, alongside the skull and crossbones, to signify the death of electoral reform. One city newspaper, the *Quizzling Glass* – part of the so-called 'unstamped press' that refused to pay stamp duty and thus was sold illicitly on the streets – summed up the rising temperature: 'Revolution is a dangerous matter, but better revolution than slavery'.

When the Whigs finally did manage to push a Reform Bill through Westminster, in July 1832, it was celebrated with fervour by the manufacturers, merchants and professional middle classes. But the mass of the population were locked out of the party. The franchise had been widened, but only to include 'ten pounds householders' – those who owned or leased property, worth at least £10 a year, at a time when the total annual wage of a worker was barely £15. In today's terms that would mean only those paying a rent or mortgage of over £1000 a month would be eligible for the electoral register.

All in all, the Great Reform Act, as it was called by the pro-government press, was a wretched setback. It meant that Scotland, with a population of 2.5 million, now had 60,000 voters in total – an improvement on where it had been before, but only just. Some 83 per cent of men and 100 per cent of women remained excluded from the franchise. Far from 'creating the political life of modern Scotland', the 1832 legislation was a kick in the teeth to those who toiled like beasts of burden and shed their blood like water to support the British ruling class – the wealthiest of its kind anywhere on the planet.

Capital against labour

One of the great watershed events in the history of trade unionism internationally was the transportation of the Tolpuddle Martyrs to Botany Bay in 1834. The six Dorset farm-workers had done nothing more dangerous than organise themselves into a Friendly Society of Agricultural Labourers, to protest against wage cuts at a time when machines were destroying the old rural ways and devouring livelihoods. Their treatment provoked a fearsome storm of protest, including a petition that gathered 800,000 signatures. The men became folk heroes, commemorated to this day at a glorious festival that includes a procession, speakers, music, drama, poetry and comedy – all in a village of just 500 souls.

One fact, however, has become a little blurred over time. The Tolpuddle Martyrs were framed not by evil Tories, but by a government of Whigs – supposedly the forward-looking, modernising, progressive wing of the British state. Whenever the interests of the rich and powerful looked to be imperilled, the descendants of the butchers of Culloden were still capable of turning up the tyranny.

In Glasgow, 30,000 signed the Tolpuddle petition – four times more per head of the population than in Britain as a whole. That reflected the strongly politicised nature of the city's working class, which was being steadily reinforced, month after month, by a continuous flow of immigration from Ireland, north and south, Catholic and Protestant. Within a month, class war erupted in Glasgow itself – and this was no gentle, rustic affair.

With the economy plunging headlong into deep depression, the city's 'Cotton Masters' announced a severe wage reduction. The three-month strike that ensued, from April through July, was vicious. According to James McElhose, in his 1886 book *Memoirs and Portraits of 100 Glasgow Men*, its effect was to 'let loose upon the already distressed community about 80,000 destitute persons'. He describes how the 280-strong Glasgow police force was simply overwhelmed, and needed the support of cavalry and footsoldiers. But even then, the peace 'was not maintained, and not only was force used to prevent the well-disposed from working, but combustibles were being thrown into the mills and houses of employers'.

The conflict came to a violent head one Saturday evening in late July, when a strikebreaker, drafted into the Houldsworth Mill in Anderston, was shot in the shoulder whilst out shopping with his wife in Clyde Street. Three days later, James Smith died of his wounds in the Royal Infirmary. He had managed to dictate a statement to the police, but had been unable to identify the gunman. The Sheriff of Lanarkshire, Sir Archibald Alison, whose jurisdiction included the north and east of Glasgow, was determined to crack down hard on those who threatened his fiefdom with chaos. He offered a reward of £500 – a colossal sum in a depressed, poverty-stricken city, equivalent to over 30 years' pay for a cotton spinner.

Given this inducement, it was no great shock when two informers came forward and arranged to meet the Sheriff in what was described in court as a 'hidden place', believed to be the vaults of the old College building on the High Street. The dubious pair told Alison that an 'assassination committee' had been formed for the purpose of picking off strikebreakers and factory owners one by one. Conveniently for the authorities, the named members of the assassination committee also happened to be the four central leaders of the Glasgow Operative Body of Cotton Spinners – the chairman, Thomas Hunter; the treasurer, Peter Hacket; the secretary, Richard McNiel; and the assistant secretary, James Gibb. Along with William Maclean, the alleged assassin, they were arrested.

The indictment ran to 26 pages. Among other things, the men were accused of orchestrating a major terror conspiracy, murders, attempted murders, arson attacks, intimidation, administering secret oaths and being part of an illegal 'secret committee'. Indeed, it seems as if the authorities decided just to throw in every recent, unsolved Glasgow crime for good measure.

The evidence against the cotton-spinners was threadbare. It hung almost entirely on the evidence of a spirit dealer who testified that he had heard Maclean claim responsibility for the shooting. But there was no corroboration. Nor was the identity of the two informers ever revealed, nor what happened to the £500 rewards, raising suspicions as to whether or not these informers even existed. After an eight-day trial, the union officials were found guilty on charges of 'conspiracy to keep wages up'; of 'disturbances at Oakbank factory'; and of 'molestation at Mile End factory'. Essentially, they had been convicted of running a strike, with a bit of mobbing and rioting thrown in. On the more serious capital charges, the verdict was Not Proven. But their punishment was severe: seven years' transportation. In pronouncing the sentence, the Lord-Justice Clerk denounced the trade union as 'an unlawful association... most injurious and dangerous in its consequences'.

The strike had the unforeseen consequence of opening up a rancorous debate at the highest levels of the reform movement. Daniel O'Connell, the figurehead of the campaign for Catholic Emancipation and the repeal of the union between Britain and Ireland, was strongly involved with the wider crusade for electoral reform. He was also a strict constitutionalist who had little time for class conflict. The events in Glasgow prompted him to demand a parliamentary inquiry into the activities of the trade unions.

His attack on the Glasgow cotton-spinners was supported by the influential London Working Men's Association which, despite its name, charged expensive subscription fees and was open only to 'persons of a good moral character'. The politics of the reform movement in the capital were more timid than in the north of England, the west of Scotland and Wales. While these were centres of mass manufacturing, with huge factories and a strong, cohesive working class, London was dominated by small-scale domestic and craft industries, such as glass, furniture, pottery and silk, all produced by skilled artisans in small workshops.

The defeat of the cotton-spinners and the transportation of its leaders was a savage blow for the entire trade union movement. Combined with the deep economic depression, it left working people at the mercy of their employers. Many of these were, no doubt, decent, honourable individuals in their personal lives. A few even had a strong social conscience – notably the owner of the New Lanark mills whose politics shifted ever more to the left as he grew older and wiser. But the collective outlook and actions of the mill owners, the backbone of the rising capitalist order, was determined by their position in a system based on the exploitation of labour. When times were good, they sought to squeeze as much profit as possible from their employees by making them worker harder and longer for little more cash. And during the inevitable bad times, they would shut factories with impunity, driving untold numbers of families into destitution with the scribble of a pen.

But as the industrial movement juddered to a halt, the political struggle began to accelerate. No-one who has ever been active in left-wing politics would be surprised to discover that the external war against the enemy outside was often relegated to the sidelines by internal conflict, the political equivalent of family squabbles.

Not that these were avoidable. Just as explorers setting off into the wilds need maps and compasses, those embarking on a quest to change society need their own route maps and direction finders: the tactics, the strategy, the policies that could get them from here to there. But the struggle to find these would take its toll, and ultimately contribute towards the failure of the great struggle for democracy.

Chartism in Scotland

The People's Charter was launched in 1838 at a series of mass rallies in Birmingham, Glasgow and several venues in the North of England. Its six-point programme demanded universal franchise for males over 21, annual parliaments, abolition of the property qualification for MPs, payment for MPs, a secret ballot, and equal sized constituencies.

On 26 May of that year, a procession – estimated at between 150,000 and 200,000 people – set off from Glasgow Green in torrential rain, accompanied by 43 bands and over 300 banners. In his book *Chartism – a New History*, Leeds University historian Malcolm Chase notes that the presence of the Strathaven Weavers flag, quartered with a Saltire, 'reinforced the occasion's nationalist undertones... in Scotland and Wales, as well as Ireland, radical reformism was fuelled by resentment that political power lay with a propertied elite ruling through institutions based in England... The delegation from Birmingham next day made a pilgrimage to the sacred field of Elderslie, the birthplace of William Wallace.'

By the 1830s, the idea of Scottish independence had receded into the background. The coming to power of the Whigs had broken the log-jam of generations of Tory rule, and for a time held out the promise of change through Westminster. Even after they had sold out the people, there still remained a sense of momentum, a feeling that parliament could still be pushed and pressurised from below into further reform. And as a huge groundswell of rebellion surged through England, Wales, Ireland and Scotland, the possibility of wholesale reform of the British state looked a more realistic prospect than at any time since the Act of Union.

That sense of a united struggle was probably heightened by the emergence of Feargus O'Connor as the leader of the Chartist movement when it was formally launched in 1838. He was an unlikely leader of the British working class. An aristocratic descendant of a Celtic high king of Ireland, O'Connor had been born in Cork into a Protestant family that was steeped in Irish nationalism. But he was an immensely charismatic figure, a powerful orator and a human dynamo, with the political skills to hold together a diverse movement which ranged from radicals, who would cheerfully send the aristocracy to the workhouse after declaring a republic, to Christian pacifists who believed that prayers to God would sort things out. The fact that O'Connor was based in the militant north of England, rather than London, augmented his appeal in Scotland. When the official Chartist newspaper, the *Northern Star*, was launched in November 1838, it was published, edited and printed in Leeds, as close to Edinburgh as it was to London.

There was always an undercurrent of national consciousness, however. At one point, the Tory *Glasgow Courier* even reported talk of 'creating a National Union of delegates from across Scotland that would eventually turn into a Scottish Workers' Parliament'. In his 2010 book, *Chartism in Scotland*, Hamish Fraser, Emeritus Professor of History at Strathclyde University, gives a flavour of that sentiment, and in his conclusion states that, within the movement, 'there was a recurring theme that Scots were a nation that had always been ready to fight for freedom whether with Wallace or the Covenanters'.

Before Chartism was launched as a coherent force in 1838, the campaign for political reform had mushroomed in cities and towns across Britain, without any central coordination or direction. Thus it was something of a jumble of organisations and publications, with a mish-mash of policies that reflected local political influences. In Scotland alone, for example, there were, at one point, 27 Working Men's Associations, six Radical Associations, five Political Unions and two Universal Suffrage Associations. Although there was some cooperation and a degree of overlap, there was also a wide spectrum of political views.

In Glasgow, the *Reformers Gazette* had been highly influential in the early

1830s. The journal was owned and edited by Peter MacKenzie, the journalist and campaigner who helped expose the spy network operating in Glasgow prior to the 1820 insurrection, and subsequently played an important role in preserving the memory of Baird, Hardie and Wilson. This latter notwithstanding, he had always advocated a moderate, pro-Whig line, and would frequently invoke the damage inflicted on the workers' movement by *agents provocateurs* as a reason to stick to constitutional methods of struggle. But after the 1832 betrayal, his dead-end strategy of concentrating on petitioning and lobbying politicians began to lose ground to those who prescribed stronger medicine. MacKenzie's newspaper soon faced a local rival in the shape of the pointedly named *Radical Reformers Gazette*, later rechristened *The Agitator*, which lumped the Whigs and Tories together as 'enemies of liberty'.

MacKenzie, and the reform movement as a whole, were prepared to compromise on the fundamental point of universal suffrage, which they suggested unrealistic. It could be achieved by instalments, they argued, but not in one fell swoop. They also maintained that the movement should explicitly oppose any tactics that went beyond peaceful persuasion. They ruled out not just violence, but any form of disruption or direct action. By contrast, the radicals demanded universal suffrage and nothing less. To dilute that demand would take the heat off the politicians. No one was advocating immediate armed insurrection, but the more radical elements had faith in neither the rigged electoral system nor the political parties that worked this system. They sought to build a mass movement from below, and believed that to rule out physical force would be to remove the only threat that could ultimately pressurise the politicians into delivering fundamental change.

The tone they struck was supportive of legal, peaceful, constitutional reform. But they went on to warn that, should the establishment refuse to budge, or counter the movement with repression, then other means would be necessary. The ambiguity of the radical position was summed up in a catch-phrase which would be popularised by Feargus O'Connor: 'Peacefully if we may; forcibly if we must'.

After the 1832 Reform Act, radicalism began to steadily gain ascendancy within the reform movement across Britain. In the west of Scotland, that trend was reinforced in the late 1830s by the deepening economic depression, and the associated wage cuts and sackings.

At the first National Chartist Convention in London in 1838, Scotland had been represented by the moderate Edinburgh Chartists. But by the end of the year, the balance of power and influence had transferred to Glasgow. This shift in the centre of gravity was prompted partly by the politicians' response to the great national petition presented to parliament in July. The public response had been phenomenal; the list of 1,280,000 signatures stretched three miles long. From Edinburgh and Lothian (the city and country areas were lumped together), 16,000 signatures had been collected, 1 in 14 of the total population, which was significantly better than the national average of 1 in 20. But from Glasgow and Lanarkshire, 78,000 signatures were raised, one in five of the total population, revealing Glasgow as one of the greatest strongholds of Chartism in the entire kingdom. Despite this surge of public feeling, MPs threw out the petition by 235 votes to 46, making a mockery of the moderates, with their belief in the politicians' innate sense of justice coming good in the end, while strengthening the hand of the radicals.

Of the 15-strong Central Committee of the Scottish Chartists, elected at a delegate conference in August 1839, all but one lived within a five mile radius of Glasgow city centre. A month earlier, just a few days before the national petition was thrown out by Westminster, the Glasgow Universal Suffrage Association had launched a new journal, underwritten by the trade union movement in the city. The *Scottish Patriot* was unashamedly radical and drew heavily on Scotland's own traditions of resistance, from Wallace and Bruce through to the 1820 rising. On its launch, the paper proudly proclaimed that it had been 'started by the working people themselves and supported by them alone'. Up until then, the principal voice in Chartism in Scotland had been the moderate, Edinburgh-based *True Scotsman*. It was passionately, and at times obsessively, hostile to physical force, prompting the *Scottish Patriot* to contemptuously dismiss it as 'a miserable apology for a newspaper'.

The *Patriot*'s editor, Ayr-born John Taylor, had founded the Scottish Radical Association in 1836, the forerunner of Chartism in Scotland. He cut a flamboyant figure, with his shoulder-length black hair and swarthy complexion which he attributed to his Indian grandmother. He had long argued that, such was the corruption of the British electoral system, physical force was 'the only weapon left to the productive classes, the last argument of free men'. Those who rejected violence were forgetting the lessons of Wallace and Bruce 'who defended their rights not by moral force but by pikes on a hillside'.

The newspaper also promoted a range of progressive social policies, such as an end to standing armies in times of peace, the abolition of the law of primogeniture (in which first-born sons automatically inherit all property), direct taxation to move the burden of payment from the poor to the rich, an end to what it called 'the feudal barbarism of military flogging', and the destruction of 'that abominable system of castes, by which fools and knaves are invested with honour and distinction irrespective of personal merit'. The *Patriot* further called for the 'Right of the Working Man to openly unite for the purpose of protecting his labour against the aggressions of Capitalism'. It was anti-imperialist, supporting the Irish freedom struggle and arguing that 'only the aristocracy and their minions gain from the colonies'. One of its reporters, James Jack, even disrupted meetings to encourage emigration to New Zealand, on the basis that Britain had no right to be there.

Another radical Chartist newspaper, the *Scottish Vindicator*, launched by Paisley activists, bore on its masthead a quotation from William Wallace: 'Return and tell your masters that we come here, not to treat, but to assert our Rights and Set Scotland Free.' It carried articles supporting republicanism, and others rejecting the 'force of petitioning'. It asked, rhetorically: 'Was it not with armies of peasants that the Swiss, the Dutch and the Americans repelled the troops of their oppressors?'

But even the most radical sections of the movement shrunk from one policy that seems perfectly reasonable today. Chartism, revolutionary as it may have appeared to the parliamentarians, dismissed half the population as unfit to vote. The women's suffrage movement would not be launched until 1872, exactly four decades after the 1832 Reform Act. Incongruously, for a piece of legislation that had progressive pretensions, this Act expressly banned all women from voting. Up until then, a few had managed to slip through a loophole by virtue of the fact that they happened to be wealthy landowners.

Despite the call for universal suffrage being rather misleading, large numbers of women did participate in the struggle, though the historical record is somewhat scant on this matter. Although membership of the National Chartist Association was open to women, they were kept strictly in their place: of the attendance list of 64 people present at the Great Meeting of Scottish Delegates in August 1839, every one was male.

Yet at least 23 specifically women's reform organisations were active during the 1830s and 1840s. Most of these, significantly, were in weaving areas with a high proportion of female labour, including a number of small towns such as Kirriemuir,

Forfar, Strathaven, Alva and Sinclairtown (later absorbed into Kirkcaldy). In Aberdeen, a woman called Mrs Legge, her first name lost to history, led a group of 18 young female activists demanding universal suffrage for women as well as men.

In a letter published in the Chartist newspaper, the *Northern Star*, in 1838, a millworker signing herself 'A real democrat' set out the case, in simple, heartfelt language, for women to have the right to education and the vote:

> 'I address you as a plain working woman – a weaver of Glasgow. You cannot expect me to be grammatical in my expressions, as I did not get an education, like many other of my fellow women that I ought to have got, and which is the right of every human being... It is the right of every woman to have a vote in the legislation of her country, and doubly more so now that we have got a woman at the head of the government [a reference to Queen Victoria's recent coronation].'

Women did, eventually, attain both. But not in that generation, nor in the next. Only in 1892, more than half a century after the weaver woman's impassioned plea, were women finally admitted to Scottish universities. And it would be a further 36 years before all women over the age of 21 were granted the vote, and only after a prolonged campaign of civil disobedience in which a thousand women were locked up in jail.

Even the Chartists' limited demand for universal male suffrage would not be granted for another 80 years. Britain may have led the world in military prowess, empire-building and profit-making. But in the race for democracy, it would be left far behind. By the time universal suffrage finally made it through the Commons, Britain had been left trailing behind a multitude of other countries, including Finland, Poland, the United States, New Zealand, Canada, South Australia, Argentina, Norway, Estonia, Latvia, Lithuania, Uruguay, Austria, Germany, Luxemburg, the Netherlands, Albania, Czechoslovakia, Sweden, the Republic of Ireland, Burma, Ecuador and Mongolia. Even the Isle of Man was decades ahead of Britain in extending the vote to women.

Days of desolation

By the end of 1842, the Chartist vision of a brave new world was already dimming. In May, yet another petition, this time with three million signatures, had been rejected by parliament. The *Northern Star* poured out its anger:

'Three and half millions have quietly, orderly, soberly, peaceably but firmly asked of their rulers to do justice; and their rulers have turned a deaf ear to that protest. Three and a half millions of people have asked permission to detail their wrongs, and enforce their claims for RIGHT, and the 'House' has resolved they should not be heard! Three and a half millions of the slave-class have holden out the olive branch of peace to the enfranchised and privileged classes and sought for a firm and compact union, on the principle of EQUALITY BEFORE THE LAW; and the enfranchised and privileged have refused to enter into a treaty! The same class is to be a slave class still. The mark and brand of inferiority is not to be removed. The assumption of inferiority is still to be maintained. The people are not to be free.'

Not only were the people not to be free; neither were they to be fed. These were times of desperation. The economy was sliding under the quicksand of yet another deep depression, and the working people of Britain were fighting, not for reform or revolution, but bare survival.

Ten years earlier the owners of the factories, mills and mines had, for a time, made common cause with the working class in pursuit of electoral reform. Back then, the industrialists had been left out in the cold by the landowners, who had carved up political power for themselves. But that precarious partnership collapsed after 1832, when the franchise was extended to include the affluent merchant class, who subsequently pulled the ladder up. And by 1843, the brief flirtation of the early 1830s had turned into a blazing class war, sparked by a cut in wages, to the tune of a shilling a week, for Staffordshire coal miners. Other employers inevitably followed suit and, in response, a general strike backed by the Chartists rolled across the industrial regions of the north of England and central Scotland.

In Lanarkshire, 10,000 coal and ironstone miners walked out, at the end of their tether after their wages had been halved to the equivalent of less than £50 a week in today's money. Desperate colliers looted company stores, seized bread and milk and dug up potato fields to feed their families. For a time, Coatbridge was under military occupation. The infamous Tory Sheriff Archibald Alison, who had hounded the cotton-spinners, reported that 20,000 people had gathered in the town in 'a state of great excitement'. He had no doubt, he added, that the Chartists were involved. In nearby Airdrie, 30,000 miners gathered at a rally where they backed a resolution calling for a general strike 'until the Charter is made law'. Eventually, seven miners from Airdrie were sentenced to ten years' transportation, and a further three Coatbridge miners sentenced to seven years.

In the meantime, strikes and disorder spread to other parts of Scotland, including the east coast, with women as well as men taking part in looting and rioting. In Fife, colliers from surrounding pit villages invaded Dunfermline, set factories ablaze, smashed machinery and ransacked shops. Across West Fife, a series of meetings of up to 20,000 were held before the state ordered the Enniskillen Dragoons into Dunfermline, where they would remain garrisoned for the next three years.

In Dundee, thousands gathered on 22 August 1842 at the Magdalen Yards, down by the riverside. A huge crowd of mainly young men and women then set off on a hunger march into the countryside, tearing up turnip fields and raiding farmhouses for food. When they arrived in the weaving town of Forfar, 2,000 locals joined them for a mass rally at Market Muir, where Station Park, the home of Forfar Athletic FC, now stands. As they dispersed, they were ambushed by police, and dozens carted off to the local jail.

In these grim times, Glasgow became a city of destitution. The Reverend William Hill, the founding editor of the *Northern Star*, came to town and could scarcely believe his eyes. He opined that its horrors could be only be remedied by razing the city to the ground. 'Of all the corruption and misery it has ever been my lot to visit surely Glasgow is the worst,' he wrote. 'I have seen London, Manchester, Birmingham and Leeds, and other great hives of human crime and human agony; but for undisguised profligacy, offensive brutality, squalid wretchedness and unbearable filth, Glasgow, to my mind, excels them all... I know of no adequate remedy for the horrors of Glasgow but that of blocking it up at one extremity and setting fire to it at the other.'

Soon, Chartism had run out of cash, ideas, and steam. Unable to move forward, it dissolved into a battleground of feuding factions, while Feargus O'Connor's mental and physical health disintegrated. The movement had already, for all intents and purposes, collapsed in Scotland long before then. There was no money to fund organisers, newspapers, conferences, rallies. Nor, in the midst of mass semi-starvation, was there much political will left to fight. The days of hope had turned into the days of desolation.

The social and economic changes ushered in by the Glorious Revolution followed by the Act of Union had benefited only the elite of Scottish society.

The upper classes had grown fabulously wealthy by any previous historical standards, and the well-to-do middle classes had expanded greatly in numbers. Life for the other 90 per cent had also changed over the previous 50 years, but not for the better. Many had been driven off the land by starvation and clearance. There had been nothing romantic about rural drudgery and a subsistence existence in a harsh climate. But there had at least been stability, community and security, and an almost spiritual connection with land and nature. The journey from the peasantry to the proletariat had been akin to departing Purgatory, only to enter Hell.

Their dwellings were squalid, overcrowded, violent and disease-ridden, the nineteenth century shanty towns of the north. Their workplaces were black canyons of back-breaking toil deep underground, or sweatshop mills where exhausted men, women and children worked 14-hour days, six days a week. Or they sought escape and adventure by joining the armed forces on the killing fields of Europe, where many ended up physically crippled, psychologically traumatised, or thrown, stone cold, into unmarked graves.

Even in the best of times, life for the masses was harsh. But the 1840s were the worst of times. And there was no light at the end of the tunnel.

20

CELTIC CONNECTIONS

Famine exodus

Exactly a century after Culloden came another Celtic catastrophe.

Britain was already an industrial powerhouse with an empire covering millions of square miles of territory, stretching from the frozen wastelands of northern Canada to the tropical islands of the Caribbean and out to the Indian sub-continent. But the United Kingdom of Great Britain and Ireland, as it was now called, was a grossly unbalanced state. The capital was awash with wealth, and in the provinces a new class of industrialists were growing richer by the day. But the marginal lands of Ireland, Wales and Scotland had been left behind.

Ireland, by now, was a full partner in the imperial union, with all the privileges that was supposed to bestow. Yet most of the country was mired in squalor. Beyond the part-fertile and part-industrialised north-east corner, the old Anglo-Irish feudal aristocracy continued to hold sway. To maximise their rents, they squeezed their tenants onto plots of land so small, the only way they could survive was to grow nothing but potatoes. These could be cultivated even on thin, meagre soil, were highly nutritious and stored well through the winter months. And they were guaranteed to produce a high yield per acre. But trouble was afoot. The first warning signs appeared in the Low Countries, during the spring of 1845, when the potato crop failed due to an infestation. By the autumn of that year, the blight had reached Ireland.

In late 1846, the first bodies were discovered in the south west of Ireland – three labourers were found on three different roadsides near Skibereen in County Cork, then a mother and her three young children in the same area. All had died of malnutrition.

All told, one million people starved to death as a result of the failed potato harvest, many already homeless after being evicted for being unable to pay their rent. Millions more boarded the 'famine boats' to Glasgow and Liverpool, or the coffin ships to North America, where passengers would be packed shoulder-to-shoulder, standing room only, starving, thirsty, and vulnerable to disease. Many died before they reached their destination.

The Great Famine was a natural disaster, like the earthquakes, hurricanes and tsunamis we are familiar with today. But its magnitude was multiplied umpteen times over by a combination of political neglect and commercial imperative.

The Prime Minister, Lord Russell, was a Whig, and therefore on the marginally more progressive wing of the British ruling elite. But he was also a staunch defender of free market forces and refused to intervene to stop the carnage. His Lord Lieutenant in Dublin Castle, Charles Edward Trevelyan, insisted that corn and other cereals produced in Ireland should be sold at market prices, not distributed free to the starving multitudes.

Huge quantities of porter, Guinness and whiskey – all brewed and distilled with grain – were shipped across the sea to England. Other ships carried butter, beans, onions, peas, rabbits, salmon, oysters, herring and honey. Meanwhile, the desperate Irish population tried to stay alive by eating grass, tree bark, ferns and seaweed.

The failure of the British Government to act was partly motivated by anti-Irish and anti-Catholic bigotry. Had the famine occurred in Kent or Norfolk, it is hard to imagine that free market dogma would have been allowed to stand in the way of famine relief. But this was Ireland, whose mutinous, treacherous people deserved everything that the good Lord threw at them. In the early days of the famine, the pro-Whig *Times* newspaper explicitly welcomed the famine and looked forward to a time when 'a Celt will soon be as rare on the banks of the Shannon as the red man on the banks of Manhattan', as quoted in *The Famine Plot: England's Role in Ireland's Greatest Tragedy* by Tim Pat Coogan.

But neither did London provide a single penny of famine relief to alleviate conditions in another part of the state, where families were reported to be living on boiled nettles and grass. The north west of Scotland and the Hebrides was like Ireland in microcosm. Its religion was different, but its language and culture were similar. Since the fertile glens had been cleared to make way for sheep, its population subsisted on small strips of land around the coast where the soil was thin and potato was the staple crop. One Church of Scotland minister, Norman MacLeod, described the heart-rending scene on a beach in Benbecula in 1847, where the whole population had gathered to forage for cockles:

> 'I never witnessed such countenances: starvation on many faces; the children with their melancholy looks, big-looking knees, shrivelled legs, hollow eyes, swollen-like bellies. God help them, I never did witness such wretchedness.'

The tragedy of the Hebrides and the north-west, however, was eclipsed by the sheer horror of what was happening in Ireland. The scale was different – in Ireland, the potato crop supported an overwhelmingly rural society of eight million people – 40 times greater than the total population of the Highlands. Scotland was also a more developed country, an industrial society with an urban population growing faster than anywhere else in Europe.

By this time the national Church of Scotland had been split, following the Great Disruption of 1843. The roots of the schism were political rather than theological. The breakaway Free Church had rebelled against the Westminster Patronage Act of 1714, which entitled wealthy patrons to install ministers of their choice, and this new anti-landlord church stood for the right of congregations to take control of the own parishes. During the famine years, the Free Church spearheaded the famine relief effort, even at one stage deploying a ship, the *Breadalbane*, to deliver food aid to the west coast and islands. It is no accident that those hardline Presbyterian sects that claim to be the legitimate descendants of the original Free Church remain strongest in the areas that suffered most during the famine years.

Famine relief helped keep the population of the north-west alive, but it could not prevent some Highland landowners using the rent arrears of their tenants as an excuse to launch a new wave of clearances. Over the next ten years, the western Highlands and Hebrides would lose one-third of its population, who left poignant memorials in the form of untold numbers of ruined townships whose gable ends and shattered walls are still visible today, all but consumed by the wilderness around them.

In his memoirs, the eminent Edinburgh geologist Archibald Geikie described an incident on Skye that remained engraved on his memory for 50 years:

> 'As I was returning from my ramble, a strange wailing sound reached my ears at intervals from the breeze to the west. I could see a long and motley procession winding along the road that led north from Suisnish... There were old men and women, too feeble to walk, who were placed in carts; the younger members of the community on foot were carrying their bundles of clothes and household effects, while their children, with looks of alarm, walked alongside. When they set forth once more, a cry of grief went up to heaven, the long plaintive wail, like a funeral coronach, was resumed... the sound seemed to echo through the

wide valley of Strath in one prolonged note of desolation. The people were being shipped to Canada.'

The small community was on its way from Suisnish in the west of the island to Broadford, from where they would embark on a voyage across the Atlantic. The landowner's agent explained that the evictions were necessary for the welfare of the souls of the tenants, because they lived too far from the church. This was one of a number of mass evictions carried out on Skye, Harris, Barra, and the Uists in the aftermath of famine. Many perished on the six-week voyage from the Celtic wastelands of Ireland and north-west Scotland.

Life on the 'coffin ships' is brought to vivid life in the novel *Entry Island* by Peter May, which is partly based on the Hebridean clearances. By the time a famine ship from Glasgow reaches the mouth of the St Lawrence River, almost one-fifth of the passengers have died of fever, their bodies thrown overboard to feed the sharks. Then they reach 'hell on earth' – the immigration control centre on Grosse Ile, where a 50-foot high Celtic Cross was erected in 1909 by the Ancient Order of Hibernians to commemorate 6,000 Irish refugees who perished *en route* to the island. There the doctor tells the main character: 'I've seen things that no man should see. I've seen suffering that no human being should have to endure. I used to be a religious man, son. But if there's a God, he's abandoned us long ago.'

The land that time forgot

In 1839, William Scrope, a Lincolnshire landowner, published a book called *The Art of Deerstalking*, after spending a few days with a rifle in his hand on the Duke of Atholl's estate in Highland Perthshire. For those who like that kind of thing, it was an entertaining read:

'Your consummate deer-stalker should not only be able to run like an antelope, and breathe like the trade winds, but should also be enriched with various other undeniable qualifications. As, for instance, he should be able to run in a stooping position, at a greyhound pace, with his back parallel to the ground, and his face within an inch of it, for miles together.'

He advised against sleep, and suggested that having a full head of hair was a serious disadvantage as it may fall over the eyes just as he had the animal in his sights:

> 'I leave it to a deer-stalker's own good sense to consider whether it would not be infinitely better for him to shave the crown of his head at once... A man so shorn, with the addition of a little bog earth rubbed scientifically over the crown of his head, would be an absolute Ulysses on the moor, and perfectly invincible.'

If Nick Hornby's 1992 best-seller *Fever Pitch* was responsible for making football fashionable among the metropolitan middle classes, it was as nothing to the impact that *The Art of Deerstalking* had on the Victorian upper classes. Overnight, everyone who was anyone in high society longed to pursue a magnificent stag across a Highland hillside. Those bitten by the bug included Prince Albert, the German first cousin, and husband, of Queen Victoria. Hardly renowned for his physical prowess – though he did have a receding hairline – he nonetheless took to the pastime like a red deer takes to the mountain-tops when pursued by bald men with guns.

With the royal seal of approval, the ancient sport of kings and chiefs took off, not just among the gentry, but also within the ranks of the *nouveau riche*, the urban merchants and manufacturers of the day. By this time, the Scottish Highlands had undergone something of a makeover, at least in the eyes of those whose only knowledge of the region was through the novels of Walter Scott. In 1822, the literary superstar had pulled off one of the PR coups of the century by enticing King George IV to Edinburgh for two weeks of royal pageantry. It was the first time in 170 years that any monarch had set foot in Scotland. As an added twist, Scott – a borderer who combined Tory unionism with a kind of anthropological fascination with the Highlands – used the occasion to carry out one of the most audacious rebranding exercises ever attempted. He dressed up the Hanoverian king, whose predecessors had outlawed highland dress, in a bright red, Royal Stewart kilt. The garment itself bore resemblance to the plaid that had been banned after Culloden, though the pattern was pure invention, loosely inspired by the colourful plant dyes traditionally used in the Highlands to create distinctive tartans.

With Culloden now a hazy memory, it was safe to indulge in this kind of patronising pastiche, a forerunner of the modern St Patrick's Day Parade in New York, with its shillelaghs and leprechaun hats, or the BBC's *Black and White Minstrel Show* of the 1960s and '70s. Following the two-week extravaganza, the Anglo-Scottish ruling elite in Edinburgh went on to create a synthetic Highland culture, stripped of the Gaelic language, which glorified the military exploits of Scottish regiments such as the Black Watch, and reinvented tartan as a symbol of British unionism.

A century on from the Jacobite Rebellion, Highlanders were no longer despised as the lawless and dangerous underclass of Scotland, but admired as a brave and steadfast warrior race spearheading the expansion of the British empire. They were the forerunners of the Gurkhas, who were incorporated into the British Army after the Nepalese resistance fighters inflicted heavy casualties upon their imperial invaders in 1815. The British Army officer John Shipp could have been referring to the Highlanders of 70 years earlier when he wrote of the Gurkhas: 'I never saw more steadiness or bravery exhibited in my life. Run they would not, and of death they seemed to have no fear, though their comrades were falling thick around them'.

Queen Victoria had come to the throne enthralled by this glamorous version of Highland history. In 1842, as colliers in Lanarkshire and millworkers in Dundee tore up turnip fields to stave off starvation, she travelled from Dunkeld to Taymouth, accompanied by 656 horsemen, at the invitation of Lord Breadalbane. There she was greeted with hilltop bonfires, cheering crowds, fireworks, gun salutes, pipe bands, Highland dancers and a flotilla of boats on the Tay. The welcome, she wrote in her diary, 'altogether formed one of the finest scenes imaginable. It seemed as if a great chieftain in olden feudal times was receiving his sovereign. It was princely and romantic'.

One of her favourite paintings was Edward Landseer's *The Monarch of the Glen*: a kitsch depiction of a stag, with marvellous 12-point antlers, surveying his kingdom of swirling mist and mountain peak, and symbolising, according to the National Museum of Scotland, 'the glory of Victorian Britain at the height of the Empire'. Victoria even took to reciting a poem by the subversive republican, Robert Burns.

'My heart's in the Highlands, my heart is not here,
My heart's in the Highlands, a-chasing the deer;
Chasing the wild-deer, and following the roe,
My heart's in the Highlands, wherever I go'.

As the great famine ravaged Ireland and the West Highlands, Victoria and Albert took over the Balmoral Estate, bringing in the builders to construct a sumptuous castle, as incongruous in the Highlands as her father's kilt had been on the streets of Edinburgh.

By this time, the sheep bonanza was over. Some people had piled up huge fortunes, but the landscape was grazed bare, and as transportation improved, the good times were finally washed away by a monsoon of cheaper, better quality wool and mutton from the New World. This could have provided an opportunity for the soil to recover, the trees to grow, and ecosystems to revitalize. Instead, the Highlands became the playgrounds of the rich.

Deer forests – which despite their name are bare, treeless landscapes – spread like lava after a volcanic eruption across the landscape. In the drier climate and thicker heather of the eastern Highlands, grouse moors became the favourite autumn hang-outs of the wealthy and their hangers-on. In 1839, there had been 28 sporting estates in the north of Scotland. By the end of the century, there were five times as many. The Duke and Countess of Sutherland, Walter Scott, William Strope, Queen Victoria, Prince Albert and various others all played a part in the expropriation of one third of Scotland's territory by the southern elites for their own entertainment.

This land grab was assisted by the transport revolution. In 1840, Britain's train network had consisted of a scattering of disjointed tracks. Eight years later, the railways reached Perth, and were then extended, first to Dunkeld where the Highlands begin, then to Inverness. By 1900, it was possible to take the train from the south coast of England to the Great Glen and beyond, all the way to the Pentland Firth.

Mill owners, coal barons, shipbuilding magnates, brewing tycoons – all hit the north for their holiday jaunts, paying big money to indulge in this new form of conspicuous consumption. Then they began buying up great tracts of land. The Highland sporting estate was the nineteenth century must-have, akin to today's yearning for a private helicopter or a luxury yacht. As the modern ecologist John Lister-Kaye puts it, 'Everybody who was anybody in 1850 wanted a Highland sporting estate. There were plenty of takers in the world of burgeoning industrial capitalism – an emergent class of nouveau riche, redolent with competitive snobbery, desperate to emulate a traditional land-owning aristocracy.'

Back in the Victorian era, few of those locals who had survived the Clearances were complaining. This luxury leisure industry did bring prosperity of sorts. It needed stalkers, ghillies, grouse-beaters, gamekeepers, pony boys, kennel boys and servants. The rich man's hobby also required intensive labour to create stalkers' tracks and dry-stone dykes, and it generated further employment in transport and tweed manufacture. But it also established an unhealthy, colonial relationship between the sporting elite and the indigenous population. As right-wing historian Michael Fry notes, 'the men transforming the wide moorlands were most of them English, with Scots appearing in their company usually as gamekeepers and beaters'.

Despite the spin-off economic benefits for the few, the upshot was a social and ecological catastrophe. The rise of the sporting estate drove Highland land values up to absurd levels, ensuring that ownership would remain concentrated in the hands of a super-rich elite. Today, an average Highland estate changes hands for between £5-£10 million, while Scotland is left with the most unequal distribution of land in the Western world, with half its land owned by just 432 individuals – mostly from outside the country. Unsustainably high deer numbers in the north and west, together with management of much of the eastern and southern Highlands for the sole purpose of breeding grouse, has left the landscape desolate.

Had nature been allowed to flourish, native woodland would by now have returned to the hillsides, along with a thriving Scandinavian-style forest economy, yielding a great diversity of wood, vegetable and animal products, and a hospitable environment in which people could live, work and seek respite from urban life. Instead, much of Scotland's landmass was frozen in time, while the once vibrant culture of the north faded, its language reduced to a whisper. The dying ecology, the warped pattern of land-ownership, the poverty of the people, all combined to drive the indigenous population out. They took with them their songs, music, stories and poetry. Back home, Gaelic was discouraged, in schools and in families, as an embarrassing relic of the past, and more compellingly as an obstacle to employment and success in the cities of the south. By the end of the century, there would be more Gaelic speakers in the Canadian province of Nova Scotia than in the whole of Scotland.

For over a century, under direct Westminster rule, the Highlands became the land that time forgot. Only after the Scottish Parliament was established did change begin. Land reform gave communities, for the first time, the right to buy the land they lived on. The right to roam was enshrined in law, making Scotland a model of open, public access that is the envy of much of Europe.

The feudal tenure of land ownership was finally abolished in 2004, more than 200 years after the Enlightenment.

After generation upon generation of repression and marginalisation, Gaelic, the language of much of Scotland's landscape, is undergoing a revival – although it is still stigmatised by some Scots. When the Gaelic TV channel BBC Alba was launched in 2008, the fervently unionist politician George Galloway made clear his loathing and contempt for a culture that had been driven to the verge of extinction by a coalition of feudal landowners and a right-wing imperial state. 'Hoots mon, Gaels have picked the pockets of the taxpayer again and Angus Og has made off with millions with the start of a new Gaelic TV station,' he wrote in his *Daily Record* column. 'If it's dying, why dig it up again… the rest of us, by a stroke of luck, are in possession of a tongue worth the weight of Ben Nevis in gold. The English language is our greatest asset and the government spends far too little spreading it even wider.'

For several generations, Catalan too was dying, and Basque, under General Franco, Spain's twentieth-century Butcher of Culloden. Fortunately, the progressive forces prevailed, and these languages are once again the native tongues of those under 30 years old.

Over the past century, Europe has lived through world wars, revolutions, counter-revolutions, general strikes, national break-ups, technological transformation, and seismic cultural and social change. During that time, Scotland has been governed by Liberals, Tories, Labour, coalitions and, more recently, the Scottish National Party. And through it all, the Victorian pattern of concentrated land ownership and ecological destruction has somehow survived, with more than 300 sporting estates covering at least 40 per cent of the total land area of the Highlands and Islands to this day.

The orange and the green

As the Highlands were being converted into an exclusive upper-class playground, legions of hungry, poverty-stricken refugees continued to pour into the central belt from the north and west, turning Glasgow into the biggest and most concentrated Celtic stronghold in the world, Dublin apart. Thousands of these new migrants bore familiar Scottish clan names: MacDonald, MacLeod, MacLean, Campbell, MacNeill, Stewart. But many more had less familiar Gaelic names: O'Donnell, Gallagher, McGonigle and Sweeney, to cite but a few.

Unlike Scotland, Ireland had never managed to establish itself in medieval times as a unified national kingdom. Lacking the strength of a fully-fledged state it had always been more vulnerable to predatory colonisation by successive English monarchs. Its refusal to join the Reformation was both a consequence of the country's national oppression by Protestant England, and a cause of its further persecution in the centuries to come. In an era of hysterical antipathy to continental popery, its Catholic majority would become, like black South Africans under apartheid, despised, persecuted and stripped of all human rights. Even Presbyterians in the north, unlike their co-religionists in Scotland, had suffered a degree of discrimination under the Penal Laws, thanks to William of Orange. Meanwhile, Ireland's industries were faltering; indeed, the only growth industries were poverty, homelessness, and starvation.

But Scotland had another decisive advantage over Ireland. In *Labour and Irish History*, the Scots-born Irish socialist James Connolly posed the question, 'Why had Scottish manufacturing advanced while that of Ireland had decayed?' His answer: 'Because Scotland possessed a native coal supply and every facility for industrial pursuits which Ireland lacked.' Across the Lowlands, from Ayrshire in the west to the Lothians and Fife in the east, a continuous belt of 'black stones' ran deep below the soil, extending far out under the Firth of Forth. And there was iron ore under the ground too, especially in Lanarkshire and Ayrshire. These two raw materials, along with the great river that flowed from the hills of South Lanarkshire to the Atlantic Ocean, would turn Clydeside into the heavy engineering centre of the world in the late nineteenth and early twentieth centuries.

Most of the desperate thousands came from the north-west of Ireland, from Mayo, Sligo, Derry, and above all from Donegal, a county with strong connections to Glasgow and the west of Scotland to this day. Their story was told with eloquence and humanity in the novel *Children of the Dead End* by Patrick McGill, who worked on the railways and the Blackwater Dam in Lochaber. In his follow-up novel, *The Rat Pit*, the Donegal-born navvy-poet exposed the harrowing conditions of destitute young Irish women through the eyes of Norah Ryan, driven to backstreet prostitution to keep alive her illegitimate child.

They came at just the right time for the owners of capital. Nineteenth century Scotland was an economic Tartan Tiger – and the industrial boom relied heavily on Gaels from the Highlands, and especially from Ireland. These new migrants were able and prepared to carry out the most difficult, dirty and dangerous work imaginable. They laid pipelines and railway tracks. They built tunnels, roads, bridges, quarries, canals, harbours, aqueducts and reservoirs. And they formed a huge part of the colossal underground army digging out the fuel that powered the industrial revolution – coal.

They had brought with them the despised old-time religion, which to contemporary Lowland Scots appeared akin to sorcery. The religious history of Scotland, from the conflict between John Knox and Mary Queen of Scots, through the violent upheavals of the Covenanting years, to the religious affiliation of Charles Edward Stuart, had all contributed to anti-Catholic sectarianism. This was overlaid with anti-Irish racism, which in turn was rooted in English and British imperial history. As a general rule of empire, those who resist and fight back against oppression are always detested by the ruling classes, whose cultural power – or hegemony, to use the word coined by the Italian Marxist Antonio Gramsci – pervades the rest of society. The Irish had dared to resist colonialism, and had refused to knuckle under to Anglicisation. They were the Palestinians of the nineteenth century, feared and vilified by their oppressors.

Scotland generally had a better relationship with the Irish nation than England. Well into the nineteenth century, mainstream newspapers would regularly refer to Ireland as 'the sister country'. The Gaels of the Scottish Highlands had a linguistic and cultural affinity with rural Catholic Ireland, while the Lowlands had strong connections with the Presbyterian north-eastern part of the island. Centuries of migration back and forth across the North Channel had reinforced that friendship, and in the late eighteenth and early nineteenth centuries, there had been a high degree of overlap between Irish and Scottish radicalism. The development of anti-Irish sentiment in Scotland had risen hand-in-hand with that of North British identity, adopted by institutions such as the Church of Scotland and newspapers such as *The Scotsman* and *Glasgow Herald*. As a general rule – although there were a few exceptions – those who fought for Scotland's national rights in the nineteenth century were sympathetic to Ireland's struggle for Home Rule and independence, while those who stood for a strong British union were hostile.

Against that wider background, the colossal waves of migration from rural Ireland into urban Scotland brought the same tensions and conflict that large-scale immigration generates to this day. In the May 2014 European elections, hysteria over immigration from Eastern Europe propelled the rabidly right-wing United Kingdom Independence Party (UKIP) into first place across England. Yet in the previous 12 months, Eastern European immigration had averaged just 770 immigrants per week into a state with a population of over 60 million inhabitants. In the first four months of 1848, 42,860 people from Ireland arrived in Glasgow – a rate of 2,500 a week into a city of less than half a million.

Apart from Glasgow, the other Mecca for Irish immigrants was Lanarkshire, especially Monklands – the most heavily industrialised parish in Scotland at that time, with hundreds of coal and ironstone pits, and 50 blast furnaces. It also had the added attraction of 330 public houses – one for every 20 adult males. By 1850, half the mining workforce in the district were first or second generation Irish, and the town of Coatbridge was already well on its way to earning the nickname 'Little Ireland'.

For people who had lived for generations on the land, the dark, dangerous collieries must have seemed like a vision of hell. But these were desperate, half-starved peasants with no possessions other than the clothes they stood up in. And they were easy prey for employers looking to drive down wages. One coal owner, James Baird, sent teams of recruiting agents to the depths of rural Ireland to hire labour for his colliery at Gartsherrie, now part of Coatbridge. Bold as brass, he then stood, and was elected, as Tory MP for Falkirk Burghs on a sectarian, anti-Catholic platform. Other employers worked hard to ensure their workforce was divided by religion or nationality as an insurance policy against collective organisation.

Bigotry ran deep in these early days of industrial society, even among the most progressive sections of the embryonic labour movement. In his book, *Conditions of the Working Class in England* – published in 1845, just before the famine – the great political philosopher Friedrich Engels, Karl Marx's right-hand man, had written:

> 'These Irishmen who migrate for fourpence to England, on the deck of a steamship on which they are often packed like cattle, insinuate themselves everywhere. The worst dwellings are good enough for them; their clothing causes them little trouble, so long as it holds together by a single thread; shoes they know not; their food consists of potatoes and potatoes only; whatever they earn beyond these needs they spend upon drink. What does such a race want

with high wages? The worst quarters of all the large towns are inhabited by Irishmen... Filth and drunkenness, too, they have brought with them. The lack of cleanliness, which is not so injurious in the country, where population is scattered, and which is the Irishman's second nature, becomes terrifying and gravely dangerous through its concentration here in the great cities... The Irishman is unaccustomed to the presence of furniture; a heap of straw, a few rags, utterly beyond use as clothing, suffice for his nightly couch. A piece of wood, a broken chair, an old chest for a table, more he needs not; a tea-kettle, a few pots and dishes, equip his kitchen, which is also his sleeping and living room... Drink is the only thing which makes the Irishman's life worth having, drink and his cheery care-free temperament; so he revels in drink to the point of the most bestial drunkenness... which places him but little above the savage.'

The prejudice that leaps forth from this passage is truly shocking when judged from the vantage point of the twenty-first century. Anyone publishing such a vituperative rant against any nationality today would be charged with racially aggravated breach of the peace. As it happens, Engels later changed his position, radically. By 1848, he was arguing that the struggle for democracy in Britain would be accelerated by the involvement of 'two million brave and ardent Irish'. And after completing a tour of Ireland in 1856, he became a fervent supporter of the struggle for Irish freedom. Nonetheless, Engels' earlier outburst provides a glimpse of the deep-rooted anti-Irish racism that infected Anglo-Saxon society, even amongst the most progressive fighters for social justice.

In Scotland, discord was complicated further by the presence of a sizeable community of Ulster Protestants. They made up between one-quarter and one-third of the total Irish-born population, and became the backbone of the Orange Order in west-central Scotland. Even into the twentieth century, the movement in Scotland was composed primarily of first or second generation Ulster Protestants. In one of the many mocking ironies that weave their way through Scots-Irish sectarian history, the Loyal Orange Order was originally formed by Church of Ireland Protestants hostile to Presbyterianism, and was rooted in the same Episcopalian religious tradition as the Highland Jacobite clans.

Most of the sectarian strife in nineteenth century Scotland seems to have been confined to the two rival camps within the Irish immigrant population. The most violent episode of all, the Partick Riots, erupted in 1875 when Orangemen attacked Catholics marching homewards along Dumbarton Road towards Clydebank after attending a huge celebration in Glasgow Green to mark the centenary of Daniel O'Connell's birthday in August 1875. For three days, the area around Partick Cross was turned into a battleground involving many hundreds on both sides. When it was all over, 70 people appeared in Partick Burgh Court to face the music. The *Glasgow Herald* expressed relief at the fact that all the combatants were Irish rather than Scottish, while the *Daily Mail* reported that the prisoners – all sporting black eyes and wearing bloodstained garments – were in 'quite a hilarious mood, endeavouring to crack jokes with one another and even with their custodians'.

This was as about bad as it got in Glasgow, and as the Scots-Irish author John Burrowes observed in *Irish: The Remarkable Saga of a Nation and a City*, it was nothing like the widespread disturbances that would convulse Belfast and Derry. The Orange Order, while able to mobilise large numbers on its annual July parade, was never as strong on Clydeside as its fearsome reputation suggests. At its peak, in the middle of the twentieth century, less than 2 per cent of Glasgow's Protestant adult male population were members of the Orange Order, compared to 7 per cent in Toronto, and 16 per cent in Belfast.

Nor was there ever the strict segregation of the population into religious ghettos as in Northern Ireland. Areas associated with Orangeism, such as Bridgeton and Govan, always had a sizeable Catholic population too, while traditional Irish areas, including the Gorbals, Calton and Anderston, were also home to large numbers of Protestants. More than 23 per cent of heads of households in Govan in 1891 were Irish-born, almost all working as unskilled labourers in the burgh's docks and shipyards.

Discrimination against Catholics in employment would persist late into the twentieth century. In the Clydeside shipyards, which by the late nineteenth century were launching a third of the world's tonnage from a dozen giant yards, the skilled trades – carpenters, boilermakers, engineers, fitters, shipwrights – were effectively reserved for Lowland Scots. That has led some historians to assert, falsely, that the Clyde shipyards were Protestant-only. That seems to have been true of the shipyard opened in 1912 by Belfast-based Harland and Wolff, but in all other yards, Irish Catholics and Highlanders worked as unskilled labourers and tended to dominate the crucial 'black squads'. These were the teams responsible for the dirty and dangerous job of riveting together sections of the iron and steel hull. The riveters themselves were respected across all trades for their bravery, strength and stamina, and, where called for, trade union militancy.

In *Glasgow – The Uneasy Peace: Religious Tension in Modern Scotland*, Tom Gallagher suggests that the existence of skilled trades helped to reduce religious tension in Glasgow, compared to Liverpool, where Irish immigrants were pitted against each other, in direct competition for the same unskilled and semi-skilled jobs. The phenomenal growth of shipbuilding and its numerous supply industries on Clydeside allowed native Lowland Scots to become upwardly mobile, leaving the Irish migrants to take on the casual, unskilled heavy labouring jobs in the docks, the building industry, the iron foundries and the shipyards that no-one else wanted. Far from throwing native Scots out of work, the arrival of the Irish filled a crucial gap in the labour market, and played an indispensable role in the rise of Glasgow to become the powerhouse of the Scottish economy and the heavy engineering capital of the world.

Mass emigration from Ireland would change Scotland profoundly in other ways too. The immigrants were physically indistinguishable from the native population, and as a result of the steep decline of the Irish tongue following the 1801 Act of Union, they spoke mainly the same language, except with a different accent. Yet in a multitude of other ways, they made their presence felt, from the Catholic Churches that would become prominent local landmarks in 200 parishes in the west of Scotland alone, to the Orange marches with their vivid banners and booming drums.

The Catholic Irish even founded their own football clubs, three of which became major Scottish institutions. Hibernian FC in Edinburgh was the first; then came Glasgow Celtic, which became one of the biggest and best supported clubs in the world; then Dundee Hibernian, which later changed its name to Dundee United. They also founded their own schools, which were eventually incorporated into the state education system. In a country where Catholicism had once been reduced to a few thousand adherents in the remote margins of the West Highlands and the north-east, Catholics would eventually outnumber members of the Church of Scotland in four major local authority areas – Glasgow, North Lanarkshire, Inverclyde and West Dunbartonshire. By the late twentieth century, intermarriage between Catholic and Protestant, once taboo on both sides, accounted for half of all marriages in Glasgow.

Irish emigration helped shape the modern Scottish nation by adding a powerful new strand to the county's fluid, ever-changing national identity. The famine, one of the biggest natural disasters any country had ever known, was a traumatic loss for Ireland. But without that mass migration across the North Channel, Scotland would today be a duller, greyer, more culturally impoverished place.

21

WATER, BLOOD AND ALE

Municipal socialism

In 1848, the English social reformer Edwin Chadwick came to the west of Scotland with a team of investigators. He was shocked by what he saw. 'The condition of the population of Glasgow was the worst we had seen in any part of Great Britain', he wrote in his *Report on the Sanitary Conditions of the Labouring Population.*

Life expectancy in the city was just 27 years, a figure that partly reflected the rampant mortality rate amongst children. Over the whole Clydeside region, dense blankets of black smoke hung permanently over the skyline, blotting out daylight and destroying the respiratory systems of those with no escape route to the suburbs. The water supply, pumped from the River Clyde by two private companies, then distributed to a couple of dozen public wells where people queued with buckets day and night, was contaminated with raw sewage and poisonous chemicals.

For the get-rich-quick private entrepreneurs, the urban lower classes were expendable. They were the sheep of the Lowlands – there simply to make money for their masters. As for the politicians who controlled the British state from their elegant townhouses in London, Clydeside might as well have been on the dark side of the moon.

In 1848, a cholera epidemic broke out. Within a year, it had spread from the slums into the more prosperous parts of the city, and over 4,000 people perished. Amid public fury against the private water companies, an idea emerged that was startling in its audacity and towering in its vision. The plan was to create a 30-mile underground aqueduct, stretching from Loch Katrine in the Trossachs to the outskirts of Glasgow, capable of transporting 50 million gallons of fresh water daily over mountain and moorland to be piped into every home in the city.

It was bitterly controversial. The two private water companies who had a monopoly on the city's water supply went on the warpath. Landowners in the Trossachs denounced what they called the 'robbery' of their land and water.

Wealthy Glasgow property owners objected to paying higher property taxes to fund the project, and warned that it would bankrupt the city. Even the Admiralty stuck their oar in, claiming the scheme would divert water from the River Forth and make it unnavigable.

Pragmatically, the council offered generous compensation packages to neutralise the opposition. The two failed private water companies received £800,000 over 30 years – in today's money, the equivalent of a rather handsome £70 million. The two major landowners along the route of the aqueduct – the Duke of Montrose and the Earl of Ancaster – received over £100,000 between them. And to placate the city's disgruntled property owners, the council promised to reduce the proposed levy on the rates by two thirds. With the most powerful opponents of the project effectively bought off, all talk of impending doom ceased. The opposition in the council was routed, and on 12 July 1855, the prosaically named Glasgow Corporation Water Works Act received royal assent in parliament. The monumental construction got underway.

The west side of Loch Katrine, where the aqueduct would begin, was well-nigh inaccessible, with few dwellings and no roads. To accommodate the 3,000-strong army of navvies, new villages of timber and mud sprang up along the shores of Lochs Katrine, Arklet, Ard and Lomond. The biggest of these, at the head of Loch Chon, had grocers' shops, reading rooms, a schoolhouse, and a church. The constant blasting of gunpowder in the surrounding hills led the inhabitants to nickname their new town Sebastopol, after the famous battle of the Crimean War.

Meanwhile, in the factories and workshops of the Lowlands, mechanics, iron moulders and blacksmiths fashioned the pipes, tubes, troughs, beams and girders that would support the elaborate structure. Eighty tunnels were blasted under the mountains, 25 bridges of iron and masonry constructed, and a new reservoir excavated at Mugdock, on the northern outskirts of Glasgow. On 14 October 1859, the city bells rang out in joyous celebration of the new dawn. In Edinburgh and Stirling, cannons roared their approval from the castle battlements. But the main stage was the lonely, eight-mile stretch of water in the wild, mountainous Trossachs, where swirling grey mists merged with soft Highland rain. As Queen Victoria turned on the tap, 400 members of the Glasgow Volunteer Rifle Corps fired off a royal salute, the volley shattering every window of the lochside cottage where she had been due to spend the night. As the sluice gates opened, the crystal clear water began its long journey south, through an 800-mile labyrinth of underground pipes, into every home in the city.

For the dropped-jaw Victorians, the new Loch Katrine Waterworks was the eighth wonder of the world. Engineers and scientists around the world hailed the structure as the finest feat of engineering since the Roman Empire. Health professionals would later declare it one of the great public health achievements of the industrial age. When a new cholera outbreak swept Britain in 1866, Glasgow escaped almost unscathed, with only 53 deaths compared to thousands elsewhere. Meanwhile, the city itself, far from descending into bankruptcy, rose to become one of the greatest industrial cities the world had ever seen, its prosperity underpinned by the fresh mountain water cascading into the city.

While all this had been going on, the private profiteers were nowhere to be seen. Nor was the Westminster Government, other than to rubber-stamp an Act of Parliament allowing the scheme to go ahead. Loch Katrine had been a triumph of social values over those of the free market, and of localism over centralism. This was a public enterprise, its aim not to make profits for shareholders, but to fight disease and extend the lifespan of ordinary people. And it was driven, not by the British state, but by local politicians – not least the Lord Provost of Glasgow, whose achievement is commemorated today by an elaborate architectural landmark in Kelvingrove Park, the Robert Stewart Memorial Fountain.

Inspired by the success of the new public water supply, Glasgow town council went on to launch one new public project after another. In 1867, the city took control of the gas supply, cutting bills by half, and providing free street and tenement lighting. Two years later, anticipating the future NHS, the council built a municipal fever hospital. It built municipal baths, wash-houses, laundry services, markets, slaughterhouses, libraries, art galleries, parks, a tram system and an underground railway. At the turn of the century, it established its own telephone network. The industrialists and merchants may have been adept at making money, and the Westminster politicians expert at waging war and seizing territories, but it was left to local campaigners to raise the quality of life for ordinary people.

Although Glasgow blazed the trail for 'municipal socialism', as it was labelled retrospectively by historians, other urban councils began to follow suit. Ten years after the opening of the Loch Katrine Waterworks, Edinburgh bought out the private company that ran the capital's water supply at a cost of over £500,000, and began to pipe in water from the Moorfoot Hills in Midlothian. Elsewhere, local councils levied rates to finance a range of public services including water, police, lighting, paving, and cleansing.

The reformism of local councils stemmed from the limited electoral reform introduced by the Whigs in 1832. The following year, the Burgh Act of 1833 saw the creation of a proper structure of local government in urban Scotland. Although the working classes continued to be disenfranchised, power at a local level was shifted away from the old elites and into the hands of the professional middle classes. The exception was the countryside, where bands of local landowners would meet as Commissioners of Supply to run the surrounding villages. Because they were also the main ratepayers, they made sure that no money was squandered on such fripperies as public transport, clean water and libraries. But in Scotland's 70 royal burghs, from Wick to Wigtown, including all the big towns and cities, the middle classes were in control. They dominated the local power structures in Scotland, and therefore had effective control over schools, public health, welfare, prisons and asylum boards.

For the British state, one unintended but welcome consequence of strong local government was that it marginalised the national question for a prolonged period. As historian Tom Devine points out, these empowered middle classes 'had no reason to seek parliamentary independence or adopt a nationalism which was hostile to the British state'.

The contrast with Ireland was glaring. There, Westminster had blocked the emergence of elected local authorities, fearing a takeover by radical nationalists. Instead, right up until 1898, each county was administered by a grand jury, composed mainly of landlords appointed by the local judge. Each county was sub-divided into units called baronies, which were run by boards chosen by the county grand jury from among the locality's highest rate-payers. According to historian Catherine Shannon, by 1880, these county grand juries and baronial boards were still overwhelmingly Unionist and Protestant, and thus unrepresentative of the local areas they controlled.

In time, the most enlightened sections of Scottish society began to draw the obvious conclusions. By the law of contrasts, dynamic local government in Scotland had laid bare the inertia and neglect of the remote Westminster parliament, and over the next half century, grievances would fester, fuelled by a sense of nationhood that continued to burn brightly long after the Act of Union had faded from living memory.

'Justice for Scotland'

In 1853, even before the Loch Katrine project had begun, the National Association for the Vindication of Scottish Rights was launched under the slogan 'Justice for Scotland'. A cross-class movement, its President was the Earl of Eglinton, an eccentric Tory lord, obsessed with horse-racing and famous for a medieval jousting tournament he had organised some years previously in the grounds of his Ayrshire castle. It boasted the support of 10 town councils, 17 Lord Provosts, and over 100 academics, as well as some of Scotland's foremost radicals. These included Patrick Dove, a land reform campaigner, and Duncan MacLaren, a Liberal Lord Provost of Edinburgh and husband of Priscilla Bright MacLaren, who would become a founder of the Women's Suffrage Movement in Scotland.

The association complained of lavish spending on the British Army and the Royal Navy, as Britain bolstered its defences against a 'feared' invasion by Russia – a threat as bogus as Saddam Hussein's weapons of mass destruction. It highlighted the fact that only £400,000 of public money was spent in Scotland in 1852, even though revenues raised north of the border totalled £6,164,804. If accurate – and the figures were culled from official parliamentary documents, and never challenged – then for every £100 of revenue raised in Scotland, over £93 went to England.

The organisation also claimed that the Westminster Government had spent £100,000 on a park in London, but had only been prepared to provide £4,000 for postal services in Glasgow. It condemned the Highland Clearances as brutal and anti-social, and attacked Westminster for its failure to provide a penny of famine relief after the failure of the potato crop. And it lamented the fact that the city of Glasgow, with over 300,000 inhabitants, was represented by just two MPs, when Oxford and Cambridge Universities were entitled to two *each*.

It argued for equality within the British state, rather than Home Rule, yet the tone of some of its publications reveals a raging sense of injustice against national oppression:

> 'The past history of England is but a long history of violations of the laws of nations, of honour, of men, and of morality... a mere enumeration of barbarous acts, from the time when Edward poisoned the brothers of Bruce, or since their boasted prince cut to pieces 16,000 unarmed and defenceless French prisoners, down to the cruel massacre of the poor Highlanders after the Battle of Culloden.'

These words, from the Edinburgh Association of the Scottish Rights campaign, does tend to put in historical perspective recent statements by Westminster politicians and London journalists extolling our 'glorious 300 years of shared history'. So too do the contemporaneous editorials carried in local and regional newspapers across Scotland.

'There is no Scotch business tolerated in the House of Commons except what Government may sanction, and that all tends towards Scotland's subjugation', said the *Edinburgh News*, while the Edinburgh *Evening Post* argued that 'Scotland has for a long period of time been systematically treated as a secondary and subordinate portion of the Empire; that her interests have been gradually merged in the wealthier and more populous section of the island, and that there is an apparent design to reduce her to the level of an ordinary province by obliterating all her ancient institutions and assimilating her laws to those of England'. The *Montrose Review* noted that 'from the day that Edward I laid claim to the crown of Scotland to the present day, the cry of English injustice has seldom ceased to reverberate across the land'. The *Elgin Courier* insisted that 'Scotland had never had anything like our fair share of public money; our public boards have been gradually diminishing and have now almost disappeared. And it is felt that when any a Scottish question is before the House, the chances are ten to one that the voice of Scotch representatives is swamped by English members. This inequality of representation is the master grievance of all.'

Over 5,000 people attended a public meeting in Glasgow to launch the movement. Another 2,000 turned out in Edinburgh, where the Earl of Eglinton received thunderous applause for noting that the government of Scotland was 'left to the tender mercies of a lawyer' – the part-time Lord Advocate – while 'the interests of England are well cared for. They have their Prime Ministers, their Lord Presidents, their Board of Trade, their Lords of the Treasury; their colonies; the army, the navy, the post office; and even that very important service, the Duchy of Lancaster [laughter] has generally a place in the Cabinet.'

Almost 150 years after the Act of Union, it would be fair to say that few Scots were bursting with pride and gratitude at being part of what a *Daily Telegraph* journalist recently assured a BBC *Question Time* audience was 'the most successful multicultural experiment in history, which for 300 years has made us wealthier, stronger and envied across the globe for the marvels and wonders and riches we have created together.'

The National Association for the Vindication of Scottish Rights was only seven months old, and on its way to becoming a serious national force. But then history flew off at a tangent, as Britain and France declared war on Russia. The Crimean War had all the ingredients needed to incite mass Union Flag-waving and Rule Britannia-singing jingoism.

It was the first mass media war in history. The invention of the telegraph system and the facsimile machine – invented by a Scot called Alexander Bain – meant that, for the first time ever, reports and images could be sent directly from the battlefield down the wires to press offices in Britain. Newspapers sold in their millions as excited readers queued up to find out the latest twists and turns in the valiant struggle between brave John Bull and the savage Russian Bear. To spice it up further, the press unearthed an unlikely new national heroine – Florence Nightingale, the 'Lady of the Lamp'.

Given the patriotic fervour aroused by dramatic naval battles on the Black Sea or the sensational Siege of Sebastopol, grievances over the diversion of funds from the diocese of Orkney to fund London municipal street-lamps seemed unbearably small-minded, not to say dull. And thus, the nearly mighty National Association for the Vindication of Scottish Rights faded into the dusty archives of history. But the imbalance of power in the United of Kingdom of Great Britain remained. And life at the bottom of the heap, where most people lay suffocating, was becoming ever more desperate.

People of the Abyss

By the end of the century, Britain had fought and won, not only the Crimean War, but the Second Opium War; the Anglo-Persian War; the Indian War of Independence; the Shimonoseki Campaign; the Anglo-Satsuma War; the Bhutan War; the Basuto-Boer War; the British Expedition to Abyssinia; the Red River Rebellion; the Third Anglo-Ashanti War; the Ninth Xhosa War; the Second Anglo-Afghan War; the Anglo-Zulu War; the

Mahdist War; the Ekumeku War; the Benin Expedition; the Tirah Campaign; and the Second Boer War. It had even lost one or two.

Through rivers of blood and mountains of corpses, Britain had marched victoriously onwards through history, collecting new territories like they were postage stamps. On the face of it, as measured by statistics, the Union had fuelled Scotland's now soaring economy. But figures can distort as effectively as words. During most of the twentieth century, the Soviet Union recorded truly sensational growth rates, far exceeding anywhere else on the planet. But these only masked what was a fundamentally a diseased economy.

Scotland in the late nineteenth century may well have been the marvel of economists and industrialists, as Clydeside became the heavy industry capital of the world, but it was a grotesquely unbalanced marvel. The role of a nation state, even in a normal capitalist economy, is to establish and negotiate terms of trade, legislate to determine priorities, create and sustain a balanced domestic market and support non-profitable economic activity. Instead, the Scottish economy was twisted and deformed to meet the needs of the British Empire. From the Clydeside shipyards to the locomotive factories on the north side of Glasgow to the Dundee jute mills, Scotland's great industries were geared not to serve the people, but to supply Britain's imperial markets. And when these markets crashed, as they did with clockwork regularity, the result was depression on a grand scale.

To make matters worse, Scotland's population became one of the most skewed in the whole of Europe. In Richard Gott's 2005 biography, *Hugo Chavez and the Bolivarian Revolution*, he describes how the man who would eventually become President of Venezuela had desperately wanted to stay forever in his home village, but was pulled away 'by a centripetal force dragging him to the city against his will. In rural areas, there was no land to work, just a shack.' In a pattern familiar across Latin American countries, 80 per cent of the population became compressed into a narrow, overcrowded, violent, disease-ridden strip of land, while the rest lay empty. By the dawn of the twentieth century, Scotland was already well down that road.

In 1909, at the height of Britain's imperial power, the American socialist writer Jack London went to the slums of the East End of London and described what he saw in *The People of the Abyss*: 'If this is the best that civilisation can do for the human, then give us howling and naked savagery. Far better to be a people of the wilderness and desert, of the cave and the squatting-place, than to be a people of the machine and the Abyss.' Across much of Scotland, conditions were even worse. While the city of London had 140 people to the square hectare, Glasgow had four times that density, rising to 2,000 people per square hectare in the main inner city. Only 7 per cent of people in England lived in houses with one or two rooms; in Scotland, the figure was 48 per cent. To this day, more than 80 per cent of Scotland's population remains concentrated in just 6 per cent of the land area.

The consequence of that distorted economy, and these swarming slums, would inflict lasting damage. The colossal, long-term, mass unemployment that ravaged the west of Scotland in the 1930s, and again during the 1980s, were part of that legacy. So too is the notoriously hard-drinking culture that persists even today, passed down through the generations from the days when alehouses and cheap beer provided an escape for the adult male population from the squalor of living 8, 10 and 12 to a room. At the start of the twentieth century, 1 in 50 buildings in London were public houses; in Glasgow, the proportion was 1 in 10. Alcohol consumption in Scotland per head was double that of England, even though wages were a third lower. And when two German students visited Scotland in 1904, they described their horror at the 'masses of ragged barefooted, unwashed and uncombed people, evidently injured by the misuse of alcohol, women as well as men, such as we have never met before in our lives.'

The other side of urban overcrowding is rural depopulation, borne of Scotland's ultra-concentrated pattern of land ownership. Recent research by Graeme Morton, Professor of History at the University of Dundee, reveals that in 1872, 93 per cent of Scotland was held in estates of more than 1,000 acres, compared with 78 per cent of Ireland, 61 per cent of Wales and 56 per cent of England. At the time, just 1,500 landowners owned 90 per cent of Scotland. Their stewardship of the land was disastrous, not just for the people, but also for the ecology. Wildlife was exterminated on a grand scale. On one sporting estate, over 2,000 otters were killed by gamekeepers in the last quarter of the nineteenth century, while across the north and east Highlands, pine martens, wildcats, and birds of prey were slaughtered indiscriminately to protect game birds such as grouse, only to be shot down by bored aristocrats with time and money to burn.

Yet landed power in Scotland remained unassailable. Throughout the nineteenth century – and the twentieth century too – every attempt at reducing the power of the great estates ran into a double dead-end. First, land reform in Scotland was hardly a priority for the English-dominated House of Commons. And second, even if the Commons had been interested, and willing, to take on this complex and highly-charged battle, the landowning classes held the trump card – the House of Lords, which they controlled lock, stock and barrel.

Under these conditions of urban squalor and rural decay, overlaid with extreme inequality, political disaffection was inevitable. It expressed itself through several channels. One was the struggle for land reform. Another was the rise of the labour movement. And a third was the cause of Home Rule for Scotland. They would soon overlap, and partially merge, as the red flag, the plough and the Saltire became intertwined in the battle for Scotland's future.

22

STRUGGLE FOR THE SOIL

Bridge over troubled waters

Alexander Robertson, or 'Dundonnachie' as he called himself, started life as an accountant in a bank, later working as a coal and lime merchant supplying the Duke of Atholl's estate in Highland Perthshire. Despite this rather conventional background, he went on to become one Scotland's first great land agitators.

From 1853, at the age of 28, Dundonnachie published a series of inflammatory booklets, including *Extermination of the Scottish Peasantry*, *Our Deer Forests* and *Hanged For the Game Laws*, in which he ripped into the elitism of the sporting estates, denounced the laws against poaching, and lashed into the feudal system of land tenure, which had created 'an incalculable amount of sycophancy and servility among all classes in Scotland'. But it was as leader of a decade-long struggle to abolish tolls on the Thomas Telford bridge over the River Tay at Dunkeld that he became Scotland's most famous, or infamous, rural rebel.

It all began when the local Free Church tried to persuade the Duke of Atholl to allow free passage over the bridge for its congregation to attend religious services. When the landowner refused to even meet a delegation to discuss the matter, a campaign was set up with Dundonnachie as convener. The former accountant then used his skills to build a compelling case for complete abolition of the toll, on the grounds that the Duke had long since recovered the £18,000 cost of building the bridge in the first place.

To force the Duke's hand, Dundonnachie initiated a campaign of direct action. Along with a dozen men, he smashed down the toll-gate and hurled it into the Tay. When a second gate was erected, that too was dismantled. Evidently rather slow on the uptake, the Duke built a third, which speedily entered the silvery waters likewise. Eventually, on 14 July 1868, an entire detachment of the 42nd Light Infantry was mobilised from Perth to sort out the situation once and for all. But they were met by a huge procession of men, women and children from Dunkeld and Birnam, the two communities on either side of the river, who marched back and forth across the bridge defiantly, led by a piper and a brass band. 'There is a state of affairs in Dunkeld which borders on revolution or rebellion', reported the socialist-leaning *Glasgow Sentinel* newspaper.

A couple of years later, as the campaign battled on, Dundonnachie was charged and convicted of 'murmuring against a judge' by accusing the local sheriff of 'assisting the Duke of Atholl to uphold a fraud'. While he served a two-month sentence in Perth Prison, collections were held across Perthshire, in Dundee and as far away as Glasgow to support his family, and 'a considerable amount of money' was raised according to press reports. The description of his liberation in the *Dundee Courier* underlines the scale of local support for the anti-toll struggle:

> 'A large crowd was collected around the prison gates to welcome him. About eight o'clock, the gates were opened, and amid deafening cheers, Dundonnachie stepped out. A procession was then formed, headed by a model [mounted on a pole] of the Dunkeld Bridge and a miniature Dundonnachie smashing the toll gate... [there] followed two pipers, blowing away with all their might... All along the line of procession, the streets were crowded with thousands of enthusiastic spectators... The cheering and shouting again became tremendous.'

The campaign thundered on for 10 years, with meetings held in Glasgow, Edinburgh and even London to rally support. In 1878, the Roads and Bridges Scotland Act was passed by Westminster, phasing out all road and bridge tolls north of the border.

Over the next decade, the centre of rural resistance would shift north and west to the ragged coastlines at the extreme edge of Europe. During the Highland Clearances, a large portion of the native Gaelic people had been banished to these narrow, coastal ribbons of inferior soil called crofts, from the Old English word meaning a small, enclosed field. Initially, the crofting communities had been established to provide a labour force for harvesting and processing seaweed to supply the fledgling kelp industry. By the later decades of the nineteenth century, the industry had been killed off by foreign competition, while the crofters themselves were left to scrape a living from small-scale agriculture combined with fishing, or any other work they could find in these lonely outposts. They were now at the mercy of the landowners, who owned their homes and whatever bits and pieces of arable or grazing land they had access to.

In 1873, a retired Customs and Excise officer from Inverness, John Murdoch, launched *The Highlander*, a radical weekly newspaper whose mission during its nine-year existence was 'to advocate the cause of the people, and particularly the right of the Gaelic people to their native soil'. It prided itself on eschewing exaggeration or shrill personal abuse, but it was uncompromising in its condemnation of the feudalised land system which caused so much misery across the Highlands. In one early edition, dated Saturday 12 July 1873, an editorial statement set out the full scale of the crisis:

> 'From one end of the country to the other, there are complaints in regard to the land... From the straths of Sutherland, from the mountain sides of Ross-shire, and from the glens of Inverness-shire, Argyllshire, and Perthshire, much the same sound reaches us; from Kintail, Lochalsh and Lochcarron; from Glenelg, Lochaber, and Badenoch; from Strathspey, Strathdearn, and Strathnairn; from the Islands of Uist, Barra, Skye, Rasaay, Mull, Islay, and Arran there is a wonderful concord of testimonies to the effect that wrong has been done to the people... by the manner in which the land is administered.'

Battle of the Braes

The Crofters' War was waged without muskets and massacre, but it was hardly a peaceable affair. The weapons were fists, sticks and stones on one side, and police truncheons backed by the full force of the law on the other. Not only that, but given the sparse population of the Highlands, with its tiny, isolated townships, the balance of forces was stacked overwhelmingly in favour of the landlords.

The central battlefield was the Isle of Skye, where a series of low level skirmishes over several years finally erupted into serious violence on the Braes peninsula, on the east side of the island, in 1882. Grievances had festered against the landowner, Lord MacDonald, for some time over the removal of the crofters' rights to graze cattle on a local hillside. Such disputes with landlords were common fare, but in Braes, several crofters had spent time in the south-west of Ireland the previous summer, working on fishing boats operating out of the port of Kinsale in County Cork. There they had become imbued with the spirit of militant anti-landlordism rampant across Ireland. Back home, they drew up a petition demanding the restoration of grazing rights on Ben Lee, which was signed up to by almost everyone in the three small townships of the peninsula.

It would have come as no surprise to the crofters when the petition was rejected by the landlord's factor. But it would have come as a serious surprise to Lord MacDonald's factor when the tenants marched on his Portree office to inform him that not a penny of rent would be forthcoming until the grazing rights were restored. Rent strikes were not unknown on Skye, but they were employed mainly for the purpose of challenging rent increases. This was more serious. This was about forcing the landowner to concede land, and was a favoured tactic of the Irish Land League, now imported into the Hebrides. It was a direct challenge to the absolute control of landowners and if it succeeded, would compromise that control, not just on Skye, but potentially across other parts of the Highlands and Islands too.

When the rents failed to materialise, Lord MacDonald dispatched a local sheriff officer, Angus Martin, to serve eviction notices on the ringleaders. When he arrived at the first township, a 150-strong crowd surrounded him, seized the warrants, and burned them. Such flagrant defiance was never going to be tolerated by the authorities. The countdown to the famous Battle of the Braes had begun.

At one o'clock in the morning of 19 April 1882, a steamboat arrived at Portree Harbour bearing 50 police officers from Glasgow, along with another dozen from Inverness. They were not told of their mission until daybreak, when they were sent off on the 11-mile march to the Braes. When they arrived, they were, according to press reports, met by a crowd of around 50 people. At that point, it must have looked like a walk-over. The herring fishing season had just begun, and thus many of the young men were out at sea. There was even some banter, as the police officers spotted a former colleague who had retired from the City of Glasgow Police. But as they shook hands and chatted about old times, the crowd swelled to over 300, mainly women.

The police were able, unmolested, to arrest the five alleged ringleaders of the burning of the warrants. But as they attempted to return to Portree with their captives, 'the scene baffled description' according to one newspaper report.

The *Glasgow Herald* nonetheless attempted description: 'The chief actors being the wives of crofters, with wonderful agility reached eminences commanding the road, from where they poured an incessant volley.' When the police finally broke through, the villagers regrouped to form a new blockade half a mile further on. The battle raged on for several hours, and by late morning, there was blood on the hillside. The *Freeman Journal* reported that 'one woman had her head cut open and lay senseless on the road, while several men were also badly beaten'. The *Glasgow Herald* reckoned 'it is doubtful she will ever recover', adding that another woman, aged 70, 'had maintained a vigorous defence' before suffering severe injuries after being thrown down the hillside. The worst injury inflicted on a police officer appears to have been 'a serious bruise on the knee, which has caused him considerable pain'.

The whole episode backfired with a vengeance. Within a few days, journalists had descended on this northern outpost from all corners of Britain. Suddenly, everyone was reading about the plight of the crofters. The pro-Tory *Glasgow Herald* wrote:

> 'Their homes as a rule are of the most miserable description. The people are clad in garments which afford scanty protection against the tempestuous weather of Skye, and even at the best, the food they are compelled to eat is neither in variety nor quantity sufficient purely to sustain the human system.'

These pen-portraits of ragged, half-starving crofters being threatened with eviction from their miserable hovels jangled incongruously with the society pages of the daily press, with their sycophantic coverage of the grand balls and hunting parties of the aristocracy. Landowners were already the most unpopular social group in Scotland. The David and Goliath struggle between them began to capture the popular imagination – and the politicians came under pressure to take action.

For the authorities, there was also a more immediate predicament. Although the villagers had failed to stop the arrests, both sides knew it had been touch and go. The crofters had refused to be intimidated, even by 50 hardened police officers from the big city, armed with heavy truncheons. And while it might be possible to mobilise such a force to deal with a one-off emergency, how could the state possibly maintain law and order if this kind of rebellion were to spread across the Highlands and Islands? The *Glasgow Herald* had already raised the alarm: 'It is an open question whether this success may in the long run prove more dangerous than defeat, because the Islemen look upon the presence of the Glasgow Police as an insult added to a former injury.'

Given these sentiments, the trial of the five crofters had to be handled delicately. One of the accused, Alexander Finlayson, was 70 years old; another, Donald Nicolson, was 66; a third, Peter MacDonald, was 48. Their charges were serious. Deforcement – obstructing a law officer in the course of his duty – was not the kind of crime that would normally be punished by a slap on the wrist or a token fine. But if these men were sent to jail, they would surely become martyrs, emblematic of the centuries of suffering inflicted on the Scottish Gaels. To avoid such impolitic provocation, the charges were reduced to common assault and, after a short trial at Inverness Sheriff Court, in which they were found guilty, the two older men were fined a modest 50 shillings (£2.50), while the others were fined just 20 shillings. 'After they were liberated, they received hearty congratulations on the way to their hotel,' reported the *Glasgow Herald*.

The Glendale Martyrs

Buoyed by widespread public sympathy for the Braes rebellion, other crofters seized the opportunity to strike back against their own landlords. Glendale, in the north-west of Skye, became the centre of the next serious wave of direct action, when crofters drove their cattle onto a local sheep farm and refused to back down, even when served with court orders. The dispute escalated when a shepherd was assaulted while clearing the cattle off the land. In retaliation, just before Christmas 1882, the authorities drew up warrants for the arrest of 20 crofters.

A few weeks later, at noon on 16 January 1883, four police officers entered Glendale to enforce the warrant and bring the illegal land occupation to an end. 'The alarm was immediately raised and a large crowd of men and women gathered to meet them... The officers were severely maltreated,' reported the *Dundee Courier*, which was generally sympathetic to the crofters. Other reports were more graphic. The *Aberdeen Journal* related that a crowd of 500 had set about the officers with sticks and bludgeons, leaving them severely bruised. 'The crofters threaten unbending resistance to any force that may be sent either to serve writs or apprehend offenders', it warned.

When the crofters marched on the nearby village of Dunvegan, armed, it was said, with clubs, scythes and other improvised weapons, the local constabulary evacuated the police station and fled across the island to Portree. 'Glendale in the opening weeks of 1883,' writes historian James Hunter, 'was passing – in a manner not seen in the Highlands and Islands since the 1740s – out of the United Kingdom's jurisdiction.' And trouble was spreading. The Dublin-based *Freeman's Journal and Daily Commercial Advertiser* reported that 'news of a very remarkable nature continues to come from Skye. The land agitation, instead of being curtailed, is spreading with remarkable rapidity across the Hebrides. The island of Barra is now in revolt.'

On Friday 9 February, a Royal Naval gunboat called *The Jackal* appeared on the north coast of Skye after a long, rough journey from Rothesay on the Isle of Bute. It carried a senior official from the Board of Supervision, the body responsible for administering the Poor Law in Scotland. His Hebridean name, Malcolm MacNeill, hints at the sensitivity of his mission. The government was now under serious pressure to both restore law and order, and do something to remedy the grievances fuelling this mini-revolution on the remote periphery of the kingdom.

That afternoon, 700 people gathered in the local Free Church to hear him out. He made a statement, translated into Gaelic by the church minister, in which he made it clear he was speaking on behalf of the government. While acknowledging that the crofters may 'have a moral right to these grazings', he underlined the seriousness of the crime of deforcement and warned that 'the Government are resolved to enforce law and order in Skye at whatever cost'. His bottom line was that the offences 'would neither be forgotten nor forgiven till four offenders – John MacPherson, Malcolm Matheson, Donald Macleod, and John Morrison – have surrendered themselves to receive the punishment they deserve'.

When the community discussed the matter without the officials present, three of the four men agreed to go to Edinburgh to stand trial, but not on a gunboat because they did not want history to record that 'Glendale men had to be taken away from their homes in a man-of-war'. A few days later the three crofters boarded the vessel called *Dunara Castle* after a tearful farewell to family and friends, who feared they would not return for a long time. A special correspondent from the *Inverness Courier* reported:

'John Macpherson, who is a man of striking appearance, bold and manly bearing, great intelligence, and considerable mental power, had a word of comfort and re-assurance for all. "If I was going," he said to them in Gaelic, "to jail for a sheep or for a lamb, you might be very sorry. But, as it is, you ought to be very glad. For we go to uphold a good cause; we go to defend the widow and the fatherless, and the comfort and needs of our hearths and homes."'

The case turned into a *cause célèbre*. John Stuart Blackie, an eminent Professor of Philosophy and Greek at Edinburgh University – later to become the first President of the Scottish Home Rule Association – had a letter published in *The Scotsman* stating: 'Our sympathies lie emphatically with the lawbreakers in this case, and we are strongly of the opinion that the real guilt lies with the law-makers.' His letter continued:

'There is no tyranny in Europe – not even in Asiatic Turkey – practically more grinding than the tyranny which, under our present Land Laws, the lord of the soil, with his commissioner, factor, and ground officer, may, in remote Highland districts, exercise over the Highland crofters. With these convictions, we have no hesitation in saying that we regard the Glendale crofters as martyrs rather than criminals – not because they are legally in the right, or because it is in any case right to break the law, but because the law is radically wrong...'

While publishing Blackie's blistering attack on landlordism, the newspaper launched a vitriolic counter-attack on the professor, accusing him of 'baseless calumny' against the landlords and factors. *The Scotsman* in turn was accused by land campaigner and writer Alexander MacKenzie of being 'the special organ of the Scottish Landocracy' and seeking to 'obliterate and destroy all traces of Celtic nationality'.

On 15 March 1883, three presiding judges at the Court of Session pronounced the Glendale men guilty of the civil offence of contempt of court by breaching an interim interdict, 'accompanied by serious violence'. More surprising than the verdict was the sentence: two months in prison, a remarkably lenient punishment in the circumstances. Their friends reported that in jail, the rebel crofters were treated as 'considerately as the regulations would allow', with comfortable bedding and a warm fire; their only complaint was that John

MacPherson, the only one of the three who was literate, was deprived of writing materials. They even had entertainment laid on by some exiled Highlanders in Edinburgh, who arrived outside the prison to play Gaelic airs on the bagpipes.

Back in Glendale, there was a further eruption of resistance when 65 notices of eviction were served on two adjacent estates. Buoyed up by widespread public support for the local men locked up in an Edinburgh jail, the community mobilised *en masse*, with between 1,000 and 1,500 people blocking the path of the sheriff officers. In his contemporaneous book, *The Isle of Skye* in 1882-83, Alexander MacKenzie detailed this latest skirmish in the Crofters' War:

> 'The sheriff-officer started on Tuesday, 10th of April, for Glendale, with the view of carrying out his instructions, but on his arrival at Skinidin, a township a few miles on his way to Glendale, he was met by a crowd of from a thousand to fifteen hundred people, ready to oppose his further progress. Angus, realising the position of affairs, and feeling that discretion was the better part of valour, decided to act upon the maxim that "he who fights and runs away may live to fight another day," at once turned right-about, and made off at full speed to Dunvegan, from whence, the same afternoon, he despatched the summonses to the Law-agent of the proprietors, at Portree, intimating that he would not, on any account, make a further attempt to serve them.'

From battleground to ballot box

As the Glendale Martyrs were released in May 1883, a royal commission began a marathon tour of the Highlands and Islands to hear evidence about conditions in the crofting communities. The Napier Commission had been established by Gladstone's Liberal government in Westminster in direct response to the rebellion on Skye. Malcom MacNeill's promise had been honoured, but the commission, chaired by Lord Francis Napier, a former acting Viceroy of India, inspired little confidence amongst the crofters of the northern townships.

The struggle on the ground continued, coordinated by a new organisation, the Highland Land Law Reform Association, which would become better known as the Highland Land League. Inspired by the Irish National League, which at its peak had 1,000 branches and 200,000 members across Ireland, the Highland Land League fought for lower rents and the break-up of the big landed estates.

The leading figure of the Irish struggle was Mayo-born Michael Davitt, who had strong Scottish connections through his close friendship with John Ferguson, a Belfast Protestant, the most prominent leader of the Irish community in Scotland. In the 1870s, Davitt had served a lengthy jail sentence for gun-running on behalf of the Irish Republican Brotherhood, the original 'Fenians', including a consignment of revolvers which was intercepted on its way to Glasgow from Birmingham. After his release, however, his politics had shifted from the conspiratorial and militaristic approach of the secret brotherhood to mass action, in which he strived to involve Protestant farmers in the north alongside the dispossessed Catholic peasantry of the south and west. On one occasion, he turned up to speak at a meeting in County Armagh, to find that the chair was the grandmaster of the local Orange Lodge. Although the meeting was 'all but exclusively Protestant', Davitt was cheered to the echo. 'The landlord organs could scarcely credit the news', he recorded in his autobiography, 'of a Fenian, Catholic and Land Leaguer being honoured by Orangemen.'

Meanwhile, the crofters' action in the north-west of Scotland escalated. 'There is a war in Tiree,' announced the London *Times* newspaper on 24 July 1886. A huge force of police officers and commissioners had been sent to the island to protect a sheriff officer as he served notices on behalf of the landowner, the Duke of Argyll. 'The people of the island gathered in such force and assumed an attitude so threatening that the invaders thought it prudent to retire to the Scarinish Inn,' said the newspaper of the British establishment. A few days later, the paper reported a meeting of around 1,200 protestors:

'At the close of it, a body comprising 800 marched to the Scarinish Inn, headed by two pipers, to deliver the resolution. They formed a circle round the house, brandished their cudgels, and rent the air with their yells. They challenged the police to go out and fight them, but of course no response was given to the challenge, and the policemen were kept carefully within the house. The mob remained... for nearly an hour hooting, bellowing, dancing, and flourishing their sticks. One of the crofters was heard to call out that when they got a Parliament of their own no police or lawyer would be allowed to set foot in the island... The whole of the expeditionary force has now left Tiree, together with the messenger-at-arms. The attempt to settle the dispute peacefully has failed and recourse must now be had to more forcible means.'

A few days later, 250 marines, each supplied with 20 rounds of ammunition, landed on the island from two warships, HMS Ajax and HMS Assistance. They were backed by a force of 50 police officers, who arrested six of the crofters identified as the ringleaders. For weeks, the small island was under military occupation.

By the time the men appeared in court, the Duke of Argyll, from his residence in Chelmsford, Essex, wrote a letter to the *Times* claiming the eviction notices were in fact 'summonses to appear before the tribunals for the violent seizure of land by members of the local conspiracy in the island'. At the High Court in Edinburgh, the judge told the men that he remembered the days when people were sentenced to deportation for deforcement, 'but of late years the punishment has been more lenient'. He told the men he had 'no doubt they were under some strange misapprehension and were ill-advised to take the steps they took'. Their sentences ranged from four to six months. Clearly, the judiciary knew they had to tread warily.

All across the north-west, similar dramas were played out. In Lewis, crofters pleaded with the widow of landowner James Matheson – a millionaire drug-dealer who had amassed his fortune smuggling opium in China – to restore some of the land her husband had cleared. Instead, Lady Matheson turned the whole area into a sporting estate, off-limits to the people who had once lived on this soil. Partly in protest, and partly to feed their half-starving families, 160 men armed with rifles occupied the estate and shot 400 deer – not to stuff and mount on the walls of draughty castles, but to eat.

Again the military were sent in – this time a detachment of Royal Scots and Naval Marines – to assist in the arrest of six crofters. They faced a bundle of charges, including trespass, poaching, mobbing and rioting, while journalists flocked to Edinburgh from across the world to report this circus of a court-case. It took the jury just half an hour to clear all six men of every single charge. Jubilant crowds greeted them at Stornoway Pier, while landowners across the Highlands drowned their sorrows with fine malt whisky.

The landed gentry had bigger problems on their plate than poached venison. The second Reform Act in 1836 had extended the franchise to all male householders in the burghs. But not in the countryside. In the entire county of Sutherland, spread over 2,000 square miles, only 329 men were entitled to vote. The landowning elite were as untouchable as the Tsar of Russia. But then Gladstone brought in the third Reform Act, in 1884. It was still a long way from universal suffrage; only 57 per cent of the male population, and 0 per cent of the female population, were now eligible to vote, leaving almost three in four adults without any political rights. But in rural areas, small tenants now had the franchise, including tens of thousands of crofters in the Highlands and Islands.

In September 1885, a conference of the Highland Land League in Portree took the momentous decision to stand candidates across the Highlands in the coming general election. They also determined to stand candidates in urban and mining constituencies. The results were enough to send a tremor shuddering through the foundations of every castle keep north of Perth. When the votes were tallied up, four Land League candidates were elected, even in the teeth of bitter opposition not just from their ancient Tory enemies, but from the Liberal Party, the Church of Scotland, and even the more radical Free Church of Scotland.

The leader of what became the new Crofters' Party, Gavin Brown Clark, MP for Caithness, had been a member of Karl Marx's First International and a founder member of the Land Nationalisation League. Two other Crofter MPs were also left wing radicals: Roderick MacFarlane, who won a landslide victory in Ross-shire, which included the Isle of Lewis; and Donald Horne MacFarlane, who became the first ever Catholic to be elected from a Scottish seat to the House of Commons, in the staunchly Presbyterian constituency of Argyllshire. In Inverness-shire, which included Skye, Barra, the Uists and Harris, Charles Fraser-Mackintosh, a defector from the Liberals, was also elected on a Crofters ticket, though he split away following year to join the newly formed Liberal Unionist party. In Wick Burghs, John Macdonald Cameron, an independent who was backed by both the Highland Land League and the Wick Radical Workingmen's Association, was returned. Indeed, almost the whole of the Highlands, with the sole exception of Sutherland, was coloured red, making the region the most radical in Britain.

The ongoing Crofters' War, together with the political earthquake that had rocked the northern half of Scotland, forced the Gladstone government to go further than the recommendations set out by the Napier Commission. The Crofters Holdings Act 1886 did nothing to break up the massive landed estates or challenge in any way the gross pattern of landownership in the Highlands. It did, however, introduce fair rents and security of tenure. The poet

Sorley MacLean, a native of Raasay, would later describe the Crofters Act as 'a poor palliative, though it removed the very worst of the abuses of the miserable status quo'.

The reform went just far enough, however, to defuse discontent for the time being, and to immobilise the Crofters' Party bandwagon. It allowed the Liberals enough breathing space to recover in the Highlands, and to make the pragmatic shift towards a more radical policy on land reform. This process was aided by the fact that as the Crofters' Party disintegrated, it tended to merge with Liberalism, the only other left-of-centre electoral force then in existence.

The Highland League and the Crofters Party nonetheless foreshadowed the imminent rise of the labour movement, while some of its key leaders went on to play a major role in the creation of Scotland's first modern campaign for national autonomy.

23

HOME RULE ALL ROUND

'A step backwards towards darkness'

In the late 1980s, as yet another campaign for a Scottish Assembly got underway, the popular newspaper cartoonist Ewan Bain produced a sketch of a boy looking up from a school biology textbook to ask, 'Dad, What's the difference between evolution and devolution?' His father's reply: 'Devolution takes longer, son.'

When the first Scottish Home Rule Association (SHRA) was founded, not even the most pessimistic of its supporters could have anticipated that Scotland would still be under the centralised control of Westminster until the final year of the second millennium. Home Rule for Scotland looked like an idea whose time had come. The only doubt was whether it would be achieved as part of a simultaneous package in Scotland, England, Ireland and Wales, or whether it would follow on soon after the delivery of Irish Home Rule.

Between 1889 and 1914, the principle of a Scottish Parliament was debated 15 times in Parliament, and each time was supported by a majority of Scottish MPs. Who would ever have imagined that it would take until the final year of the 20th century before a parliament of sorts would finally be established?

The early movement for Home Rule in Scotland was partly inspired by the struggle in Ireland, a country already burning with righteous anger after centuries of oppression, even before the trauma of the Great Famine. Scotland's grievances were of a different magnitude, but they were real nonetheless.

One stimulus was the slow pace of political reform in Britain, and a widespread feeling that Scotland was being held back by a reactionary state. 'There is not one single item in the whole programme of Radicalism or social reform today, which if Scotland had powers to pass laws, would not have been carried out long ago,' wrote one Liberal parliamentarian. Another, referring to haemorrhaging of Scotland's population, told the House of Commons that 'the country has become a reservoir for the filling up of Canada', and blamed the exodus on the fact that 'feudalism, unchecked by legislation, survives in Scotland.'

Since the first extension of the franchise, Scotland had already begun to diverge politically from England. In an electoral pattern which looks familiar today, Toryism was reduced to a marginal force north of the border. In 16 general elections, between 1832 and the end of the 19th century, the Liberals had an average 34-point lead in Scotland – two and a half times wider than the 13-point gap in England. In four of these elections, the Tories had won power at Westminster despite being rejected north of the border. Fortunately for the stability of the British state, the Liberals had won the other 12 general elections, otherwise the national movement in Scotland would almost certainly have crystallised, becoming a more urgent political priority.

The long road to devolution and beyond started gingerly enough, with the establishment of the SHRA as a small propaganda group distributing leaflets and posters with the message, 'Scotland can never be free and prosperous whilst her Laws are made in England.'

Not long after its launch, the *Aberdeen Journal* of 19 August 1886 reported a meeting of Aberdeen Trades Council – the umbrella body for all trade union branches in the city – at which the SHRA's James Reith delivered 'a rousing address' and received an equally rousing response. The only note of dissent was sounded by a Mr Milne, blacksmith, who was concerned that the president of the organisation, Edinburgh University Professor John Stuart Blackie, 'appeared to be a man of queer ideas, and at best an eccentric, dreaming kind of poet.'

The blacksmith's reservations were well-founded. The 77-year-old was a celebrity academic – genial, erudite and charismatic, and a useful public figurehead for a movement trying to establish itself. Blackie was strong on land reform, as demonstrated by his robust defence of illegal direct action by the Skye crofters in the letters pages of *The Scotsman*. But he was in essence a right-wing liberal with an antiquated mish-mash of opinions and prejudices that combined sentimentalism, cultural nationalism and a hint of racial superiority. He was also hostile to the Irish national movement, whose turbulence and occasional violence was rooted in a very different climate from the rarefied circles of Edinburgh academia.

But over time, as the movement found its feet, he would become an increasingly isolated figure. By the time of the first national conference, in 1888, he was removed from the post of president in favour of Gavin Brown Clark, the Crofters MP from Caithness, and future founder of the Scottish Labour Party. By 1890, Blackie was bitterly condemning what he called the 'extreme radicalism' of a section of the leadership of the SHRA, whose 'crimes' included glorifying the manual working class, proposing 'to sweep away in unceremonious fashion the House of Lords,' and wanting to 'throw aside like an old rag the sentiment of nationality which makes Scotsmen Scotsmen'.

Interestingly, the pro-union press intervened robustly on the side of the ethnic nationalism advocated by the professor. The *Aberdeen Journal* contrasted his 'poetic, idealistic and wholesome nationalism' with the 'destructive Radicalism [of the] Scottish Home Rulers who are, in the main, men impressed with revolutionary notions, which are socially of the most dangerous type.'

The Scotsman, which a few years earlier had flayed Blackie mercilessly over his support for crofters' direct action, also rushed to his support. 'There is nothing in common between these spouting gargoyles and the Professor's clear well-springs. Everyone but himself knew that the Professor was out of place in the Scottish Home Rule Association... It has from the first aimed at political revolution. It has set itself out to undo the union of 1707.'

The establishment press in Scotland and London was generally hostile to this new expression of Scotland's sense of nationhood. The establishment press joined in the fear-mongering. In one editorial, the right-wing *Morning Post*, based in London, taunted 'simple-minded Scotsmen' with 'sentimental grievances' who had taken up 'a dangerous weapon borrowed from the armoury of Irish discontent'.

Yet there was also sympathy, from the radical press. The left-wing *Reynolds News*, also based in London, had long been a scourge of the establishment. It had been a staunch supporter of the Chartists, and continued to proclaim on its masthead: 'Devoted to the cause of freedom and the interests of the enslaved masses.' It also came out strongly in support of both Irish and Scottish Home Rule. In one major article, headlined 'Scotland for the Scots', it praised Scotland's progressive politics and international outlook, ascribing them to the legacy of Andrew Fletcher, and argued:

> 'Apart from the general soundness of federal government, so splendidly illustrated in the United States and Switzerland, Scotland's claims to autonomy in domestic legislation are invincibly strong... Scotland's demand for Home Rule makes Irish Home Rule as certain as anything in the future. It is the first important and irrevocable step in the reconstruction of the British constitution on the basis of a federal as opposed to an incorporating union. Nay, it is the first step to a United States of Britain.'

From the other side of the political spectrum, the Tory Party remained ferociously hostile. One Conservative Lord Advocate warned that Scottish Home Rule would be 'a step backwards towards darkness', and that 'anything more dismal than a Scottish Parliament had never been conceived.'

Arthur Balfour, the Secretary of State for Scotland and a future Tory Prime Minister, attacked 'the growing sentiment in Scotland, not merely in favour of Home Rule, but in favour of those socialistic opinions which are really at the basis and root of the Home Rule cry in the country'. He added that every nation in the world was drawing closer together – a spectacularly inept forecast at a time when there were just 72 sovereign states in the world, compared to the 192 member states of the United Nations we know today.

The most eloquent enemy of Scottish Home Rule, however, was Randolph Churchill, the father of Winston. In the north of Ireland, he had, in his own words, 'played the Orange Card' when he went to Belfast and coined the slogan, before a massed rally of Unionists, 'Ulster will fight and Ulster will be right'.

On Home Rule for Scotland, he told the House of Commons:

> 'There are those who seriously recommend to the Scottish people a disturbance – a profound disturbance – of the arrangement of the Parliamentary Union which has worked for such splendid advantage to Scotland. They advocate change, a change which, mind you, amounts in its magnitude to a revolution... Such is the frightful and wanton recklessness engendered by a sense of utter irresponsibility'.

'A Celtic Protestant of the Irish race'

The term 'Home Rule' was originally coined to define the goal of the constitutional movement in Ireland for greater autonomy within the British Empire. The Irish National League, led by Charles Parnell, was like the ANC of its day, a diverse movement whose support extended across a wide social spectrum, from the Catholic Church hierarchy, to militant republicans and direct action land activists. By 1885, the movement had 85 MPs in the House of Commons under the name of the 'Irish Parliamentary Party.'

The national question in Ireland dominated much of the business in the House of Commons around the turn of the century. The Liberal leader, William Gladstone, was driven by a burning commitment to 'pacify Ireland,' as he put it, and not with the sword, as so many had tried before. Eventually his party split, when a 'Liberal Unionist' faction broke away. In Scotland, the breakaway – whose leaders included the Duke of Argyll, from the old Whig dynasty – eventually merged with the Tory Party, rescuing Conservatism in Scotland from oblivion under the name the Scottish Unionist Party (the forerunner of today's Scottish Conservative and Unionist Party). With the backing of the *Glasgow Herald* and *The Scotsman* newspapers, the new party attracted substantial support from the worlds of business, the professions and academia, and made some inroads into the skilled Protestant working class, especially around the Orange Order. It never did, however, become the biggest electoral party in Scotland, except for a temporary spell during the 1950s.

By this time, the Irish national movement was already strong in Scotland. It had an unlikely figurehead in John Ferguson, a Belfast-born Protestant who had built a successful publishing business. Ferguson had family connections with the struggle for Irish freedom; his paternal grandfather had fought at the Battle of Antrim Bridge under Henry Joy McCracken, during the revolt of 1798. But he had never personally taken much interest in politics before he came to Glasgow, a hotbed of political activism and debate around a multitude of issues, including Ireland.

His adherence to the reformed religion rendered him a target for sections of the Catholic clergy – one parish priest in Pollokshaws, for example, exhorted his congregation to 'beware false Protestant leaders and renegades'. Ferguson in turn accused the priest of 'Catholic Orangeism.'

For 30 years, until his death in 1906, Ferguson remained a highly respected and popular leader of Scotland's huge, working class Irish Catholic community. A self-proclaimed 'Celtic Protestant of the Irish race', he offered a strong antidote to the jibe that Home Rule meant Rome Rule, and helped the Irish national struggle gain broader sympathy in Presbyterian Scotland, especially in progressive circles such as the land reform and labour movements.

As well as helping straddle the religious divide, Ferguson was an astute tactician who helped unite all wings of the Irish national campaign in Scotland, from cautious constitutional reformers to radical republicans. He was a close friend and political ally of Michael Davitt, the giant of the Irish Land League, who would, in 1892, lay the first sod of turf at Celtic Park. On his regular visits to Glasgow, Davitt always stayed at Ferguson's villa, 'Benburb,' in the suburb of Lenzie, north of Glasgow.

Ferguson had initially been sceptical of Scotland's claim to national autonomy; the country already had a high degree of independence, he believed, through the legal system, the church, and the financial institutions. But as he studied the issues more thoroughly, he became convinced of the cause of Scottish Home Rule and its connection with the struggle in the land of his birth. In 1888, he was elected vice president of the SHRA at its first conference, providing a vital bridge to the Irish community. And he would soon become one of the pioneering figures of the early Scottish labour movement too.

Michael Davitt, through his connection with John Ferguson, also became a supporter of the Scottish Home Rule Association. He tendered his apologies to the 1890 conference, due to pressure of work in Ireland, regretting that he must miss this important meeting 'to once again proclaim my faith in Home Rule all round.'

The boundary of a nation

Davitt's message to the SHRA conference alluded to what had now become the central slogan of the national movement in Scotland. 'Home Rule All Round' aimed to achieve the absolute equality of the four nations, irrespective of size. As John Ferguson put it: 'Give England, Scotland, Ireland and Wales national parliaments for purely national purposes. Call into an existence an Imperial Parliament for purely imperial purposes. Let each of the nations, as in the United States, have 50 seats each and thus combine national (or state) independence with an imperial or federal structure.' Such talk was incendiary.

The idea that Wales, Scotland, and Ireland should have full equality with England, not just at home, but on the international stage, struck at the heart of the centralised, top heavy, British state, whose power structures had always been concentrated in a few square miles of territory around central London. It had little in common with later notions of devolution, in which Westminster bestows a lower tier assembly or parliament upon one or two of its provinces.

The use of the term 'imperial' has been misinterpreted by some commentators as an endorsement of colonialism. It is further offered as evidence that the Scottish Home Rule movement was founded on an ideology christened 'unionist-nationalism' by modern historians.

But in the context of the times, federal Home Rule was by far the most radical option available – so advanced that it provoked frenzied hostility from dedicated unionists. The phrase Home Rule within the empire was commonplace, not just in Scotland, but in Ireland too. Even the pro-independent republican currents there generally recognised that the achievement of Home Rule within the empire, along the lines of Australia, Canada or New Zealand, would be a great leap forward. Although deprived of sovereignty in international affairs and matters of war and peace, these self-governing dominions had used their substantial legislative autonomy to create democratic structures far in advance of the sclerotic British state. New Zealand, for example, became in 1893 the first country in the world to grant women the right to vote in parliamentary elections.

Even Marx and Engels recognised that the movement led by Parnell offered the best medium-term solution for Ireland. Engels further argued that the Irish Home Rulers, despite their limited programme, had a more revolutionary outlook than many London Marxists. Moreover, concepts such as imperialism and empire had not yet been fully analysed or understood, even within radical circles. Only with the carnage of the First World War would the word empire lose its vaguely altruistic gloss. Lenin's book *Imperialism, the Highest Stage of Capitalism* – in which he denounced the model as 'annexationist, predatory, plunderous' – was not published until 1916, by which time Europe was in turmoil.

In general, Scottish Home Rule activists were, along with Irish Home Rulers, instinctively anti-imperialist. During the second Boer War, for example, many of the SHRA's members, including President, Gavin Brown Clark, stood against the tide of jingoism to denounce British colonialism.

The association was a product of its time and place, yet the dominant strand of its politics was progressive; it was in essence a broad alliance of left-of-centre forces. As a national movement, it inevitably attracted all sorts, including the occasional right-wing dissident, such as Maltman Barry, a bizarre character, who stood as a serial candidate for the Tory Party while describing himself as a Marxist, and tried to challenge, unsuccessfully, the SHRA's support for Irish Home Rule.

There was even the odd aristocrat, such as Lady Florence Dixie – although, it has to be said, she was hardly a typical daughter of the landowning elite. Although skilled with a shotgun, she opposed bloodsports. A radical, feminist and suffragette, she passionately championed gender equality in all walks of life, even founding the first women's football association. She rejected religion, and was a friend of the controversial naturalist, Charles Darwin. Most treacherously of all, from the standpoint of the social class from which she sprang and into which she married, she backed James Keir Hardie when he stood as the first ever independent working-class candidate in the historic 1888 Mid-Lanark by-election, writing to tell him: 'If the miners put you in they will know that, at least, they have a representative who will be the slave of no Party, but who will speak fearlessly for Scotland and her people's interests.'

The SHRA officially threw its weight behind Keir Hardie, its London branch passing a resolution stating, 'That this meeting hails with gratitude the appearance of Mr. J. K. Hardie, the tried and trusted champion of the rights of the Scottish Miners, as a Labour candidate for Mid-Lanark, and trusts that the working men in that constituency will rally round him and do themselves the honour of returning the first genuine Labour representative for Scotland.'

The by-election did generate some friction, however, between the national movements in Scotland and Ireland. Charles Parnell, anxious to maintain good relations with Gladstone, publicly urged Keir Hardie to stand down to avoid splitting the Liberal vote in the constituency with the biggest Irish vote in the country. John Ferguson, a socialist as well as an Irish nationalist, was none too pleased. Through Michael Davitt, he tried, but failed, to persuade Parnell to back Hardie. Without the Irish vote, the Scottish Labour campaign was doomed, and the Liberal candidate stormed to victory. But a spark had been generated that would, in time, ignite a generation.

Later that same year, another legend of the left, the flamboyant scourge of the British establishment, Robert Cunninghame-Graham, was elected a vice-president of the SHRA, alongside John Ferguson and others. Nicknamed Don Roberto, Cunninghame-Graham had made a fortune as a cattle rancher in Argentina before being returned as the Liberal MP for North West Lanarkshire.

His politics were far to the left of his party. A self-proclaimed socialist, he was elected on a platform which included Home Rule for Scotland and Ireland; universal suffrage, including votes for women; nationalisation of land, the mines and other major industries; free school meals; the separation of church and state; and an eight hour working day, as opposed to the normal 10-16 hour day. He was also an uncompromising opponent of racism, corporal and capital punishment, the House of Lords, child labour and profiteering by landlords and industrialists.

In one debate, he told the House of Commons: 'A legislature in Scotland would find the working classes more largely represented than they are in the present House of Commons,' at which point the future Tory Prime Minister, Arthur Balfour, interjected. 'He wants Home Rule for Scotland because he wants socialism for Scotland.' To which Don Roberto roared out, 'Hear, hear!' On another occasion, he was asked in the Commons whether he preached 'pure unmitigated socialism.' His reply: 'Undoubtedly!'

Cunninghame-Graham's passionate belief in a Scottish Parliament was matched by his sense of social justice and spirit of solidarity with working people everywhere. In 1887, he was arrested, charged and sentenced to six weeks' hard labour at the Old Bailey, along with the London dockers' leader John Burns, for leading an illegal march on Trafalgar Square in support of the famous London match girls' strike, which had been banned by the authorities. He was also actively involved in the 1889 London dock strike.

The same year, he attended the Marxist Congress of the Second International in Paris, and the following year was expelled from France after making what the French Government believed was an outrageously revolutionary speech in Calais. Don Roberto would go on to be a founding figure of the Scottish Labour Party and, in 1928, the first president of the National Party of Scotland, the forerunner of the SNP.

Despite its efforts over a quarter of a century, the Scottish Home Rule Association eventually faded away. Although it failed to achieve its stated aims, it left a strong legacy. Under its influence, the Liberal Party in Scotland adopted the policy of 'Home Rule all round' in 1888 – a position it never relinquished, though in later years its support for federalism became tokenistic rather than earnest. The Labour Party too, from its foundation in the early years of the 20th century, maintained its formal commitment to Home Rule for Scotland right up until 1948; three decades later, in 1978, under pressure from a resurgent SNP, it dusted down its old policy, tore the guts out of it, and presented it to the electorate under the bland, managerial label 'devolution' – a word which essentially meant delegation of power from a higher to a lower authority. It wasn't quite what Keir Hardie and the early pioneers of the Scottish labour movement had in mind.

In June 2014, in the heat of the referendum campaign over Scottish independence, the old idea of federalism was revived in an unlikely quarter. Murdo Fraser, deputy leader of the Scottish Conservative and Unionist Party, displayed a certain political *chutzpah* by flying in the face of his party's entire history to promote the radical demand of Andrew Fletcher of Saltoun, Robert Cunninghame-Graham, Charles Parnell, James Keir Hardie, Michael Davitt, Jimmy Maxton and the early SNP.

Federalism had been a progressive idea in its time. It was more radical than devolution because it meant national equality rather than subordination. It stopped short of full independence to minimise the risk of isolation in a fast-changing, rapidly industrialising world, which had as yet few international interconnections other than top-down empire.

But times have moved on. In the age of the internet, global markets, social networking, mobile communications, the European Union, the United Nations, international NGOs and other worldwide institutions, sovereignty no longer means separatism. In the world of the 21st century, it would be no more possible for Scotland to lock itself away from the rest of the world than for Robert Burns to have boarded a 747 at Prestwick Airport. The slogans of a century ago are not necessarily the slogans of today.

And in any case, had federalism ever been agreed – against all the forces ranged against it, in the House of Commons, the House of Lords and Buckingham Palace – the momentum may well carried Scotland all the way to full national statehood at a later stage, for, as Charles Parnell once said of Ireland, 'No man should have the right to fix the boundary of a nation.'

24

DREAMS ON THE ROAD TO HELL

Guru in a cloth cap

Until sometime in the late 1990s, the Labour Party in Scotland had as its headquarters a four storey Victorian townhouse in Glasgow's Charing Cross area with a name steeped in working class legend and folklore.

Keir Hardie House had been christened in 1974 in honour of the man who was once the most revered figure in Scottish Labour history. He was a giant of the socialist movement: a visionary whose flowing rhetoric matched his biblical appearance, and whose personal kindness, granite integrity, coal dust voice and austere lifestyle won him the respect of tens of thousands. But by the dawn of New Labour, he had become the political equivalent of Banquo's ghost, haunting the conscience of a party now slashing and burning the principles he had preached until his dying breath.

James Keir Hardie was born in 1856 in a single-roomed cottage, still standing today, between the former mining villages of Newhouse and Holytown in Lanarkshire. Scandalously, for the times, his mother, a farm servant called Mary Keir, was unmarried. Two years after his birth, she wed a ship's carpenter, David Hardie, who was, by all accounts, an abusive binge drinker. It would instil in the young Hardie a lifelong commitment to the cause of temperance.

The family moved around, living for a time in Water Row, the little street that still runs from Govan Road to the old ferry pier on the banks of the Clyde. There, he started work, at seven years old, as a message boy for The Anchor Line Shipping Company – the first of a series of jobs that included heating rivets in a shipyard and working in a printers' before going to work in the Lanarkshire coalfield, the oldest, biggest and most treacherous in Scotland, aged just ten.

He was employed as a trapper, opening and closing trapdoors for ten hours a day, to keep the air circulating. He later moved on to become a pony driver, then a hewer of coal, before becoming a fully-fledged miner. Intelligent and well-read – having taught himself to read in his teens – he was elected leader of the Lanarkshire Miners' Union at the age of 23. The colliers he represented were mainly Irish Catholics, a point that was driven home early to the young firebrand when he unwittingly provoked uproar at a rally after introducing a veteran campaigner as 'the Martin Luther of the miners'.

In April 1888, now in his early 30s, and living with his young family in Cumnock, Ayrshire, he quietly strode onto the stage of national history. Like many radical activists of his generation, Hardie was a member of the Liberal Party, but he was reaching towards the idea of creating a political organisation that would specifically address the interests of the working class. In contrast to the diehard reactionaries of the Tory Party, the Liberal Party championed progressive policies on land reform, Home Rule for Ireland and Scotland, and extension of the franchise. It was also imbued with a paternalistic philosophy that insisted that those at the top of society had a duty of care to the weak and the poor. Fortified with these values, the party had dominated Scottish politics for more than half a century.

But there was another side to Liberalism that became more apparent with the rise of heavy industry. At its heart, it was a free trade, free market party, which sanctified wealth and profit. It was the party of Scotland's richest and most ruthless industrialists, such as the Coats family of Paisley, who had built a multinational empire of thread mills, based on young female labour, where trade unions were banned.

When the seat of Mid-Lanark fell vacant after the local MP resigned, Keir Hardie sought support from the Liberals for his candidature. A reasonable request, all told, given that this was possibly the most proletarian constituency in Britain, a black and grey jungle of collieries and ironworks, eternally engulfed in a dense fog of smoke and toxic fumes. But the Liberals were having none of it. Instead, they invited in a wealthy young London barrister, educated at Winchester and Oxford, who would eventually wind up in the House of Lords.

Despite pressure and attempted bribery by the Liberal establishment – including the offer of a £300-a-year salary should he stand aside – Hardie declared himself an Independent Labour candidate. He was backed by an assortment of groups, including the Highland Land League, the Glasgow Trades Council, the British Steel Smelters' Association, and the Scottish Home Rule Association.

His manifesto included an eight-hour day for miners, and a land value tax directed against the landowning elite. He vowed to 'support the Irish Party in winning justice for Ireland, and in the event of a difference between them and the Liberal Party, I would vote with the Irish,' adding, 'I am also strongly in favour of Home Rule for Scotland, being convinced that until we have a Parliament of our own, we cannot obtain the many and great reforms on which I believe the people of Scotland have set their hearts.'

His main appeal, however was that he was different from anything that had ever been sent to Westminster before. He pointed out that, of Scotland's 72 MPs, not one was from a working class background. He asked:

> 'Why is it that in the richest nation in the world, those who produce wealth should alone be poor?... Few save the poor feel for the poor, the rich know not how hard it is to be [denied] needful food and needful rest. I ask you therefore to return to Parliament a man of yourselves, who being poor, can feel for the poor, and whose whole interest lies in the direction of securing for you a better and a happier lot?'

It was a bitter campaign, in which the full weight of the national Liberal machine, and its newspapers such as the *North British Daily Mail*, mobilised to destroy Hardie's credibility. Parnell's support for the Liberal candidate was perhaps the decisive factor. When the votes were announced, Hardie had won a respectable, but disappointing, 618 votes – far behind the two main parties.

Yet as one early biographer of Keir Hardie notes, 'the election had cleared the air, and had settled one thing for ever: the impossibility of a Labour Party within the Liberal Party... From that day onward, the coming of the Independent Labour Party was a certainty, and that it should be a Socialist Party was equally certain'.

One month later, on 10 May 1888, a group of 27 left-wing activists gathered in Glasgow, at a meeting chaired by the veteran Highland Land League campaigner and Scottish nationalist, John Murdoch. It began preparations for the founding conference of the Scottish Labour Party in Glasgow's Waterloo Rooms, later the site of the famous Alhambra Theatre, now an office block.

James Keir Hardie was elected General Secretary. Scottish Home Rule activist and socialist, 'Don Roberto' Cunninghame-Graham, who had been elected Liberal MP for North West Lanarkshire, now switched allegiance to Scottish Labour and became president of the new party. Two other activists from the SHRA, John Ferguson and Gavin Brown Clark, were elected joint vice-presidents. James Shaw Maxwell, an activist with the Scottish Land Restoration League, which campaigned for a land value tax, was elected chair of the executive committee. Another key figure in the party was Robert Smillie from Larkhall, the Belfast-born son of a Scottish crofter who would go on to become the first president of the Scottish Miners' Federation, and a major driving force in the establishment of the Scottish Trades Union Congress.

'Liberalism is one thing, Socialism is quite another, and the new Labour Party is Socialistic,' Keir Hardie told the conference, which adopted an 18-point programme, including wholesale nationalisation of the railways, waterways and tramways, land, minerals and the banking system; abolition of the House of Lords; disestablishment of the Church of Scotland; full adult suffrage, including for women; an eight-hour working day; and Home Rule for Scotland, Ireland, England and Wales.

The political genealogy of the labour movement in Scotland and across Britain can be as tangled and confusing as any family tree. The first point to note is the pioneering role of the Scottish Labour Party, which was the first ever attempt to create a broad, left-wing electoral force to fight for the distinct interests of the working classes. Five years after its launch, its leader, Keir Hardie, accepted an invitation to stand in a parliamentary seat in London as a labour candidate (with a small 'l'). When he won the seat in 1892, to become MP for West Ham South (in circumstances which we explain in the next section), the idea of creating a Britain-wide equivalent of the Scottish Labour Party was born. The result: the cross-border Independent Labour Party (ILP), launched at a conference in Bradford in 1893. Three of its four main leaders, including Keir Hardie, were exiled Scots based in England, and pro-Home Rule. The Scottish influence was strong from the start, and Clydeside, in particular, remained a stronghold of the party right up until the Second World War.

So far, so straightforward. But to anyone familiar with left-wing politics, it should come as no surprise that things start to become complicated. In 1897 the Scottish Trades Union Congress (STUC) was formed as a left-wing breakaway from the British TUC, and, two years later, established a broad electoral umbrella called the Scottish Workers Representation Committee (SWRC). The following year, 1900, the TUC in England and Wales set up a similar body, the Labour Representation Committee (LRC). The ILP affiliated to both, along with a number of trade unions on either side of the border. Two separate electoral alliances operated independently of one another for the best part of a decade, before finally merging in 1909 to form the British Labour Party. (If you've managed to follow us up to this point, you might as well carry on.)

The ILP then affiliated to Labour Party, but retained its own separate membership and structure, held its own conferences, and set its own policies. It was, in effect a party within a party. It provided dynamism, ideas, and, most importantly of all, footsoldiers. But from the beginning, there was serious political tension between the LRC/Labour Party and the ILP. In the early years of the century, the division revolved around women's suffrage (which we explain in a later section of this chapter). In 1914, there was a cataclysmic fall-out over the First World War. And later still, in the 1930s, the ILP – now led by Glasgow MP Jimmy Maxton – walked out of the Labour Party, along with almost the entire Glasgow membership. But in the meantime, in the years before the First World War, the two managed to set aside their differences and work together, in an uneasy coalition.

There were also differences within the ILP. In his 1966 book *Left in the Centre*, labour historian Robert Dowse succinctly sums up the eclectic character of the organisation: 'Fervent and emotional, the socialism of the ILP could accommodate, with only a little strain, temperance reform, Scottish nationalism, Methodism, Marxism, Fabian gradualism and even a variety of Burkean conservatism'.

The moral and political authority of Keir Hardie managed to hold the organisation together, his legend almost sanctified within the broad labour and trade union movement after flouting the conventional dress code of the House of Commons on his first day there. According to one observer, he wore a 'blue serge double-breasted jacket and waistcoat, fawn-coloured trousers, and, in the place of the decorous starched linen, a striped flannel shirt, with a coloured scarf tied round its collar in a sailor knot.' Topping it all, literally and metaphorically, was a traditional working man's cloth cap, known colloquially in Scotland as a 'bunnet'.

That bunnet would become a symbol of the incorruptibility of James Keir Hardie. A century after his death, his values continue to resonate, along with the political ideas he fought for: wealth redistribution, women's equality, republicanism, peace, anti-racism and the right of nations to control their own destiny.

Labour with a tartan tinge

One of the conundrums of the early Scottish labour movement is the contradiction between its pioneering dynamism and its lack of electoral success. Many historians, particularly those of a pro-union bent, have drawn attention to the fact that Keir Hardie was first elected to parliament from a London constituency, and contrast that with his resounding defeat in his own backyard in Mid-Lanark. They further highlight the 1906 general election, which returned 27 labour candidates in England, but only two in Scotland – Blackfriars, in Glasgow's Gorbals area, and Dundee. On the face of it, surely these statistics demonstrate that Scotland lagged behind when it came to radical left-wing politics?

But the bare facts conceal more than they reveal. Keir Hardie was actually invited to stand in West Ham South by radical Liberals, up in arms after having had a wealthy city financier, James Hume Webster, foisted upon them as Liberal candidate in one of the most solidly working class constituencies in the country. West Ham had been a stronghold of the recent London dock strike, when 100,000 workers had fought and won a historic battle over low pay, casual labour and union recognition. Hardie might have spoken with a different accent, but he talked the same militant, socialist language as the East London dockers.

Even with a divided Liberal Party, however, he would have faced an uphill struggle to win the seat. But before the election was called, James Hume Webster committed suicide, leaving a straight fight between the Tory candidate and Keir Hardie, now backed by the Liberals. This was an altogether different contest than the fiercely fought, three-way Mid-Lanark by election.

Moreover, the victory of 27 labour candidates in England in the 1906 general election was a product of a series of electoral pacts between the Liberals and the various labour organisations across England, especially in the mill towns of Lancashire and Yorkshire. Only one of these victories – in Bradford, where the ILP's founding conference had been held – was achieved via a three-way contest including the Liberals and Tories. In Scotland, the two Independent Labour seats were won without deals or pacts with the Liberals. That is not to devalue the significance of the labour breakthrough in England, but to place the comparative results in context.

But that context in turn demands an explanation. Why was there no electoral deal between the Liberal Party and the forces of labour in Scotland?

One reason was the different character of the movement north and south of the border. In England, the more moderate influences tended to be stronger, especially the Fabian Society, whose most prominent leaders, Beatrice and Sidney Webb, saw a major part of their role as persuading the Liberals, and even the Tories, to become more socially responsible. Although the couple did not actually become members of the until 1914, their influence permeated the early Labour Party, which in turn developed the psychology of a pressure group, rather than a potential rival to the two traditional political blocs. The Scottish ILP, in contrast, tended to be more strongly rooted in the working class and more militant in their politics. North of the border a river of clear red water separated labourism from liberalism. Thus, from its inception, the labour movement in Scotland tacked more strongly to the left.

But the primary reason for the absence of any electoral pact was the sheer dominance of Liberalism in Scotland. The party was a mighty machine, and it operated everywhere. It also had the majority of sitting MPs, who would rather bite off their own tongues than stand aside to allow proletarian upstarts to take their place in the hallowed halls of Westminster. The Scottish Liberals had neither incentive nor need for labour support.

Their strength was further reinforced by the support of the huge Irish Catholic population in Scotland. The Liberals were the Home Rule party, in a parliamentary alliance with Parnell to deliver Gladstone's mission. Anything that might threaten to split the Liberal vote and allow unionist candidates to be elected was anathema to the Irish organisations.

Even the voice of John Ferguson was drowned out by the thunderclaps of pro-Liberal propaganda reverberating from the pulpits and the Irish press. In 1894, the *Glasgow Observer* newspaper was vehement in its opposition to the Scottish Labour Party, describing it as 'a set of the most venomous enemies that Ireland and the Irish people have... It is a dishonest party. Every man with Irish blood in his veins should shun it, as he would the bitterest enemy of his race.' It mattered not that the Scottish Labour Party was simultaneously under attack from the Orange Order, and other unionists, for supporting Home Rule. But for the Catholic Church – perhaps understandably, given the high stakes in Ireland – labour had to wait until Irish Home Rule was settled.

In local elections, things were different. In 1896, an assortment of Independent Labour and other pro-labour candidates contested every seat in the

Glasgow elections, and won 11. They formed a group under the leadership of John Ferguson, who had been elected as an Irish National League candidate for Calton, known as the 'Stalwarts'. The Irish vote had already begun to break with Liberalism at a local level.

The Boer War drove the Irish vote further into the Labour camp, after the Liberals, under Sir Henry Campbell-Banner, backed the imperial crusade of the Tory Government. Although it would later be eclipsed by the events of 1914-18, this was a brutal, shameful episode in the history of the British Empire. This was a war for gold, literally, in which Britain seized the mineral wealth of southern Africa by pouring in 450,000 men to carry out what Lord Kitchener called 'total war'. One in ten never came home, five times more than the combined loss of all coalition forces in the twenty-first century wars in Afghanistan and Iraq.

Kitchener's scorched earth policy included the destruction of 30,000 Boer farms and the transportation of captured Boer guerrillas to the far-flung islands of Bermuda, St Helena and Ceylon. It also involved incarcerating 300,000 civilians in a hundred concentration camps, hell holes of starvation and disease where 28,000 Boers and 14,000 black Africans perished. More shocking still was the revelation in an official report that 22,000 of the Boers who died were children under 16 years old, their immune systems weakened by deliberate starvation, a tactic designed to pile pressure on fathers, uncles and elder brothers on the battlefield. 'Every one of these children was purposefully murdered', wrote the celebrated newspaper journalist and editor William Stead, who later died on the Titanic.

After creating the Union of South Africa, Britain co-opted the Boer population and began to introduce segregationist legislation which would ultimately lead to the horror of Apartheid. The total cost to Britain of the war was a mind-boggling £220 million – as a proportion of GDP, the equivalent of a modern UK government spending £185 billion. But these were not cabbage fields they were fighting over: it was the misfortune of the Boers and Africans that vast canyons of gold and diamonds had been discovered underneath the land on which they lived.

Two years into the war, in August 1901, the Scottish Workers Representation Committee stood Robert Smillie, the miners' union leader and ILP member, in a by-election in North East Lanarkshire. With the backing of the

Catholic *Glasgow Observer* and the Irish organisations in Scotland, Smillie took a healthy 21 per cent of the vote, even after the *Daily Record* had falsely accused him of being a secret member of the Orange Order.

As well as the broader labour organisations, Scotland also had several smaller, more hardline socialist parties. The Social Democratic Federation (SDF) was a Britain-wide Marxist group led by Henry Hyndman, an autocratic ex-Tory who would go on to split his party in 1914 after coming out in support of the First World War. Its main rival on the far left, the Scottish Land and Labour League, was created as an offshoot of the London-based Socialist League, led by William Morris, the famous textile designer, poet and pioneer of the fantasy genre, who split from Hyndman's party. Less dogmatic than the SDF, its name recognised the strength of national feeling in Scotland, and, according to one of its founder-members in Edinburgh, the need for an image that was more 'homely, concrete, alluring and less abstract'. It made little impact on the working class, however. With the exception of some Russian Jewish cigar-makers, German glass-blowers and a few other artisans, its main activist base was made up of middle class men, including writers, artists, businessmen, lecturers, and other professionals.

A further schism from the SDF was established in 1903 by the Irish Marxist, James Connolly. The Socialist Labour Party, inspired by the ideas of the American revolutionary socialist, Daniel de Leon, concentrated on workplace struggles and attracted a number of shop stewards from the shipyards and engineering factories, but its membership would only ever be numbered in hundreds rather than thousands.

Although these organisations attracted some of the brightest and most dedicated activists, they made little progress. Later, earth-shattering events across Europe, and colossal class conflict at home, would raise up the spectre of Red Clydeside and turn revolutionary Marxists such as John Maclean and Willie Gallacher into popular heroes. But in the meantime, within radical and left circles, the main show in town was the Independent Labour Party. In the 1906 general election, when the ILP secured two seats in Scotland, the Liberal Party won a landslide victory. A few years later, however, a Liberal memorandum noted that 'the Socialist and Labour movements are steadily gaining adherents in Scotland', and contrasted the 'extraordinary enthusiasm' of the left with the demoralisation of their own forces.

The ILP was still a small-scale operation, but it had one powerful advantage over its more theoretically-steeled Marxist rivals. It was a home-grown party of the Scottish working class, with its finger on the pulse of the people.

Forward together

Nowhere was the north-south divide within the labour movement more clearly illuminated than in the two newspapers produced by the Independent Labour Party on either side of the border.

In his memoirs of the time, *No Mean Fighter*, Harry McShane, a member of the Marxist Socialist Labour Party, pithily summed up the differences. *Labour Leader*, the official party and published in London, was 'negative, dull and bland'; *Forward*, the newspaper of the Glasgow ILP, 'was a very lively paper...It carried marvellous exposures... it was as different from the official paper as the Glasgow members were from the rest.'

Forward was launched as a weekly in 1906 by Tom Johnston, with capital of £60 he had borrowed after inheriting a small printing press. He remained editor of the paper until 1932, when the ILP disaffiliated from the Labour Party, taking with it the newspaper and almost the entire Glasgow membership, including most of the city's MPs.

But in the early days especially, *Forward* was a trail-blazing publication. Its content was bold and broad, dealing with almost every subject from a socialist perspective. It was splattered with vivid, first-hand reports from the frontline of workplace and community struggles, and spearheaded local campaigns in favour of measures such as free school meals and rent control. Although a Glasgow paper, it dealt comprehensively with the plight of rural communities as well as urban squalor. Johnston himself wrote a major series of articles on the aristocracy and how they acquired their land and titles, which became a best-seller when it was a published as *Our Scots Noble Families* in 1909.

Forward also carried features that would never have seen the light of day had they been submitted to the mainstream press, on subjects such as sexual morality; the arguments around vegetarianism; spiritualism and socialism; alcohol abuse; the rising incidence of insanity; the case for and against a land value tax; the case for Esperanto; and features with such eye-catching headlines as 'Was Jesus Christ a Tramp?' or 'Glasgow's Murder Rate and How to Decrease It'. By today's standards, perhaps, its correspondents were not always of the right side of progress, but they weren't backward at coming forward.

Vibrant and varied, *Forward* was impressive and influential. Its correspondents hailed from across the spectrum of left-wing thought, and included John Maclean, destined to become the most famous Red Clydesider of them all, but then still a primary school teacher in Govan. He was contemptuous of the Labour Party: 'Its representative men are anxious to flatter Liberal ministers, Liberal measures and Liberal policy, and to keep the Liberals in power.' On the other hand, he supported an amalgamation between his own Marxist Social Democratic Party (previously 'Federation') and the ILP, of which he estimated that 'the rank-and-file hold the same ideas and the same principles as the SDP'.

Forward also carried regular reports from Ireland, from the future leader of the Easter Rising, 'Jim' Connolly, and from James Larkin in Belfast, who led a famous dockers' strike in the city in 1907, uniting workers across the religious divide. Keir Hardie, now in exile in Wales and London, was another regular contributor. He had lost his West Ham seat three years after his breakthrough, but had subsequently been returned to parliament in 1900 as a 'junior' MP in the two-seat Merthyr Tydfil and Aberdare constituency, in the heartland of the South Wales iron and steel industries. Although he had left Scotland, his old passion for the rights of small nations had never diminished. As MP for Merthyr, he became a standard bearer for Welsh culture, language and autonomy. As one current Labour Shadow Cabinet Minister, Jon Cruddas, pointed out a few years ago in a piece in the *New Statesman*, 'He was a dedicated supporter of feminism and Welsh nationalism – the red dragon and the red flag'. The final phrase is a reference to the publication produced by Keir Hardie, and his statement that he 'looked forward to a time when he would see the red dragon emblazoned on the red flag of socialism'.

Forward never wavered in its commitment to the cause of Home Rule in Scotland, Ireland and Wales. Issue number three carried a major front page feature in support of federalism by the Arran-born radical Liberal MP for Tyneside, John M Robertson, who wrote a follow-up article the next week calling for the abolition of the House of Lords. Six years later, in the months before the First World War, it ran a series of 11 full-length essays on Scottish history by historian Morris Davidson, lambasting 'the sale of Scottish nationhood' in1707 and the 'disastrous Union of Crowns'. It concluded with a condemnation of the 20th century British state, and a call for the United States of Scotland, England, Ireland and Wales.

A column called 'Catholic Socialist Notes' appeared weekly. Although unsigned, it was usually written by John Wheatley, originally from Waterford, whose socialist beliefs were strongly influenced by Marxism. A coal miner turned businessman, he had, since the death of John Ferguson in 1906, become the most influential political figure within the Irish community, and played a decisive role in winning the mass of Scottish Catholics over to the side of the labour movement.

Reflecting the broad labour and socialist movement in Scotland, the pages of *Forward* brought together divergent traditions that included Calvinism, Catholicism, radicalism, republicanism and Marxism. Although the word itself was not yet familiar, one other 'ism' featured prominently in almost every issue of *Forward*. 'Suffrage Notes' was another weekly column that ran for years on end. It focused on the immediate struggle for electoral equality, but it also inevitably strayed into more controversial territory by championing the cause of women's emancipation. Whatever it was called back then, feminism had arrived, and would forcibly make its presence felt in the Scottish labour movement.

Suffragette socialism

The word 'suffragette' was originally coined as a term of derision by a *Daily Mail* journalist, but Britain's right-wing male establishment would soon stop laughing. The Women's Social and Political Union, formed in 1903, would go on to lead a tremendous crusade for equality – the biggest mass campaign of civil disobedience ever seen in the UK.

Yet as the author Maggie Craig points out in her highly readable social history, *When The Clyde Ran Red*, the suffragettes have acquired something of an image problem over the years, as result of their portrayal in the modern media as 'well-off ladies with plenty of time on their hands for smashing windows, pouring acid into pillar boxes, tying themselves to railings and otherwise making mischief'. She points out another 'curiosity' – 'that the depiction of suffragettes in popular culture seems always to show them doing what they did only in London.'

The movement did draw much of its strength and dynamism from the middle classes. Working class women were doubly oppressed by dint of their gender and social status. They tended to marry young and have large families, leaving them crushed under the twin weight of household drudgery and pressure to know their place in society. When they did rise up, it tended to be within the workplace or local community.

One of the landmark industrial battles of the early twentieth century was fought out in Clydebank, famous for building some of the world's greatest ocean liners. The rapidly growing new town was also home to the Singer sewing machine factory, owned by a Tennessee-based multinational corporation. The giant workplace, reputed to be the biggest industrial plant in the world, churned out a million sewing machines a year. In 1911, women made up around 30 per cent of a 10,000 strong workforce.

That year, the American bosses began to experiment with new techniques designed to maximise profit. One Monday morning in March of that year, a manager arrived in the polishing department, which comprised a dozen women employed to finish the sheen on the wooden cabinets. The manager ordered that three of them be transferred to another department, leaving their nine colleagues to carry out the work previously done by twelve. And just to rub it in, he announced that their pay would be cut from 14 shillings a week, to 12 shillings. Outraged, the dozen walked out, leaving their dusters and polish. As the word spread through the factory, they were joined by another 2,000 women, and by the following day, the entire operation was at a standstill.

They stayed out for weeks, but it was an unequal contest. Working people lived from week to week, always just a wage packet away from starvation. And they were up against one of the biggest and wealthiest commercial operations in the world. When the strike was over, the American company took its revenge by sacking the strike leaders and circulating a blacklist to prevent them working again.

Yet the industrial action had other, more progressive consequences. Over the next few years, trade union membership on Clydeside doubled. During the next three years, there would be 400 industrial strikes in Scotland, mostly on Clydeside. And the leading role played by thousands of women in the strike helped to galvanise the wider struggle for women's rights across Scotland, and root it more strongly in the working class. That year, Helen Crawfurd set out on a speaking tour of the pit villages of the Lanarkshire coalfield to promote the case for women's suffrage, along with two colleagues from the Women's

Political and Social Union (WPSU). The wife of a Church of Scotland minister, her speeches, tinged with socialism, were also in her early days peppered with biblical references. By all accounts, she got a great response from the colliers, who would refuse the normal fee for their miners' social clubs, and donate generously to the WSPU's collections. As Maggie Craig puts it, 'the suffragettes were fighting to right an injustice and they understood all about that'. And as another historian, William Ferguson, notes in *Scotland 1689 to the Present*, 'the suffragists' most consistent supporters were the socialists'.

Keir Hardie had been a long-standing supporter of votes for women. It had been part of his manifesto in Mid-Lanark, back in 1888. When it came to women's rights, he was decades ahead of mainstream Liberalism. Gladstone had conspicuously excluded women in the 1885 Reform Act which widened male suffrage. Years later, in 1892, he continued to justify his position on the grounds that giving a woman political rights would 'trespass upon the delicacy, the purity, the refinement, the elevation of her own nature'. During the years of the most intense suffragette agitation, from 1905 to 1914, the Liberal Party was in power and denied women the franchise. By contrast, Keir Hardie's support for women's equality was unwavering and – no doubt influenced by his close friendship with Sylvia Pankhurst – hardened into feminism. In an essay published in 1905, he wrote:

> 'It is only by removing the disabilities and restraints imposed upon woman; and permitting her to enter freely into competition with man in every sphere of human activity, that her true position and function in the economy of life will ultimately be settled. We can at present form no conception of what woman is capable of being, or doing. We have no data upon which to base any real conclusions. Nowhere is woman treated as the free and equal companion of man.'

He even resigned as leader of the Labour Representation Committee in England and Wales – the forerunner of the Labour Party – after the 1907 conference overwhelmingly voted down his proposal to put women's suffrage at the centre of its manifesto. Of the 300 delegates present, only one was a woman. A furious Hardie said: 'If it is necessary for me to separate myself from what has been my life's work, I do so in order to remove the stigma resting upon our wives, mothers and sisters of being accounted unfit for citizenship.'

Part of that debate had revolved around the conflict between women's equality and full universal suffrage. The 1885 Reform Act had left a significant portion of the male population disenfranchised, especially younger, unmarried men who were not householders. The Labour Representation Committee (LRC) opposed votes for women unless it was part of a package for full adult suffrage. It was a pseudo-radical policy, based on simple sexism combined with a fear that women might be less inclined to vote Labour than men.

Keir Hardie, and the ILP, especially in Scotland, had no such qualms. For them, equality of human beings was a matter of principle, so they backed the suffragettes' position demanding 'votes for women on the same terms as it may be granted to men'. This did not mean opposing universal suffrage; but neither did it mean insisting that women should put their fight for equality on hold until Westminster was ready to abolish all qualifications for voting.

Forward was a strong supporter of the movement for women's equality. Tom Johnston wrote a pamphlet, *The Case For Women's Suffrage and Objections Answered*, which was heavily promoted in the newspaper. It also carried a continual stream of reports of the suffragette campaign in Scotland, along with in-depth features on women's oppression. One regular contributor, Isabella Bream Pearce, was joint secretary of the WSPU's Scottish Council, as well as a seasoned socialist activist and member of the ILP. Under the *nom de plume* Lily Bell she wrote some of the most hard-hitting pro-feminist polemics ever carried by the paper. In one piece, *The Women's Fight For Freedom*, published in November 1906, she wrote:

> 'The attitude of men all through the present agitation... has been simply that of the master to an insubordinate servant. To realise that a woman cannot take a stand against an injustice to her sex without bringing down upon herself torrents of abuse and contempt can have only one serious result – that of stirring up the latent womanhood in women to eventually enable them to overthrow the male autocracy...Refuse any longer to recognise such authority and claim for yourselves the full right to determine your mission in life.'

In another piece, dated 15 December 1906, she called time on the assumption that women's emancipation would automatically follow the achievement of socialism, before putting the male fraternity of the socialist movement in their place:

'Examine the attitude of socialist man to woman...You will not find it a whit better than that of any other men. Woman is not one bit higher with them and will not be until she asserts herself independently of them and takes the place that belongs to her instead of waiting to see if it will be given.'

For a decade, the struggle for women's equality raged on. But it repeatedly collided with a brick wall in the human form of Liberal Prime Minister, Herbert Asquith, who would later gain a reputation during the First World War as a weak-willed, vacillating ditherer. But when it came to denying women the vote, he was resolute.

Although it was never general public knowledge at the time, Asquith had something of a reputation for being an inveterate sex pest. Clementine Churchill, the young wife of Winston, objected to his persistent habit of peering down the tops of women's dresses. One woman complained about his 'drooling, high thigh-stroking advances', while another alleged that the Prime Minister would 'take a lady's hand as she sat beside him on the sofa, and make her feel his erected instrument under his trousers'. His interest in women stopped there.

When Asquith shelved yet another parliamentary bill in 1911, anger erupted and peaceful direct action escalated into serious vandalism. In Scotland, Leuchars railway station was burned down, as was a medieval church in West Lothian. One group of militant suffragettes planted a bomb in Glasgow Botanic Gardens, and attempted to blow up Burns' Cottage.

They were making a wider point, however, that crimes against people, including the rape and abuse of women and children, were treated leniently by the authorities, while the destruction of property would bring the skies crashing down on the heads of the perpetrators. Helen Crawfurd served two prison sentences for attacking property. After smashing the windows of the Liberal Education Minister's London residence, she was sentenced to a month in Holloway Prison. Two other inmates of the North London prison were suffragette socialists from Glasgow: Margaret McPhun, press secretary of the WSPU in Scotland, and a socialist, and Janie Allan, from the wealthy Allan Shipping Line family, also a socialist and ILP member. While incarcerated in Holloway, Crawfurd went on hunger strike, ultimately barricading herself into her prison cell, in protest at the brutal force-feeding procedures.

Back in Scotland, some of the suffragette actions would be classified as terrorism in the twenty-first century, despite the fact that they stopped short of violence against the person. Dundonian Ethel Moorhead and Dorothea Chalmers Smith – a doctor, mother of six, and wife of a church minister – were sentenced to eight months in prison for breaking into an empty house in Glasgow's exclusive Park Gardens, and setting it alight.

Then in the early hours of 8 July 1914, an Alloway night-watchman doing his rounds spotted two shadowy figures, wearing men's tweed caps, lighting a fuse in the thatch above the window at the back of Burns' Cottage. After a tussle, one of the women fled and escaped either by bicycle or car. The other turned out to be the niece of Lord Kitchener, of 'Your Country Needs You' fame. The evidence against her was pretty conclusive, and included gunpowder and tins of oil. The next morning, the story was plastered on newspaper front pages around the world.

The nation was outraged, and as luck would have it, Helen Crawfurd was scheduled to speak at a public meeting in Perth that evening. Bravely, she faced the audience and explained that the two women responsible were English, and had been unaware of what this building meant to the people of Scotland. She then won the meeting over by quoting the bard himself:

'While Europe's eye is fixed on mighty things,
The fate of Empires and the fall of Kings;
While quacks of state must each produce his plan,
And even children lisp the rights of man;
Amidst this mighty fuss just let me mention,
The Rights of Women merit some attention.'

The verse was timely in more ways than one. Ten days earlier, the heir to the Austrian throne, the Archduke Ferdinand, had been assassinated in Sarajevo, along with his wife, Duchess Sophie. In the weeks to come, Europe's eye would be fixed on mighty things, and the fate of empires would hang in the balance.

The years between the Boer War and 1914 had been a time of optimism. The Edwardian era, was, according to historians a time of 'peace and plenty'. There was certainly plenty for the merchants, industrialists, landed gentry and burgeoning middle classes. Britain had grown rich on the spoils of the empire, paid for by the blood and tears of generations of the poor.

Now some of that wealth was even beginning to trickle down. The Victorian culture of subservience was dying, as governments came under siege from suffragettes, socialists, trade unionists and the progressive middle classes.

Even the old two-party system, split between the landowning Tories and the capitalist Liberals, was crumbling. After the 1910 general election, 42 Labour MPs held the balance of power in the House of Commons, forcing the Liberal Government to introduce an embryonic welfare state through legislation such as the National Insurance Act, which allowed people access to free medical treatment, sick pay and unemployment pay in return for fixed weekly payments. It stopped short of the free universal insurance system that Keir Hardie and the Scottish Labour had first demanded 25 years earlier, but at least it provided peace of mind for those who could afford the weekly payments.

Even Home Rule, for Scotland, as well as for Ireland, began to look as though it might be within grasp. In May 1913, the House of Commons passed the second reading of the Scottish Home Rule bill by 204 votes to 159, vehemently opposed by the Tories and Unionists, but supported by a coalition of Liberal, Labour and Irish Parliamentary Party MPs.

Winds of change were blowing and old ways seemed to be going. But then… cataclysm. 'The lamps are going out all over Europe,' said Sir Edward Grey, the Foreign Secretary. 'We shall not see them lit again in our time.'

25

FLOO'ERS O'THE FOREST

Armageddon

It all began with a carnival of naïve excitement. In his book, *Revolt on the Clyde*, Willie Gallacher, who would later represent West Fife for 25 years as a Communist MP, captured the mood on the streets at the start of the Great War.

> 'What terrible attraction a war can have! The wild excitement, the illusion of wonderful adventure and the actual break in the monotony of working class life. Not because of the high feelings of 'patriotism' but because of the new, strange and thrilling life that lay before them.'

Leon Trotsky, exiled in Austria, experienced a similar scenes. The chaos and excitement on Vienna's *Ringstrasse* reminded him of the first, unsuccessful Russian Revolution in 1905, when the masses poured onto the streets in a frenzy of excitement at the prospect of a new world dawning. In his memoirs, *My Life: An Attempt at an Autobiography*, he tried to explain the psychology, on both sides of the conflict, of these first, heady days of what would soon turn into Armageddon:

> 'The people whose lives, day in and day out, pass in a monotony of hopelessness are many; they are the mainstay of modern society. The alarm of mobilisation breaks into their lives like a promise; the familiar and long hated is overthrown and the new and unusual reigns in its place. Changes still more incredible are in store for them in the future. For better or worse? For better, of course; what can seem worse than 'normal' conditions?'

This sense of euphoria soon fused with fear and hatred, whipped up by a frenzied press in full xenophobic flow. 'Man, some of these editors are right rough creatures,' says one character in Lewis Grassic Gibbon's *Sunset Song*, as news of the war reaches rural Aberdeenshire. 'God pity the Germans if they'd their hands on them.'

From the day Britain joined the war – 4 August 1914 – grotesque tales of German atrocities reached a crescendo when newspapers published a photograph of a Belgian baby without hands. A few days later, the story had escalated: not only had German soldiers chopped off the hands: they had eaten them like they would chicken legs. The report had been fabricated by the French propaganda agency, the *Bureau de la Presse*, but nobody bothered to check its veracity until after the war was safely over.

Rudyard Kipling was hired by the government as an official propagandist. For several years, the master wordsmith churned out pamphlets and articles glorifying this crusade of civilisation against savagery. And churned they were, in unashamedly over-seasoned style: 'There is no crime, no cruelty, no abomination that the mind of men can conceive of which the German has not perpetrated, is not perpetrating, and will not perpetrate if he is allowed to go on. Today, there are only two divisions in the world: human beings and Germans.' From the press, the pulpit and the political platform, the message was deafening: our islands are about to be over-run by Teutonic monsters. It was hard to resist the epidemic of invasion fever that rampaged through every village, town and city in the land.

In the first weeks of the war, Vice-Admiral Charles Fitzgerald founded the Order of the White Feather, which mobilised a network of young women across the land to publicly shame young men in civilian clothes, by handing them a white feather, the symbol of cowardice. Clergymen preached demagogic sermons against sinful pacifism. And in the factories, young workers were given a stark choice: enlist – or be sacked in disgrace.

In Glasgow, 22,000 signed up in the first week. In pit villages, young colliers stampeded to the recruitment centres; by February 1915, one in five Scots miners had enlisted. Nine out of ten sons of Church of Scotland ministers signed up. In *Sunset Song*'s fictional township of Kinraddie, one of the first to volunteer is the staunch socialist and opponent of war, Chae Strachan. The British Labour Party backed the war from the start. So too did Henry Hyndman, the veteran leader of the Social Democratic Federation, now renamed the British Socialist Party. The Women's Social and Political Union, under the formidable influence of Emmeline Pankhurst, and her daughter Christabel, also threw its weight behind the British war effort – though Sylvia and most of the leading suffragettes in Scotland campaigned against the war.

It would be all over by Christmas, insisted the politicians and the press.

Britain was the greatest warrior state on the planet, with a colossal global empire at its command and a Royal Navy that controlled the world's sea routes. And we had God on our side, they said. Nobody anticipated a global bloodbath. Nobody imagined in their worst nightmares that Europe would be strewn with the bones and burning flesh of nine million corpses.

Keir Hardie had clearer vision as well as a stronger backbone. In the first days of the war, he issued an *Appeal to the Working Class,* co-authored by another key Labour leader, Arthur Henderson.

> 'Men and women of Britain, you have an unexampled opportunity of showing your power, rendering a magnificent service to humanity and to the world. Proclaim that, for you, the days of plunder and butchery have gone by. Send messages of peace and fraternity to your fellows who have less liberty than you. Down with class rule! Down with the rule of brute force! Down with war! Up with the peaceful rule of the people!'

Henderson soon crumbled under the twin pressures of isolation and ambition, and accepted an invitation to join Asquith's war cabinet. But the veteran ex-miner from Lanarkshire didn't flinch, even when most of his friends refused to shake his hand and turned their backs on him, literally as well as politically. With tears in his eyes, he told his comrades in Merthyr that the war would escalate, and lead to conscription. 'My own boy may be taken,' he said, 'and I would rather see him in his grave than compelled to fight against other workers.'

He never lived to see the full apocalypse unfold. He passed away in a Glasgow hospital on 26 September 1914 at the age of 59, broken and defeated, his life's work reduced to smoking ruins to the discordant music of machine guns, mortar shells and hand grenades. 'He died of a broken heart,' wrote Tom Johnston in *Forward.* James Connolly also paid his tributes: 'By the death of Comrade James Keir Hardie, labour has lost one of its most fearless and incorruptible champions, and the world one of its highest minded and purest souls... he never faltered in the fight, never failed to stand up for truth and justice as he saw it, and as the world will yet see it.' The same could have been written of Connolly himself seven months later, when he was shot by firing squad for his part in the Easter Rising – a brave, defiant and doomed attempt to turn the tables against the men in Whitehall, with the blood of millions on their hands.

In the excitable first weeks and months of the Great War, it took enormous bravery to admit to fear. And it took towering courage to stand against the seething tide of patriotism by condemning the war. In Scotland, there were plenty prepared to do so. They were almost all on the socialist left. And such was their authority, built over years of campaigning on behalf of the working class and the poor – especially on Clydeside – that they were neither stoned nor lynched, but given a respectful hearing.

The first issue of *Forward*, on Saturday 8 August, ran a banner front-page headline: 'CIVILISATION SUBMERGED'. Underneath, it lashed into the politicians who had sided with the tyrannical Russian Tsar in the name of freedom:

> 'So, at the command of Russia, we go to war in a cause in which we have no interest, in which we were never consulted and from which by no possible conceivable result can we derive any advantage – only starvation, hungry children crying in the streets, bones lying in the battlefields, widows, orphans, tears.'

To illustrate its point, the newspaper carried a photograph from the Boer War, of a heap of mangled corpses on Spion Kop. The caption read: 'Notice the dismembered bodies. They don't show you this at the recruitment offices; the Harmworths [publishers of the fervently pro-war *Daily Record*] won't be in the next batch for the trenches.'

The following week, *Forward* led with a front page attack on the *Clarion*, the influential English socialist newspaper, which had come out strongly in support of the war: 'Whether or not the *Clarion* speaks for the socialist movement in England, it certainly does not speak for the socialist movement in Scotland.' In opposition to the Labour Party, to which it was still affiliated, the ILP opposed the war, and nowhere more strongly than in Scotland. According to *Forward*, a conference of 500 delegates had voted for an anti-war stance, with only one dissenting voice, while the East of Scotland ILP had unanimously adopted the same policy. After visiting Scotland a few months into the war, Fenner Brockway, the editor of the London-based ILP paper *Labour Leader,* said that when he 'met Maxton, Wheatley, Shinwell and Johnston, I realised the distinction almost immediately. They were speaking a different language from the British ILPers'. A fervent pacifist, Brockway strongly approved of the 'outspoken campaigning' of the Scottish socialist leaders.

Forward paints a more complex picture of the wider mood in Scotland than that of later historians, who draw predominantly on accounts from the mainstream, pro-war press.

> 'One comfort we have in these dolorous days is that the socialist movement in Scotland keeps its head, and the democracy [ie the general populace] we feared would be swept off its feet is keenly critical, calm, chafing at the war, feared at its consequences, dumbly feeling that our leaders have led the country unnecessarily into the broiling pots of hell. There is a dull, sickening sense of horror at it all, and a determination that in the clearing up of this mess, a great many aristocratic perquisites [perks] will be carted to the dunghill.'

There was no mass anti-war movement north of the border, but neither were meetings broken up by angry mobs, as was routine in England. On 15 August, eleven days after the declaration of war, *Forward* reported public anti-war meetings in Ayrshire, and a similar number in Lanarkshire, which were 'all orderly and undisturbed', with 'attentive and non-Jingo audiences'. At a further public meeting in Glasgow, James Maxton had 'stated the case against the war to an audience of 500 people and suffered no interruption'.

With his flowing mane of black hair and soaring oratory, Maxton was the charismatic showman of the ILP in Scotland. But he was also a man of steel. Along with John Maclean, James MacDougall, Willie Gallacher, Arthur Woodburn and others, he would end up behind bars, a prisoner of principle. His indefatigable opposition to the slaughter in Europe would help transform Glasgow and the Clydeside into the mightiest stronghold of socialism in the empire.

So too would the educational work of John Maclean, of whom the poet Hugh MacDiarmid wrote:

> 'Scotland has had few men whose names
> Matter – or should matter – to intelligent people,
> But of these MacLean, next to Burns, was the greatest.'

A school teacher whose parents had been Gaelic-speaking victims of the Highland Clearances, Maclean became the most famous anti-war campaigner of all, immortalised in song, drama and poetry for generations to come. He would serve two jail sentences for his anti-war activity. Before being sentenced to five years' penal servitude for attempting to cause mutiny, sedition and disaffection amongst the civilian population, he delivered an epic speech from the dock which would echo across Europe, including the famous passage:

> 'I wish no harm to any human being, but I, as one man, am going to exercise my freedom of speech. No human being on the face of the earth, no government is going to take from me my right to speak, my right to protest against wrong, my right to do everything that is for the benefit of mankind. I am not here, then, as the accused; I am here as the accuser of capitalism dripping with blood from head to foot.'*

Reverberations

By the time Maclean walked free, just seven months later, following a mass campaign for his release, the war was over. In 1914, Pope Benedict XV had declared the neutrality of the Vatican, warning that the Great War marked 'the suicide of Europe'. By the time it was done, few disagreed with that verdict. Even some of the most die-hard reactionaries were left shaken.

As the chief spin doctor of the war machine, Rudyard Kipling had, in the early days of the conflict, spat out his contempt for those wretched creatures who shirked their duty. He had even used his influence to bend the rules, in order to allow his own physically disqualified son to join the glorious fight for freedom. Two weeks later, at the age of 18, John Kipling lay dead on the Loos battlefield. With the guns now silent, a more sober and reflective Kipling wrote 'If any questioned why we lied; tell them, because our fathers lied.' His grief-stricken epitaph betrayed more than a hint of guilt.

In 1914 another writer, HG Wells, had predicted this would be 'the war to end wars'. Unlike Kipling, he was on the left, but like much of the British labour movement, he argued that only the defeat of Germany could bring to peace to Europe. Instead, it heralded social collapse, revolutionary upheaval, communism in the Russian empire, and Nazism in Germany. 'The First World War explains the Second World War', said historian AJP Taylor, 'and in fact caused it, insofar as one event causes another.'

---

* The story of Maclean and Red Clydeside will be more thoroughly described in the second volume of this work.

The backlash against the slaughter would have dramatic political consequences in Scotland. In January 1919, just two months after Armistice Day, Glasgow was under military occupation, with tanks on George Square and 12,000 armed troops ready to quell what was rapidly turning into a workers' uprising. The *Glasgow Herald* estimated that 'the revolutionaries could call on the support of 100,000 people'. These included radicalised women on Clydeside, who had taken on profiteering landlords in the biggest rent strike that Britain had ever seen.

The Liberal Party in Scotland would never recover from the war. From unbroken dominance since 1832, the party reduced to just 15 seats out of 71 in 1922. Never again would it win a majority north of the border. The Labour Party had gone along with the war, albeit with less enthusiasm. But in Scotland, the old guard who had backed military action would be cleared out by the ILP anti-war brigade, led by Maxton and Wheatley. In 1914, their stance had made them pariahs within the British labour movement. Their zealous opposition had brought embarrassment and even shame to the left, it was said. But the rebels were vindicated by history.

At the 1922 general election, Labour became the biggest party in Scotland, with 29 MPs, including 10 out of 15 in Glasgow, mostly members of the ILP. When they set out for parliament, 200,000 people gathered to give them a heroes' send-off. Among other things, they pledged to fight for Home Rule for Scotland. Within a decade the ILP, led by Maxton would leave the Labour Party forever, taking with them most of the Glasgow membership, not to mention the socialist-pacifist legacy of Keir Hardie. Thus, the labour movement lost its heart and soul.

Home Rule would not have saved Scotland from being sucked into the 1914-18 catastrophe. Independence could have. Some socialists, and others, began to shift in that direction. One group left the ILP in 1928 to help found the National Party of Scotland, the forerunner of the modern SNP. John MacLean called for 'Scotland to be torn out of John Bull's blood-soaked empire', and launched a new party that pledged to fight for a Scottish Workers Republic. In November 1923, he died aged just 44, and the dream of Scottish socialism seemed to die with him. It would be revived, but not for many generations.

In the meantime, Scotland hobbled on, out of the Great War and into the Great Depression. In 1914, its population had been 4.75 million; by the final year of the century, that figure had crept up to just over 5 million. In the same period, the populations of Norway, Sweden, Denmark and other small independent countries had more than doubled, a testimony to their vibrancy and vitality.

In the 10 years before 1914, 600,000 emigrated. After the Great War, that exodus of talent would continue. One of those exiles, Eric Bogle, had shuffled various dead-end jobs after leaving school, before emigrating to Australia at the age of 25. There he became a successful folk-singer, composing one of the most powerful songs ever written about the glorification of slaughter. *And the Band Played Waltzing Matilda* ends with an old man who lost both legs at Gallipoli watching the annual parade of war veterans, 'renewing their dreams of past glories':

> 'I see the old men all bent, stiff and sore
> Those weary old heroes of a forgotten war
> And the young people ask "What are they marching for?"
> And I ask myself the same question.'

Scotland provided more than its share of what Bogle called 'lambs to the slaughter'. Per head of population, the number of Scots who fought in the war was marginally higher than in the UK as a whole, reflecting the working class composition of the country and the desperation among young men to escape the deserted glens, the desolate slums, the suffocating pits, the blazing furnaces. But the fatality rate soared above the average: 26.4 per cent of Scottish soldiers were killed, as compared with 11.8 per cent for the rest of Britain and Ireland. Of the dozens of nations that became entangled in the war, none bar the Serbs and the Turks suffered a higher proportion of deaths per capita.

More than 1 in 10 of the entire male population of Scotland between 15 and 49 died on the butchered battlefields or in the sordid trenches, consigned to their graves by greed, arrogance and cold-blooded stupidity. They left behind tens of thousands of young women, widowed and single, and countless children unborn. All that would remain were names engraved on a thousand monuments, where each November their dwindling numbers of descendants gather to lay wreaths, while a lone piper plays the haunting melody composed in the wake of the Battle of Flodden.

> 'The Floo'ers o' the Forest, that fought aye the foremost
> The pride o' oor land lie cauld in the clay.'

Selected Bibliography

GENERAL

Armstrong, Allan, *From Davitt to Connolly*, Intfrobel Publications, 2010

Barrow, GWS, *Robert Bruce and the Community of the Realm of Scotland*, Edinburgh University Press, 1965

Barrow, GWS, *Kingship and Unity: Scotland 1000-1306*, Edinburgh University Press, 1981

Benson, John, *British Coalminers in the 19th Century: A Social History*, Longman, 1989

Bewley, Christina, *Muir of Huntershill*, Oxford University press, 1981

Brown, Gordon, *Maxton*, Mainstream, 1986

Burrowes, John, *Irish: The Remarkable Saga of a Nation and a City*, Mainstream, 2003

Cameron, Ewen A, *Impaled Upon A Thistle: Scotland Since 1880*, Edinburgh University Press, 2010

Clark, GN, *The Later Stuarts 1660-1714*, Oxford University Publications, 1963

Connolly, James, *Labour in Irish History*, Ulan Press, 2012

Cornell, David, *Bannockburn: The Triumph of Robert the Bruce*, Yale University Press, 2009

Craig, Maggie, *Damn Rebel Bitches: The Women of the '45*, Mainstream, 2000

Craig, Maggie, *Bare Arsed Banditti*, Mainstream, 2010

Craig, Maggie, *When the Clyde Ran Red*, Mainstream, 2011

Davidson, Neil, *Discovering the Scottish Revolution: 1692-1796*, Pluto, 2003

Davies, Norman, *The Isles: A History*, Pan MacMillan, 2008

Devine, TM, *Clanship to Crofters War*, Manchester University Press, 1994

Devine, TM, *The Scottish Nation: 1700-2000*, Allen Lane, 1999

Devine, TM, *Scotland's Empire 1600-1815*, Smithsonian, 2004

Donaldson, Gordon, *The Scottish Reformation*, Cambridge University Press, 1960

Donaldson, Gordon, *Scotland: James V-James VII*, Oliver & Boyd, 1965

Dowse, Robert E, *Left in the Centre: The Independent Labour Party 1893-1940*, Longmans, 1966

Ellis, Peter Berresford & Mac a' Ghobhainn, Seumus, *The Scottish Insurrection of 1820*, John Donald, 2001

Ferguson, William, *Scotland: 1689 to the Present*, Oliver & Boyd, 1968

Ferguson, William, *Scotland's Relations with England: A Survey to 1797*, Saltire Society, 1994

Fisher, Andrew, *William Wallace*, Birlinn, 2002

Forster, Sally, *Picts Gaels and Scots*, Batsford, 2004

Fraser, Lady Antonia, *Mary Queen of Scots*, Delta, 1993

Fraser, Lady Antonia, *King Charles II*, Phoenix, 2002

Gallacher, William, *Revolt on the Clyde*, Lawrence & Wishart, 1942

Gallagher, Tom, *Glasgow: The Uneasy Peace*, Manchester University Press, 1989

Herman, Arthur, *The Scottish Enlightenment: How the Scots Invented the Modern World*, Fourth Estate, 2003

Howell, David, *British Workers and the Independent Labour Party,* Manchester University Press, 1984

Howell, David, *Lost Left: Three Studies in Socialism and Nationalism*, Manchester University Press, 1986

Hunter, James, *The Making of the Crofting Community,* John Donald, 2006

Hunter, James, *The Last of the Free, a History of the Highlands and Islands of Scotland*, Mainstream 2010

Johnston, Thomas, *The History of the Working Classes in Scotland*, Forward Publishing, 1922

Kenefick, William, *Red Scotland!: The Rise and Fall of the Radical Left, 1872 to 1932*, Edinburgh University Press, 2010

Lenman, Bruce, *The Jacobite Risings in Britain*, Scottish Cultural Press, 1995

Lister-Kaye, John, *Ill Fares the Land*, Scottish Natural Heritage, 1994

Lynch, Michael, *Scotland: A New History,* Pimlico, 1992

MacInnes, Allan, *Union and Empire*, Cambridge Studies in Early Modern British History, 2007

Mackenzie, Alexander, *The History of the Highland Clearances*, Mercat, 1986

MacKenzie, Peter, *An Exposure of the Spy System Used in Glasgow 1816-1820*, Muir, 1833

MacKenzie, Peter, *Old Reminiscences of Glasgow and the West of Scotland*, John Tweed, 1865

MacLeod, John, *Highlanders: A History of the Gaels*, Hodder & Stoughton, 1997

MacMillan, Hector, *Handful of Rogues*, Argyll Publishing, 2005

Madden, Richard Robert, *The United Irishmen, Their Lives and Times*, J Madden & Co, 1842

McFarland, Elaine, *John Ferguson - 1836-1906: Irish Issues in Scottish Politics*, Tuckwell Press, 2003

McLynn, Frank, *The Jacobites*, Routledge & Keegan, 1985

McLynn, Frank, *Bonnie Prince Charlie*, Pimlico, 2003

McLynn, Frank, *The Road Not Taken: How Britain Narrowly Missed a Revolution*, Bodley Head, 2012

McShane, Harry & Smith, Joan, *No Mean Fighter*, Pluto, 1978

Middlemass, Keith, *The Clydesiders: A Left Wing Struggle for Parliamentary Power*, Hutchinson, London, 1965

Milton, Nan, *John Maclean*, Clydeside Press, 2002

Morgan, Kenneth, *Keir Hardie: Radical and Socialist*, Faber and Faber, 2010

Oliver, Neil, *A History of Scotland*, Hachette, 2009
Parkhill, John, *The History of Paisley*, Robert Stewart, 1857
Pittock, Murray, *The Myth of the Jacobite Clans: the Jacobite Army in 1745*, Edinburgh University Press, 2009
Prebble, John, *The Highland Clearances*, Penguin, 1969
Prebble, John, *Glencoe*, Penguin, 1973
Prebble, John, *The Lion in the North*, Penguin, 1981
Prebble, John, *Culloden*, Pimlico, 2002
Richards, Eric, *The Highland Clearances*, Birlinn, 2008
Scott, Paul Henderson (ed), *The Saltoun Papers*, Saltire Society, 2003
Smout, TC, *History of the Scottish People, 1560-1830*, Fontana, 1972
Smout, TC, *A Century of the Scottish People, 1830-1950*, Fontana, 1986
Smout, TC, *Scottish Woodland History: Essays and Perspectives*, Scottish Cultural Press, 1997
Smyth, JJ, *Labour in Glasgow, 1896-1936: Socialism, Suffrage and Sectarianism*, East Linton, 2000
Stewart, William, *J Keir Hardie: A Biography*, Cassel, 1921
Watson, Fiona, *Scotland: A History: 8000 B.C.-A.D. 2000*, Tempus, 2001
Wightman, Andy, *The Poor Had No Lawyers*, Birlinn, 2011
Woolf, Alex, *From Pictland to Alba 789 – 1070*, Edinburgh University Press, 2007
Young, James D, *The Very Bastards of Creation*, Clydeside Press, 1996
Young, James D, *The Rousing of the Scottish Working Class*, Clydeside Press, 2009

NEWSPAPERS AND OTHER ARCHIVES

Aberdeen Journal
Daily Record
Dundee Courier & Advertiser
Edinburgh High Court Reports and Transcripts
Evening Times
Forward
Glasgow Courier
Glasgow Herald
Glasgow Observer
Hansard (online)
Inverness Courier
The National Archives of Scotland
Spartacus Educational (online)

Index